Understanding Social Lives
Part 1

The Open University

Understanding Social Lives
Part 1

Edited by John Allen and Georgina Blakeley

This publication forms part of the Open University module DD102 Introducing the social sciences. Details of this and other Open University modules can be obtained from the Student Registration and Enquiry Service, The Open University, PO Box 197, Milton Keynes MK7 6BJ, United Kingdom (tel. +44 (0)845 300 60 90; email general-enquiries@open.ac.uk).

Alternatively, you may visit the Open University website at www.open.ac.uk where you can learn more about the wide range of modules and packs offered at all levels by The Open University. To purchase a selection of Open University materials visit www.ouw.co.uk, or contact Open University Worldwide, Walton Hall, Milton Keynes MK7 6AA, United Kingdom for a brochure (tel. +44 (0)1908 858793; fax +44 (0)1908 858787; email ouw-customer-services@open.ac.uk).

The Open University, Walton Hall, Milton Keynes MK7 6AA

First published 2014

Edited, designed and typeset by The Open University.

Printed and bound in the United Kingdom by Halstan & Co. Ltd., Amersham, Bucks.

ISBN 978 178 00 7333 0

1.1

Contents

Preface

Understanding Social Lives, Part 1 is the first module textbook for *Introducing the social sciences* (DD102). As with other Open University materials, *Understanding Social Lives, Part 1* has been produced by a 'module team' of academic and production staff that included the authors and editors named here, but also many others. This wider module team played a key role in shaping the module, the book and individual chapters through successive drafts. Professor Dale Southerton, our external assessor, was a valued source of critical and supporting advice, and we very much appreciate all his careful work on our behalf.

The academic staff at The Open University are unusually lucky in being able to benefit from the expertise and professionalism of the best production and administrative colleagues. Lesley Moore, our Module Coordinator, was a model of efficiency, 'unflappability' and good humour, and provided strong support to the module team. Production colleagues and editors – Melanie Bayley, John O'Dwyer, Katie Belcher and Salia Nessa – did far more than edit and compose this book and the range of online study materials with care, attention to detail and goodwill: they must take a large share of credit for the clarity, coherence and accessibility of this book and all of the other study materials. Thanks are also due to Jo Mack and Roshni Amin, both consummate professionals, whose years of experience ensured the quality of the films and audio materials. Paul Hillery and Howie Twiner, Graphics Media Developers, are due our collective thanks for their creative work on the design and artwork of the book. And last, but certainly not least, thanks must go to Ann Tolley and Eileen Potterton, who worked as Curriculum Managers on *Introducing the social sciences*. They are the best in the business and oversaw the production of this book and the rest of the module with such enthusiasm, efficiency, goodwill and patience that our lives were made much easier than we had any right to expect.

Unusually, perhaps, DD102 builds on its predecessor module – DD101 – through trying to both incorporate what worked on this previous module and improving what worked less well. In this regard, the DD102 module team also owe their thanks to the DD101 module team and particularly to its chair, Dr Simon Bromley, who laid such excellent foundations for our work here.

Understanding Social Lives, Part 1 is divided into two sections: the introductory chapters; and 'Making lives'. These were edited respectively by Georgina Blakeley and John Allen. With years of experience at his fingertips, John Allen, the strand editor for 'Making lives', worked to shape and refine this text and much of the module besides. We are truly grateful for all his creative efforts, which have made the module far better than it would have been without his invaluable participation.

Georgina Blakeley and Matt Staples
Chair and Deputy Chair of the *Introducing the social sciences* module team

The street

Contents

Introduction

Where do you live? One answer to this question is to provide your address, but an address provides a lot more information than simply where you live. Addresses convey messages about whether or not they are desirable places to live, as the headlines in Figure 1.1 demonstrate.

Ten best places to live in the UK: Solihull comes top
The Independent, 14 November 2013

Poignant pictures of a decaying, crime-ridden housing estate which has fallen into ruin and now the remaining residents await the bulldozers
Mail Online, 28 April 2013

£1.5bn revamp of sink estate reveals 'social cleansing' plan
The Independent, 6 February 2013

Residents fear BBC documentary 'makes their estate look like Shameless'
The Telegraph, 12 September 2012

Hands off our land: housing estates will not be 'plonked' next to villages, pledges David Cameron
The Telegraph, 12 January 2012

Britain's most expensive address feels the pinch as house prices tumble
Sunday Mirror, 28 November 2010

130 houses .. 120 dead; welcome to the country's most dangerous housing estate
Sunday Mirror, 28 November 2010

Orchard Park housing estate was to be aspirational. Locals now call it Beirut
The Guardian, 19 November 2010

Figure 1.1   Selection of headlines

Such headlines communicate various ideas about the places where people live, the types of people who might live there and the kinds of lives they might lead. This is why the street has long been used as a starting point from which to start asking questions about the nature of society and the ways in which people live their lives.

Streets are a familiar part of contemporary social life in different ways. They are reproduced in traditional board games like Monopoly, in computer games, apps and television programmes. *Coronation Street* is a soap opera based on an urban street in the fictional suburb of 'Weatherfield', in the real city of Manchester in northern England. Alongside its London-based rival, *Eastenders*, the programme is a fixture at the top of the television viewing figures, and for many people, a vital part of their weekly routine. Even if you never watch it yourself, you probably have a friend, relative or colleague who does.

Streets are also replicated in shopping malls, such as those in Bicester Shopping Village in Oxfordshire and at the Trafford Centre in Manchester.

Figure 1.2   Bicester Shopping Village and Trafford Centre

Activity 1

Think of a street with which you are familiar and list the different ways in which you use it.

Although you may not live on a street, it is likely that you will use streets for a variety of activities: working, cycling, shopping, walking, jogging, parking, using a wheelchair, meeting friends, visiting the pub, cinema, cafés or restaurants. It is this widespread familiarity that makes the street a good place to start out on a journey of social scientific inquiry, even if not everyone lives on a street.

In the contemporary UK, people live in a wide variety of dwellings in different locations – from tower blocks to farms, from caravans to canal boats. Some people are homeless and may literally sleep on the street.

Figure 1.3 Variety of dwellings in the contemporary UK

The street is, therefore, a familiar enough place for it to be a useful starting point to begin describing how people live together as **social beings** and observe various aspects of society. Many viewers of television programmes such as *Coronation Street* or *Eastenders* empathise with programmes like these because they see something of their own lives within the fictional accounts of everyday life in these communities. Such programmes provide some insight into social life in the contemporary UK, even though they are based in fictional settings.

Programmes such as *Coronation Street* reflect the changes and continuities that have characterised UK society over the past half century. They do this through storylines as diverse as the decline of traditional manufacturing industry and the growth of a more service-based

Social beings
The idea that humans, by their very nature, are best suited to living together in communities rather than alone.

7

Neighbourhoods will be discussed in detail in Chapter 6 of *Understanding Social Lives, Part 2*.

Microcosm
Something that illustrates on a small scale, or is representative of something larger.

Trends and patterns
'Trends' refers to the general direction in which something is changing or developing; 'patterns' refers to a social situation or event that happens in a regular or repeated way.

economy, the increasing diversity of family life and the introduction of subjects that were previously considered to be personal and private, such as domestic violence and gay/lesbian relationships. They also reflect changes in the material fabric of neighbourhoods, such as the more modern houses built to replace the older Victorian housing stock, as in Figure 1.4.

Both fictional streets and real streets provide a window to a range of social issues that is of interest to social scientists. In this sense, streets act as a **microcosm** of society from which it is possible to begin to think about broader **trends and patterns** within society.

Figure 1.4   Old and new housing on *Coronation Street*

1   Doing social science on the street

Social scientists use a range of methods to explore society. Door-to-door **surveys** are one tried and tested method to find out about the street, for example the number of people and what kind of people live on what types of street.

In the nineteenth century, people such as Joseph and Seebohm Rowntree, Beatrice and Sydney Webb, and Charles Booth carried out door-to-door surveys to document the lives of people in each street. They were motivated by a concern about poverty and the condition of the working classes. Seebohm Rowntree conducted a survey of streets in York. Booth and his team of researchers visited every street in London and produced detailed notebooks, surveys and poverty maps describing the inhabitants of London.

Booth's study was published between 1886 and 1903 in 17 volumes under the title *Life and Labour of the People in London* (Booth, 1902–03). What was novel about his approach was the rigorous nature of the way he researched and gathered evidence. Using the street as the basic unit of investigation, he was able to systematically build up a street-by-street picture of much of Victorian London, allocating a colour code to each specific street to indicate its socio-economic position. These can be seen on the map of East London (Figure 1.5) with different colours representing varying levels of poverty in different districts across London:

- black stands for 'Lowest class. Vicious, semi-criminal'
- dark blue stands for 'Very poor, casual. Chronic want'
- grey stands for 'Poor. 18s to 21s a week for a moderate family'
- brown stands for 'Mixed. Some comfortable, others poor'
- pink stands for 'Fairly comfortable. Good ordinary earnings'
- red stands for 'Middle class. Well to do'
- white stands for 'Upper-middle and Upper classes. Wealthy'.

Booth's study took into account a wide variety of subjects – working conditions, education, wage levels, workhouses, religion and the police – to name a few. As part of his research, Booth lived with working-class families for several weeks at a time. This process of observation enabled him to see that for poor families disease, hunger and death were an ever-present danger. These studies were some of the earliest

Surveys
A method of investigating the behaviours, opinions or experiences of groups of people by asking them questions.

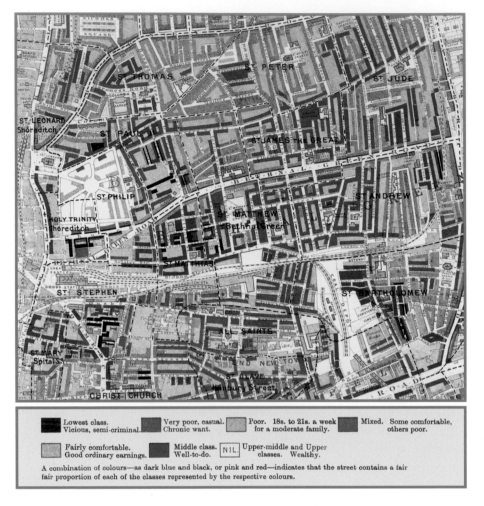

Figure 1.5   An extract from one of Booth's maps of East London

examples of doing social science on the street and a good illustration of the way that social science inquiry can lead to changes in public policy – the work that Booth did in measuring poverty was one of the factors leading to the introduction of means-tested, old age pensions in 1908.

It is worth pointing out, however, one key difference between Booth's study and doing social science today. Despite the systematic nature of Booth's study, the notebooks did not just count the people in each dwelling: they included many moral comments about the workers and their living conditions. For example, in Figure 1.6 Booth's comments on Simpson Road were:

Dirty tumbledown houses should be condemned. People very poor dirty drinking lot.

However, he described Harrow Lane inhabitants as:

Respectable working people. Not migratory.

Such moral comments are not appropriate when doing social science today.

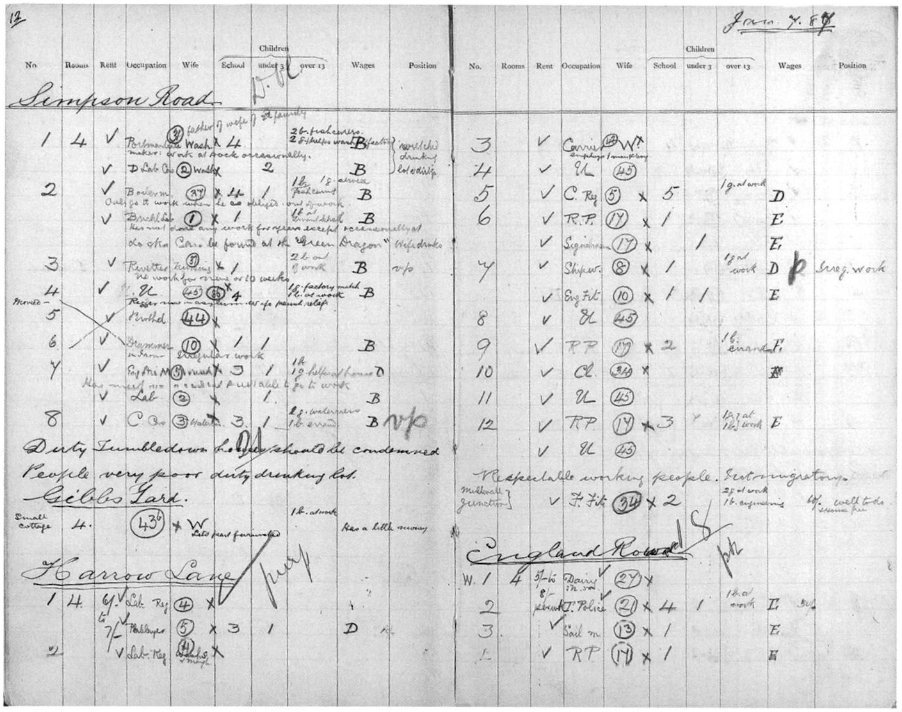

Figure 1.6   Excerpt from Booth's notebooks

Many people and organisations are interested in where people live, from latter-day social investigators like Booth to today's opinion poll surveyors, insurance companies and market researchers. The government is also interested in where people live. The first census was carried out in England and Wales in 1801 and, since that date, the government, through the UK Statistics Agency, has counted the population every ten years by delivering by hand questionnaires to every house or dwelling for people to complete. The most recent census was carried out in 2011, and for the first time people could choose to complete it online.

By studying individual streets, the people who live on them, what happens on them, identifying similarities and differences between streets, and organising all of this information in a systematic way, social scientists (including early ones like Charles Booth) can start to observe and describe common patterns and trends. This is what you are going to do at the start of this module using City Road in Cardiff, the capital city of Wales and one of the largest cities in the UK. Yet, it could have been any street in any city, town or village, as any street in the UK can open a window to a range of key social science issues.

From an initial process of observing and describing streets, and what is happening on them, social scientists can start to ask questions about what can be observed on a street and what this might tell us about people's social lives more generally. Many people, for example Lloyd Robson on City Road, do social science all the time in the sense of observing, describing and asking questions. This is what John Clarke refers to in *The Life and Times of the Street: Part 1* as 'doing everyday social science' (The Open University, 2014a). He also suggests, however, that there are small, but nevertheless significant, differences between doing everyday social science and the work of social scientists:

- The first point is that social scientists try to make the questions they ask more systematic and explicit.

- The second point is that social scientists are interested in looking for patterns, regularities and trends that underlie the individual stories on the street.

- Finally, social scientists are looking for explanations for these wider patterns and for why some things stay the same and how others come to change.

Another difference is that social scientists use *concepts*. Concepts are words that are in regular use, but not everybody uses a concept in the same way. Using concepts is also part of doing everyday social science – it is impossible for anybody to think or to speak without using concepts. The difference is that social scientists try to think about the concepts they use and reflect on them. Social scientists also contest the meanings of concepts, so reflecting on *how* concepts are used is important.

To return to the example of Booth, when he colour-coded the streets of London and described each category, he used concepts – 'lowest class', 'middle class' and 'upper class'. These concepts served to simplify the detailed features and complexity of the categories of people he was describing. Concepts put to one side complicated or less relevant details to leave a term that acts as a kind of shorthand – a simplification of what is a far more complex idea. Concepts make a difference to social science inquiry. They affect how social scientists describe the social world and the questions they ask. For example, the concept of 'shopping mall' is a relatively new concept despite the fact that variations on malls, from markets to arcades to bazaars, have existed for centuries. But having a new concept, that of 'shopping mall', draws the attention of social scientists to new aspects of the ways in which people shop. It also leads to new questions about how shopping becomes combined with other leisure activities, and what kinds of people are included in or excluded from these new practices and places.

Broadly speaking, it is useful to divide questions into two kinds:

- **Description**: who, what, where and when? For example, who lives on City Road? What do people do on City Road? Where on City Road do the activities take place and when?

- **Explanation**: why and how? For example, why do some people have more money than others on City Road? How do social scientists start to find out about people's lives on City Road?

Concepts are particularly helpful in moving from the first type of description questions to the second type of explanation questions. For example, an observation that people have differing levels of income and therefore different opportunities in terms of what they can buy and consume on the street is underpinned by the concept of **inequality**. As you progress through the study materials, you will develop a larger vocabulary and greater understanding of what concepts are and how they underpin social science inquiry – from observing, describing and questioning, to attempting to understand and explain society.

Description
A written or sometimes visual depiction of a social scene, situation or event. Descriptions are attempts to represent something without necessarily trying to explain or account for it.

Explanation
An attempt to give reasons for society taking on particular characteristics or qualities. Explanations attempt to answer 'why?' and 'how?' questions.

Inequality
The unequal distribution of valued social resources within a society or between societies.

Summary

- The street offers a window to many aspects of social lives (such as the family and workplace), which social scientists are interested in.

- The street provides a familiar and approachable starting point from which it is possible to begin observing and describing various aspects of people's social lives.

- Descriptions and observations of what is happening on streets can reveal how people live together as social beings.

- Streets can reflect broader patterns and trends within society.

- Social scientists try to:
  - be systematic and explicit in the questions they ask
  - look for patterns, regularities and trends beneath individual stories
  - look for explanations for these patterns and regularities, and why some of these change and others persist
  - think and reflect on the concepts they use to describe and ask questions.

2 'Your' street

When looking at City Road and thinking about what you have seen, the emphasis should be on using this and applying it much more widely to streets that you know.

When you think of a street, you might initially imagine a street with which you have a close connection. You might go along this street on a regular basis and take what happens on it for granted. It is when you encounter a less familiar street that you might start to observe things that are different. Following this process, it makes sense to return to the street or streets that you know and see if there is anything that you can identify that now appears less familiar. For example, perhaps you have never really looked at the pavements to see if they are easily accessible for people who have mobility difficulties, or perhaps you have never noticed the buildings and whether they are all similar or whether there are some differences between them. Social scientists are often interested in exploring what makes up the taken for granted – they try to make the familiar unfamiliar by asking questions such as: why are things like this? How did they come to be like that?

No two streets are exactly the same. All are distinctive in some way, and you will see and encounter things in them that you won't see anywhere else. In other respects, streets around the world have similarities as well as differences. Social scientists look for patterns in social life that exist alongside those distinctive characteristics that are often the most obvious aspect of any given society.

Activity 2

Some examples of things that are often taken for granted might include:

- people's behaviour
- the things that people buy
- how people dress.

Can you list some more things that you think are taken for granted? You might wish to share your list with your tutor and other students on your forum.

Looking for the patterns that lie beneath individual stories on the street is one way of beginning to ask what social lives on the street can reveal about life in the contemporary UK more generally. As you move from City Road to asking questions about streets that are familiar to you, it is also helpful to ask questions about society as a whole. In particular, there are three module questions to bear in mind, both over the period of your studies on the 'street' and over the module as whole:

- How is society made and remade?

- How are differences and inequalities produced?

- How do social scientists know?

As you progress through the materials, these are questions that you will return to at regular points in your studies. At this very early stage in the module, it might help to keep one aspect of each of these questions in mind.

- In relation to the first question, it is worth thinking about the idea that societies are not just there or given – they are made by people, and by the relationships they have with each other and the world around them.

- The second question highlights that, in making societies, people are not all the same, and the rewards and costs of our social lives are not equally distributed.

- The last question points to questions of how social scientists inquire about the world.

These module questions are explored through the three strands of study materials:

1   Making lives

2   Connecting lives

3   Ordering lives.

2.1   Making lives

Making and remaking
The various activities and practices that people engage in, and the relationships they have with each other and things, that help to shape society in particular ways.

People are not finished products: lives are always in the making. This strand looks at how people go about **making and remaking** themselves, their lives and the society in which they live through trying to make the best of the opportunities that come their way, and responding to change and challenges as best they can. Yet, people do not start with a blank sheet of paper: individuals have to make their lives within a society that is already made as a **consumer society**, in

Consumer society
A society that is defined as much by how and what people purchase and use, as by what they make or do.

which people's ability and desire to consume is a key feature. People therefore face both choices and constraints in making and remaking their lives. This strand examines how and why some individuals and groups in society have greater opportunities than others to make their lives and the lives of those around them.

2.2 Connecting lives

When you look at City Road it can seem like a set of individuals, maybe small groups of friends or a family, people doing a job or going shopping, but these things are connected and sometimes disconnected. The street is not just a collection of isolated individuals – people are connected to each other, to places, to things and to the social world around them. Yet there are also disconnections. Individual lives and the society in which people live are made and remade through these different connections and disconnections.

This strand looks at the different ways in which people relate to each other and to the places where they live and work, and how they are sometimes disconnected. It examines the choices and constraints people face in making connections and disconnections, and how these both shape people's sense of who they are and who other people think they are.

2.3 Ordering lives

Without some kind of order, it would be very difficult for people to live together. This strand looks at the daily, and often mundane, practices, routines and behaviours that make **social order** work smoothly in the ways that people expect. Yet, 'Ordering lives' also explores the ways in which social order is disrupted and how social order gets remade in the face of **disorder**. The strand looks at who gets to define and contest different ideas about order and disorder, and the relationship between order and disorder. It explores how disorder can often reveal much about how the social order it is disrupting is supposed to work. Finally, it questions whether disorder might be more than just a lack of order: might disorder offer different visions of social order?

Social order
A stable social situation in which connections are maintained without change, or else change occurs in a predictable way (often contrasted with social disorder or chaos).

Social disorder
An unstable social situation where behaviour is unpredictable and labelled as contrary to a desired or imagined social order.

Summary

- The street is a place from which social scientists can begin to observe how people live their social lives.

- Social scientists are often interested in asking how the things that are taken for granted are made up – why are things as they are and how did they come to be like that?

- Social scientists look for patterns in social life that exist alongside distinctive characteristics.

3   Observing City Road

We have already made the point that observation is a starting point in the social sciences, but that there is a difference between the kind of 'everyday' social science that people do and what social scientists try to do. One distinguishing element is that social scientists try to look for patterns, trends, themes and regularities, which lie beneath the details of people's individual stories. When watching the films and observing City Road in Cardiff, it will be helpful to consider four ways in which you can begin this process of observing like a social scientist.

1   *Look at the people you see and the activities that they are engaged in, as well as what they say about what they think and experience.* For example, people's perspectives of City Road may differ depending on whether they are young or older people, able-bodied or disabled, rich or poor, or whether they use City Road for different purposes. Some of the people you see work on City Road, for example as shopkeepers, refuse collectors, café proprietors, market traders and sports centre staff; some are there to shop and buy things; some live there and are retired; and some, such as the police officer, are there in an official capacity. Each person has a different story to tell, but social scientists look for patterns. For example, a number of the shopkeepers or café proprietors talk about their job not only as selling goods and services to people, but also in terms of their role in helping to make a sense of **community**, a point that is highlighted in the commentary by Kath Woodward in *The Life and Times of the Street: Part 1* (The Open University, 2014a).

2   *Focus on what is going on behind the scenes, which helps to keep the street running.* Sometimes this might involve the infrastructure of the street such as the street signage, electricity, water and other utility networks, and the use of CCTV and other technologies. Sometimes this might involve the activities of people who work on the street to keep it running smoothly such as the street cleaners, the community police officers and the refuse collectors.

Community
A group of people living in the same place and/or having particular characteristics or interests in common.

Figure 1.7   Refuse collector on City Road

3   *Look for connections.* One set of connections might be between City Road and other places. Some of these connections may not be directly observable, but they are visible in other ways. City Road is connected to places across the world through the products that are sold there, the people who come to City Road from other parts of the UK and from overseas, and through technology. For example, in *The Life and Times of the Street: Part 2*, Janet Symmons talks about her connections to Africa and these connections are visible in the types of product that she sells in her shop (The Open University, 2014b).

Another set of connections might be between the present day and the past. The past cannot literally be seen in contemporary City Road, but it leaves traces in the memories of those who live and work there, for example the men in the Municipal Club who are nostalgic about the past in *The Life and Times of the Street: Part 2* (The Open University, 2014b). The past also leaves its trace in the buildings themselves. One example is the Gaiety Cinema, Cardiff's oldest surviving cinema building, which has since been converted into use for bingo, a bowling alley, and most recently, occupied by anarchist squatters whom you will meet in the *Ordering lives* film (The Open University, 2014c).

4   *Focus on the differences across time and space.* City Road looks very different in the daytime and night-time: different people use it for different activities. The women who have their coffee in Taste Buds Café during the day (The Open University, 2014a) experience City Road differently from the younger people visiting the takeaway

restaurants at night (The Open University, 2014b). The time aspect can also refer to different historical periods, and the ways in which City Road displays both **change and continuity** over time. City Road was a street of small businesses for much of the twentieth century, but the car showrooms of the 1960s gave way to a greater variety of restaurants, takeaway outlets and shops. A more recent addition to the street is the proliferation of nail bars, which are becoming familiar on many high streets in the UK.

City Road is a physical space made up of buildings, places of various kinds and the material infrastructure of the road and pavements. This same physical space may be used differently by different people at different times. Space on City Road is used by an assortment of vehicles, pedestrians, parents pushing prams and people in wheelchairs. A bus shelter that is used by passengers waiting for a bus during the day may well be used by younger people at night as somewhere to hang out, or by a homeless person looking for a sheltered place to sleep.

Buildings on City Road also have different uses at different times of the day. Perhaps the most dramatic contrast in this respect is the Mackintosh Centre, discussed in *The Life and Times of the Street: Part 1* (The Open University, 2014a). First, there is its historical transformation from the home of a local landowner to a community sports centre. But second, there are its contemporary uses: during the week it is a sports centre that is seen – imagined – by some local people to be exclusive, as not for them, and then at weekends, it becomes the site for a farmers' market that attracts a range of local people.

There are also very different experiences and imaginations of City Road: in *The Life and Times of the Street: Part 2* both the men in the Municipal Club and one of the young women playing pool describe it as 'dangerous' or 'rough' (The Open University, 2014b). But this is denied by other users of City Road. The ideas people have may be based on experiences and they may also be imagined, as Kath Woodward observes when she talks about the nostalgia with which the men in the Municipal Club talk about the past (The Open University, 2014b). As the street changes, different groups of people feel different senses of belonging to the street.

Change and continuity
'Change' highlights those aspects of social life that differ over time; 'continuity' refers to those aspects of social life that stay the same over time.

3.1   How is society made and remade?

The first module question, which has already been briefly referred to is: 'How is society made and remade?'. 'Making' and 'remaking' refer to the activities people engage in and the relationships they have with other people and things. It is these activities and relations that help to make up society. Sometimes these activities and relationships are everyday, taken-for-granted activities, such as going shopping, taking children to school, helping people to cross the road; sometimes they are less frequent activities, such as occupying a disused building; or sometimes they are activities that only a few experts engage in, such as politicians making new laws – but they all *make* society in certain ways.

There are many examples of making and remaking on City Road. All of the shopkeepers, café proprietors and customers who use these facilities make and remake social life on City Road through the activities they engage in, and the relationships they have with each other and the world around them. Janet Symmons contributes to making social lives on City Road through the particular products she sells in her shop, Xquisite Africa, and the clientele she tries to attract. Moreover, because she brings various products from Africa and China to sell in her shop, she contributes to making social lives in these countries as well as on City Road (The Open University, 2014b).

Social life on City Road is also made and remade by the material infrastructure that is often hidden from view such as the electricity cables, sewers and water pipes. Many individuals' relationship to City Road is characterised by trying to keep City Road running smoothly, for example people in *The Life and Times of the Street: Part 2* such as Tim Masters who clears blockages of fat in the sewers, or the refuse collectors who have to deal with the huge amounts of waste generated by the restaurant trade on City Road (The Open University, 2014b).

You will learn more about migration in Chapter 4 of *Understanding Social Lives, Part 2*.

The process of migration is another factor that contributes to making and remaking the street in different ways. Indeed, it is the migration of people that makes streets in the first place, as it is only when people come to settle in particular areas that streets are created. Although the origins of the different groups of migrants change, City Road, like many others in the contemporary UK, continues to be made and remade by migrants both from other parts of the UK and from overseas.

Figure 1.8   The sari shop on City Road

The making and remaking of society, however, does not always proceed smoothly. Disruptions can occur – a car accident perhaps, a disagreement between neighbours or a larger-scale event such as the economic crisis of 2008 – which challenge people's routines and expected behaviours, and require people to engage in activities to smooth over the disruption. Sometimes disruptions can lead to change, such that social lives are remade in different ways. Sometimes disruptions reinforce existing patterns. In making and remaking society, there is both change and continuity, as some things may change and others remain the same.

Economic changes have always been part of making and remaking City Road and people's lives on the street in particular ways. City Road's very creation resulted from the impact of the coal industry in Wales, which by the end of the nineteenth century had made Cardiff into one of the world's busiest ports. City Road was thus remade from a country lane into a busy shopping street and thoroughfare. Subsequent economic changes remade City Road again from a street where car showrooms predominated to a street characterised by restaurants, shops and other services. City Road therefore does not operate in a vacuum, but rather is subject to national and global economic changes. Influences from beyond the street shape City Road and people's lives and, in turn, what people do and don't do make City Road what it is.

In the making and remaking of society, there are tensions and conflicts, as people and things compete or press in different directions. For example, not everyone is equally able to make and remake their lives in the face of change. People make individual choices, but not in circumstances of their own choosing. For example, in *The Life and Times of the Street: Part 1*, Mark Hocking was able to change his line of work in the face of wider economic change, which saw the demise of the car trade on City Road and in the UK as a whole (The Open University, 2014a). Yet, Colin Buttwell's newsagent business eventually closed in the face of increasing competition from supermarkets (The Open University, 2014a).

The power of supermarkets is explored in Chapter 6.

There is, then, work to be done to remake society in the face of what has been unsettled or broken – from the literal repair of sewers and the collection of rubbish, through to the work of shops, cafés, clubs and sports centres to include people and foster a sense of community. Much of this activity is conducted by people in the course of their day-to-day lives, but sometimes it is also deliberately planned and fostered by particular authorities, such as the local council. Yet, even as society is remade, some inequalities persist or new ones appear, as the food bank in *The Life and Times of the Street: Part 1* demonstrates (The Open University, 2014a).

Activity 3

Think about the following:

- the activities that you do in a typical day
- the relationships that you have with different people you come across
- your interaction with material things.

Try to list at least one example in each category. How does each of your examples contribute to making and remaking society?

3.2   How are differences and inequalities produced?

It is important to note that a focus on making and remaking highlights that societies are not just there or given – societies are actively made and remade in particular ways. The active nature of this process highlights two important elements:

- First, there can be both continuity and change in the process of making and remaking social lives. Although society is often made and remade in taken-for-granted ways, which suggest continuity rather than change, the fact that it is what people do or don't do that makes and remakes society always holds the possibility of change.

- Second, because making and remaking society is an active process involving people, and their activities and relationships with others, some groups of people will have a more prominent role in making and remaking society, such that the ways in which society is made and remade will favour the interests of some groups of people over others.

A focus on making and remaking, therefore, highlights the second module-wide question, which is: 'How are differences and inequalities produced?' Social lives include **differences** among people as well as similarities, and the things people value and the resources they have are unequally distributed. Differences can refer to variations between individuals – these may be physical, behavioural or related to attitudes and preferences. Social science, however, tends to use difference to focus on contrasts between groupings of people, such as those based on gender, class, age, sexuality, and race or ethnicity.

Difference
Contrasts between groupings of people, such as those based on gender, class, age, sexuality, and race or ethnicity.

Difference is not the same as inequality, although some differences are often associated with inequalities. 'Inequality' refers to the unequal distribution of valued social resources within a society or between societies. The social resources people value can change over time and differ from place to place, but the term generally includes money (economic resources), time, access to education, cultural facilities, and so on. Social scientists are interested in studying the processes that turn some differences, and the ways in which they are experienced by different groups of people, into inequalities.

A good example of the relationship between difference and inequality can be seen in the experience of somebody with a physical impairment. A physically impaired person in a wheelchair is different from a person without this physical impairment, but this difference only becomes an inequality in the face of a material barrier such as steps without a ramp, or in the face of **prejudice** from people without physical impairment. Other examples of the relationship between differences and inequality are:

- differences in age may be linked to inequalities in mobility and access to places
- racial and gender differences may be linked to inequalities in income and access to education

Prejudice
Opinions that individuals might hold towards groups of people identified on the basis of difference, which are not based on reason or actual experience.

- class difference is generally linked to economic inequalities, although it is sometimes associated with different ways of thinking and behaving.

On City Road, there are many examples of differences and how they relate to inequalities. There are different kinds of shops on City Road, which attract different kinds of clientele. These differences may relate to inequalities in economic resources. For example, different people may use the charity shop, Islamic Relief, compared to those who use Tesco. People may use different types of transport and wear different clothes. Sometimes these different types of transport or clothes may be indicators of inequalities in wealth. Some places on City Road, for example the Mackintosh Centre or Xquisite Africa, might appeal to people from different ethnic groups, but these examples of difference do not necessarily produce inequalities unless groups of people feel excluded, or are actively discouraged, from these premises.

Inequalities are often about people's unequal access to economic resources. On City Road, for example, John Arthur, the homeless man, and the various people who use the food bank experience economic inequality (The Open University, 2014a). Economic inequality is a key constraint on the choices people can make in making and remaking their lives. Those who use the food bank have no choice in the food they are given. This contrasts sharply with the people who attend the farmers' market and can choose which types of food they want to buy. People going to the Taste Buds Café or the farmers' market are also choosing to support particular lifestyles and ways of living in contrast to those who go to the food bank out of necessity.

Inequalities can also refer to other social resources such as time, mobility or access to places. These, however, are often linked to economic resources. Remember that in the making and remaking of society some groups of people are able to be more active in this process than others. City Road may be more accommodating or welcoming to young people rather than older people, or able-bodied people over people with mobility difficulties (which might relate to a physical impairment or the difficulties of manoeuvring a pram). People of all different ages use City Road, although young people tend to be the main users at night. Different facilities on City Road may provide for different age groups.

Figure 1.9   The food bank

The material world also shapes the relationship between difference and inequality. Differences in age can become an inequality when buildings and streets are designed for those who find it easy to get around. Steps, cobbled streets and uneven pavements can make mobility difficult for older people. However, local councils can take steps to ensure differences do not become inequalities, for example by making sure pavements are smooth for wheelchair users or painting white strips on bollards, so that they stand out more for people who have poor vision. Such interventions can stop differences, in this case physical differences, from becoming inequalities.

Perception also plays an important role in producing differences and inequalities. In *The Life and Times of the Street: Part 1*, the head coach at the Mackintosh Centre notes that local people can feel excluded from the sports club (The Open University, 2014a). It looks expensive and exclusive even though it tries to be inclusive and open to everyone. Janet Symmons' Xquisite Africa shop is designed to attract a predominantly African clientele who might feel excluded from other shops on City Road (The Open University, 2014b). Older people feel welcomed at the Taste Buds Café (The Open University, 2014a), while they may think that they would not feel as welcomed in the Pool Hall. This is not because the Pool Hall deliberately excludes older people; rather, it is about how places are designed to attract specific groups of people.

The activities of some groups are sometimes perceived as threatening or out of order by others, for example think of the contrasting views of nightlife on City Road expressed in *The Life and Times of the Street: Part 2* and the different senses of belonging to City Road that people express (The Open University, 2014b). As the street changes, different groups of people feel varying senses of belonging to the street. The men in the Municipal Club feel that the street no longer belongs to them, as it once did in the past (The Open University, 2014b). The sense of nostalgia they feel reflects the changes in City Road – from its original roots, when it was home to large numbers of the male working class who used to work in the docks and factories, to its role today, as home to a largely transient student and migrant population.

Activity 4

Think about a particular street that you know well and jot down some brief notes on the following:

- Identify two differences amongst people on the street, for example, differences of age, gender or race.
- Think about how these differences relate to inequalities: for example different shops/restaurants can cater to different clientele and indicate unequal wealth; different ages can mean inequalities in terms of mobility and access to places; and different modes of transport sometimes relate to inequalities in wealth.

3.3   How do social scientists know?

The final module-wide question is 'How do social scientists know?'. That is, how do social scientists inquire about the social world? In addition to the various social scientists talking, here are some of the things that you encountered in Parts 1 and 2 of *The Life and Times of the Street* (The Open University, 2014a; 2014b):

- people engaged in activities of various kinds
- people – students, shopkeepers and restaurant owners – talking about themselves
- people in various official roles, for example the commentary of the narrator and guide, Lloyd Robson
- historical archive material.

All of these provided information about what is and was going on, and all of them – not just the social scientists talking to camera – offered some kinds of explanation of why things are as they are or why they saw things the way they did. That is to say, many people you saw in and around City Road were involved in both describing and explaining aspects of its social life. They were involved in making sense of it. Yet social scientists, like the people you saw in the films, do not always agree. They argue for particular explanations, make certain claims about what they see and try to find evidence to support the claims that they want to make.

Social scientists try to go beyond what people can generally see in their everyday lives in order to construct and argue for explanations that go beyond the stories that individuals might tell. For example, in *The Life and Times of the Street: Part 1* (The Open University, 2014a) John Arthur's story about homelessness is both an individual story about his life and a story about a wider pattern of homelessness within the contemporary UK. What individual stories like John Arthur's can do is to bring such patterns to life and, in so doing, draw attention to these wider patterns. In this way, they provide a starting point to begin asking questions about these individual experiences and what they might reveal about society.

Social scientists try to be explicit about how and what they know, and they may draw upon and assemble a range of ideas and evidence in support of their explanations. Yet, social scientists often begin with the same kinds of question as those that interest the people they are studying, and build upon what is seen and the stories that they are told. As John Clarke says, what Lloyd Robson is doing in talking to people about their social lives is one of the things that social scientists do as well and there is only a small, albeit significant, difference between what Lloyd Robson is doing in the film and what social scientists are trying to do (The Open University, 2014a).

Figure 1.10   Lloyd Robson talks to Gareth Joshua who helps to keep the street running

Social scientists try to see differently in order to account for trends, connections, patterns and themes. While there are many different stories and experiences that you have come across on City Road, the aim of the social sciences is to assemble these into a picture of more general patterns. The changes visible on City Road – from its role as the centre of car showrooms to the contemporary dominance of nail bars and takeaway restaurants – serve as examples of change on a number of levels:

- at the level of individual lives, such as those of Mark Hocking and Colin Butwell
- at the level of City Road
- at the level of the wider UK economy, from manufacturing to services.

The next stage, of course, is to take the step from City Road to streets with which you are familiar. While City Road has many stories and characteristics that are distinctive, much of what you can see and learn from observing City Road can be applied to almost any street, anywhere.

Summary

- One way in which social scientists try to see the world differently is by looking for the trends, patterns and connections that underpin individual stories and experiences.

- Although City Road is distinctive (as are all streets), the patterns you can discover or assemble from it are likely to have much in common with many other streets elsewhere in the UK and beyond.

- Streets and social lives more generally can be viewed in different ways. For example, through people and their activities, and what they say about what they think and experience; through the interactions and connections between people and the material infrastructure around them; through the connections between people and things in one place and time, and those in other places and times; and the different and competing uses of spaces and times, as the people, activities and experiences change.

- Observing and describing City Road is one way of beginning to look for answers to the three module-wide questions:
  - How is society made and remade?
  - How are differences and inequalities produced?
  - How do social scientists know?

References

Booth, C. (1902–03) *Life and Labour of the People in London*, London, Macmillan.

The Open University (2014a) 'The Life and Times of the Street: Part 1' [Video], *DD102 Introducing the social sciences*. Available at https://learn2.open.ac.uk/mod/oucontent/view.php?id=443760&section=2.3 (Accessed 10 March 2014).

The Open University (2014b) 'The Life and Times of the Street: Part 2' [Video], *DD102 Introducing the social sciences*. Available at https://learn2.open.ac.uk/mod/oucontent/view.php?id=443760&section=2.7 (Accessed 10 March 2014).

The Open University (2014c) 'Ordering Lives' [Video], *DD102 Introducing the social sciences*. Available at https://learn2.open.ac.uk/mod/oucontent/view.php?id=444610&section=2 (Accessed 10 March 2014).

Chapter 2
Making lives

Matt Staples

Contents

Introduction

A busy street is a good place to view how the everyday lives of people are made. You can start to get a sense of people going about their lives, the clothes they are wearing, the shops they go into, the things they might buy and how they interact with each other in different ways – a brief chat between customer and shopkeeper, a longer chat between people who know each other on the pavement, or pedestrians weaving past one another on the way to somewhere else, going into buildings, taking journeys in the car, by bus or on foot. The interactions and activities that can be seen on the street are the first clues as to how social relations are made. It is possible to get a sense of the **choices** and **constraints** that people encounter in their everyday lives through the things that people do, what they buy, how they present themselves and relate to each other and the physical environment in which these all happen.

Choices
The ability to make decisions concerning the way a person lives their life.

Constraints
Limits on the ability of people and groups to make decisions over various facets of their lives.

Figure 2.1   City Road, Cardiff

'Making lives' explores the bustling commercial centre of City Road in Cardiff where it is possible to observe the different ways in which people make their lives and how these observations prompt questions about wider society. As you learn about the lives of the people in the film *Making Lives* (The Open University, 2014a), the focus is on the ways in which contemporary society makes people's lives and how, in turn, people make society through their actions and practices – through a process of **social construction**. For example, what can be seen on

Social construction
Something that is socially constructed is, at least in part, dependent on the society and social relations in which it is made and used.

Socio-economic position
The position of an individual or group based on a range of factors, including occupation, income level, education and cultural background.

City Road, the different activities on the street and the interactions between people on it, provides a good starting point to think about whether people have choices in all aspects of their lives, or whether for some people choices are quite constrained. Do some groups in society have more opportunities than others to make their lives in a manner of their own choosing and, if so, what are the factors that shape this? Is it **socio-economic position** or class, race or ethnicity, gender or disability? Or are many of the free choices that people make subconsciously made for them? It is this two-way relationship between the individual and society that you should keep in mind as you watch the hustle and bustle of
City Road.

By observing City Road, it is also possible to think about how the street is characterised by both continuity and change. Much of what takes place is a product of routine and repetition, yet the street is also a site of change. Change can be the product of subtle and barely noticed changes, or the product of more obvious, larger-scale shifts in society.

These are some of the issues and questions raised in the 'Making lives' strand.

1   Change and continuity

The history of City Road is typical of many streets in the contemporary UK. It highlights the changing nature and the continuities evident in everyday life, and how these impact on the making and remaking of social lives. **Consumption** provides a useful way into observing and thinking about how lives are made and remade. Consumption can be about the everyday trip to the corner shop or the supermarket or it can be a less frequent one, such as new clothing or a visit to the beauty salon. In its different forms and in the meanings people give to specific objects and activities, being able to consume offers people opportunities in terms of defining themselves and the image they wish to project. In short, being able to consume opens up the possibility of making lives in specific ways and of shaping relationships by linking or separating people from each other. Through its shops and restaurants and through advertising on hoardings, bus stops, buses and taxis, the street offers numerous opportunities for observing various forms of consumption, and for thinking about consumption in different ways.

Starting as a rural lane, through its role as a centre for the car trade to its current role during the day as a busy shopping street, and as a night-time destination for those visiting pubs and restaurants, City Road emphasises how *what* people consume and *how* they consume are subject to both continuity and change. The social lives of people and the ways in which they are made and remade are not static – they change and have their own histories. Indeed, social scientists often try to read some of the social history of society by looking at how lives have changed in the context of consumption. As the services and things that people buy change, this impacts on the way people relate to each other and to the street around them.

City Road, once a street of car showrooms and car workshops, has become a street of ethnic restaurants, takeaway outlets, fabric warehouses, barbers and beauty salons. These changes on City Road are perhaps a sign of a wider shift in consumption patterns in society. Some will gain from these changes, while some changes may result in new inequalities or the embedding of existing ones. Old things may acquire new uses and support new activities and forms of consumption. The changing use of buildings on City Road is not only bound up with a redesign of the physical spaces involved, but is also a conscious attempt to adapt to the changing nature and demands of the consumers who live in or come to the area.

Consumption
The purchase and use of products and services, and one of the defining features of contemporary society.

Despite these changes, the essential purpose of City Road has not altered. Although the businesses might change over time, as might the products sold, City Road remains a place of commerce and consumption. One illustration of both change and continuity is the effect that the changing nature of the population has had on the ways in which lives are made on City Road. Like many streets across the contemporary UK, City Road has been, and continues to be, made and remade by migration and the new forms of consumption this can bring with it. As John Allen argues in *Making lives* (The Open University, 2014a), the mix of different shops on City Road is the product of diverse cultural influences drawn from around the world. This reflects the openness to global influences that is a characteristic of shops across the UK and the products within them.

In *Making lives* (The Open University, 2014a), Mark, a student at Cardiff University who decided to stay and make his home and business on City Road after his studies, is indicative of the importance of global connections. Although his shop Jing Xing Express Asian Grocery is aimed at Asian students at Cardiff University, he attracts customers from the wider community as well. This highlights the changing appetites and choices being made to consume different food among the wider population. Although some of his products are made in the UK, others are from China, Hong Kong, Thailand and Taiwan, emphasising how working and consuming on City Road are connected to the making and remaking of other social lives in other streets across the world.

Mark's story is interesting in two ways:

- Moving to City Road and opening his business there has changed social lives on City Road. Mark's shop is the first Chinese food shop on City Road and provides people with a greater choice in food.
- Mark's life has also been remade by coming to the UK, opening his business on City Road and having the opportunity to try food from other cultures. Yet, he emphasises that he still prefers Chinese food!

Activity 1

Think about a street that you know well. Have you noticed changes taking place? Are there continuities as well? List two changes and two continuities that can be observed on this street. Think about which groups of people (for example, older, younger, richer, poorer) might be the winners and losers from these changes and continuities.

Each street, although it may share some characteristics with others, is distinctive. For example, your street might have its own mix of shops, businesses and residential housing, or it might just have a few houses and no commercial outlets. As each street is distinctive, it will have its own set of changes and continuities. As shops come and go, different groups who use specific shops will win, while others will lose. People might have to go much further to access the products that they want or they may not be able to get certain types of product at all. If businesses close down, those who rely on them for employment will lose out and, if they remain unemployed, they may be limited in their ability to participate in the life of the street.

The emphasis on how the making and remaking of lives on City Road is connected to social lives elsewhere is also illustrated in *Making lives* (The Open University, 2014a) in the discussion with Hannan Mumood, the manager of the Clare Food Superstore. To appeal to his customer base, Hannan goes to Southall in West London to get specific products, emphasising the links with the wider Asian community located in the UK and beyond, and the ways in which culture can influence and underpin consumption. For his meat, Hannan goes to the very 'English' setting of Gloucestershire, where the needs of Muslim consumers have led to farmers producing meat according to halal requirements. In this example, the way people on City Road conduct their lives has also impacted on the ways in which some people in Gloucestershire make theirs as well.

Figure 2.2 Clare Food Superstore

Economy
The range of activities that gives rise to the production, distribution, exchange and consumption of goods and services.

Social scientists are also interested in the way that economic and social change impacts on people differently, leading to new inequalities or embedding inequalities that already exist. Recession in the **economy** has impacted heavily on many groups within City Road. The question of economic inequality and how this affects the ways in which lives are made is shown in *Making lives* (The Open University, 2014a) through the focus on Deals Wales and its proprietor, Malcolm Taberner. Deals Wales is a contemporary form of pawnbroker: people bring in material goods in return for a cash payment. Their goods can be returned to them if the original sum, plus an agreed amount of interest, is repaid. Malcolm says that his clientele is fairly mixed, but divided between people who use the service in two main ways:

- There are customers who use the service as a buying service: they sell their goods and use the money on alternative forms of consumption and do not return to reclaim their original goods.

- There are those who use the service as a buy-back scheme: they sell their goods for cash, but then return within a given period to buy back their original goods.

Figure 2.3   Deals Wales

What the example of Deals Wales emphasises is how the street can be remade in ways that have historical echoes. Economic recession in the contemporary UK has highlighted the wide scale re-emergence of pawnbrokers – a form of financing that had largely disappeared from the high street until the arrival of payday lenders and buy-back schemes such as Malcolm's. As people lose their jobs or suffer a fall in income, their socio-economic position declines, and what can emerge are inequalities in access to conventional and ultimately less expensive forms of credit. Pawnbroking has re-emerged to cater for this need within specific groups in society and for many people it is again a legitimate means by which lives are made and remade.

Deals Wales also highlights the role of technology and how it has changed the reality of buying and selling, and the changing role of the street. Malcolm's description of his internet-based business and the role it has come to play alongside his shop on City Road illustrates how online shopping has changed, and to an extent undermined, the traditional high street. Not the least the very physicality of shopping changes as consumers make purchases from internet sites rather than shops. This also highlights the issue of inequalities, as those with the resources and skills to access the internet may benefit from new ways of shopping, and often access cheaper goods and services, while others who do not have the means or the knowledge may be restricted to the physical high street. Deals Wales and the changing nature of what consumers are interested in buying and selling in the shop, is also illustrative of wider societal trends. As different products rise and fall in popularity and new technologies emerge, the stock in the shop changes to reflect and respond to these trends.

Summary

- The consumption, production and disposal of material goods play a key role in making and remaking social lives on the street and in wider society.

- The making of individual lives is linked to the wider making of the street and of society.

- The ability of people to make and remake their lives on City Road and beyond is subject to both continuity and change, with some people benefiting and others losing out.

2   The individual and society

As individuals, people try to consciously make something of their lives. Individuals choose to do certain activities, go to specific places and look a certain way – these can be seen as individual acts and individual choices. Yet the ways that people on City Road and beyond wish to project their individual identities, and their ability to make and remake their lives in ways of their own choosing, is linked to wider social phenomena and issues beyond the street.

The importance of how individuals make themselves and how the social makes personal lives can be explored through the emergence of the many hairdressers, beauty salons and tattoo artists on City Road. As the owner of Physical Graffiti, Dan Walters, explains in *Making lives* (The Open University, 2014a), tattoos, which were once the preserve of 'sailors and criminals', have become much more socially acceptable over the past few years. Tattoos are now a legitimate way to express and establish individual identities, with people requesting patterns and styles of tattoo that are personalised and have specific meaning to them. Although the phenomenon is primarily associated with young people, the tattooist has also noticed older people choosing to have them as well.

Activity 2

Think about a street that you know and note down:

- people's appearance – their clothes, hairstyle and body art, such as tattoos
- the activities that people are taking part in.

Once you have written these down, think about wider society. Are there links between what you have observed and wider trends or popular culture?

Connections between street trends and wider society can be subtle – brands of sports shoes emerge as fashionable to the extent that they become very visible on the high street, popularised by music stars, magazines and online 'trending', or much more obvious – particular products run out in the supermarket because of their popularisation in cookery programmes.

The increasing fashion for tattoos, and the sacrifices that students like Connor Wall in *Making lives* (The Open University, 2014a) will make to have them, highlights how the consumption of tattoos on City Road is connected to the making and remaking of social lives elsewhere. Tattoos have been popularised by celebrities such as David Beckham and Megan Fox, and have become a mainstream part of 'celebrity' youth culture in the contemporary UK. What is also interesting is the way in which the desire for individuality can, over time, lead to a sense of uniformity. In *Making lives* (The Open University, 2014a), Connor specified a carp fish design over a Polynesian sleeve design because so many of his friends and acquaintances already had the latter design.

Figure 2.4 The tattoo parlour

The desire to be individual is often seen as a 'free' choice, yet sometimes decisions on how individuals make their own lives are affected by the views of others, by friends, family, peer groups and, ultimately, wider society. This is further emphasised in *Making lives* (The Open University, 2014a) by the interviews with the girls shopping on City Road who talk about their dreams of designer clothes and perfume. In clothing and cosmetics, as for many other things, it is possible to get a sense of how individual lives are consciously influenced by social lives and how people's choices are subtly, and sometimes less subtly, directed through advertising and other forms of persuasion.

You will explore advertising and forms of persuasion in Chapter 7.

The scene in *Making lives* (The Open University, 2014a) of the man talking about the designer clothing rail in the Islamic Relief charity shop, however, highlights the way in which people have to find alternative means to create a lifestyle they aspire to and how life chances are connected to, and sometimes defined by, access to resources. Although Connor had to miss out on a holiday, he was, as a consequence, able to pay for a tattoo, while the shopper in Islamic Relief has to buy his designer clothes second hand in order to make a lifestyle and his identity on the street. Others may not be able to do either.

The Islamic Relief charity shop is also interesting in the way it shows how people use such shops for different ends. Some might use it because they have to in order to make ends meet. Others might use it to make a different kind of statement about themselves and their identities. Consuming from charity shops raises issues of inequalities on the street: some consumers are drawn to the shops because of sheer necessity and the socio-economic position they hold, which prevents them shopping elsewhere; for others, however, charity shop purchases are used to establish difference from others on the street, using them to establish an identity around 'vintage chic'.

Charity shops rely on different forms of material transactions to maintain themselves, taking in donations of mainly second-hand goods and selling them at lower prices than conventional shops selling the equivalent new product. Charity shops also provide a very tangible example of how making lives on the street can impact on social lives elsewhere, as their profits go to help communities in the developing world. In turn, other people go to charity shops specifically to establish a form of extended social relations, and a link between the personal and the social with those they may not know or see, but with whom they are expressing solidarity through their charity purchases or through donations of clothing and other goods.

Summary

- Individuals make and remake their lives, but not necessarily in circumstances of their own choosing.

- Making individual lives on the street can impact on making social lives elsewhere and, in turn, wider society shapes individual lives on the street.

- Many of the decisions concerning the making and remaking of society result from choices and constraints, with different people having more or less freedom to make their own choices depending on a variety of factors, for example class and socio-economic position, gender, race and ethnicity, disability and sexuality.

3   Choice and constraint

For many people, consumption enables a better quality of life or opportunities to emphasise specific forms of self-expression. Yet many people will have constraints on what, how and how often they consume. Some constraints might be self-imposed or imposed subtly through the desire to conform or 'fit in'. Yet often these constraints are a consequence of socio-economic position or result from the way in which the street environment is designed. One way of thinking about choices and constraints is through the relationship between the individual and the social: individuals make their lives, but not necessarily in circumstances of their own choosing. For example, choices are sometimes made for people and constraints can be imposed against a person's will. Constraints can be economic or cultural, or linked to issues of race, ethnicity, disability, sexuality and gender.

The way in which the choices and constraints of some of the people on City Road are made and remade unequally, as a consequence of wider economic events, is shown very vividly in *Making lives* (The Open University, 2014a) through its focus on the food bank just off City Road. Ryan Watkins, who uses this food bank, highlights how losing one's job has multiple consequences. In particular, the choices he once had are now constrained. What he perceived as everyday acts of consumption, such as trips to the cinema and buying ice creams for his family, are now not possible. Moreover, his ability to make decisions about how he makes and remakes his life, like many others who use the food bank, have in some ways been taken over by others. For example, he is no longer able to decide what foods he can choose to consume: this is primarily due to his socio-economic position and the lack of **power** this gives him in society.

Power
A complex term used to denote influence, control or domination.

Patterns of consumption on City Road and other streets also influence the jobs that people do on the street, and this can shape the choices and constraints that affect the way people's lives are made. The presence or absence of work and the types of work that people do is important for the making of individual lives and for wider society. Work connects to consumption in that many of the jobs that people do involve the provision of services and the making of products that people want. In this way, the types of job that people do on the street exhibit both continuity and change over time. In shops, offices, workshops and in occupations on the street itself, the kinds of work people do, the salaries they earn and the connections made through the workplace open up or close down the ability to make lives – specifically where and how people live. Similarly, the absence of work or under-employment on the street can reduce the ability to actively make choices as well as contribute to the emergence or maintenance of socio-economic inequalities. Long-term unemployment, in particular, can impact on life chances by imposing constraints on future generations who are born into families where successive generations have suffered from the absence of work or low-paid work.

Figure 2.5   The food bank – where food is chosen for those who use them

This restriction of choice is evident in other ways on City Road. The making and remaking of lives on the street is never straightforward, and is often contested. Consumption in its many forms also has a political dimension and can become a site of resistance. For example, in *The Life and Times of the Street: Part 1* (The Open University, 2014b), the student making the chocolate orange cake is obviously concerned with the lack of choice available to consumers who might wish to make purchases on an ethical basis or in smaller, more 'local' shops than Tesco. On City Road, as on other high streets across the country, constraints have been imposed on the ability of people to make choices through a lack of alternatives to shopping in the outlets of the big supermarket chains. Issues of power begin to emerge as smaller businesses are unable to compete with the bigger supermarkets. The processes of standardisation, of increasing uniformity and the perceived lack of choice in particular areas of consumption have been very significant in terms of change across many high streets across the UK. People's varying reactions to this highlight how the personal experience is linked to wider societal concerns about specific issues. What it also highlights is how choices taken by some in society, in this case Tesco's decision to site a store on City Road, can impose constraints on others, such as the 'reluctant Tesco shopper'.

Activity 3

Think about your relationship with a street that you know well. What are the constraints that you have in terms of your ability to make your life on the street? What are the choices that you have on the street?

Everybody's circumstances are different, so you will have your own set of choices and constraints. However, in writing these down for Activity 3, it is useful to think about how these choices and constraints link to some of the factors discussed in the chapter. For some it might be their socio-economic position or cultural or ethnic background that enables or constrains choices; for others it is the street itself, either through the lack of choice or the difficulties in accessing the street.

People also interact with, directly and indirectly, the material infrastructure of the street: the buildings, shops, cafés, pavements and road. This physical environment can provide both opportunities and constraints for how people want to live their social lives on the street. In *Making lives* (The Open University, 2014a), Stephen Sweetman is a wheelchair user on City Road and has first-hand experience of the difficulties that socially constructed understandings of how the street is made can have for the personal. Yet, he also talks about how these understandings can be subject to change. Through negotiating pavements, roads and buildings, all designed with walking pedestrians and cars in mind, what comes across is Stephen's frustration at the constraints placed on him and others. These physical constraints limit the ability of some people to fully participate in the social life of the street because of their disability. Barriers, such as shops with stairs or steps or raised kerbs on pavements, may constrain the opportunities for where and how people are able to make and remake their own lives. Barriers may lead to a process of self-imposed constraints, whereby people choose not to do certain things or go to certain places because of the difficulties of the material environment they might encounter.

However, Stephen is also keen to stress that activism by disabled people has improved the provision for them over time. As John Allen indicates in *Making lives* (The Open University, 2014a), Stephen's willingness to ensure his personal access to the street is part of a wider campaign to make public and private spaces accessible. This emphasises the role of the personal in engaging with others to make a political issue out of the social, in this case public infrastructure and street furniture. Stephen's story also illustrates the wider change in social attitudes to people with disabilities, and the opportunities that now exist on and beyond the street for wheelchair users like Stephen. Through the politicisation and campaigning against unequal access to the street and other elements that enable social lives to be made and remade, physical differences might simply remain differences rather than become inequalities.

Summary

- People face a range of both choices and constraints in making and remaking their lives.
- The making and remaking of social lives on the street and in wider society is characterised by both differences and inequalities.
- Choices and constraints may vary over time and space, with some being fluid and others being more fixed.

4   Module questions

4.1   How is society made and remade?

This chapter has shown that society is made and remade through the two-way relationship between the individual and society. Lives are made both consciously, through the choices and constraints that people are aware of, and subconsciously, through more subtle forms of choices and constraints that may be external and self-imposed. How lives are made can in some aspects seem fixed, but in other aspects be more fluid, changing over time and space. Yet, some people have a greater ability to fashion their lives in ways and forms of their own making than others, and this too can vary as a result of a range of factors such as socio-economic position, race, ethnicity, age, disability, sexuality and gender.

4.2   How are differences and inequalities produced?

The ways people make their social lives on the street, and the changes and continuities that are part of this, also have consequences for who benefits and who loses out. In their social lives, people both cooperate and compete with others and, to an extent, with the street itself. People compete for resources, opportunities and power on the street with other individuals and groups, and making the street in one way rather than another has implications for who gains and who loses out in contemporary society.

Looking at the role of consumption is one way of seeing how differences and inequalities are produced. Sometimes differences may simply be an expression of different groups wanting different products, services or environments with which to make their lives. In other cases, differences become inequalities, as consumption produces winners and losers: specific shops appeal to certain groups, limiting choice for others; the physical street is made in ways that facilitate the ability of some groups to make their lives as they choose, while hindering the ability of others to do so; large companies can exert economic power over smaller retailers; some people have to use facilities – the food bank or payback schemes – because of their socio-economic position, so that the choice over how they participate in decisions about their lives is taken out of their hands altogether. These are just some examples of how lives are made and remade in unequal ways on City Road.

4.3   How do social scientists know?

In this chapter, the street provides a place from which to observe the interactions and activities that shape and make the lives of people and those around them. From observation, social scientists can describe the factors that enable people to make choices in their lives, and start to ask questions about how they exercise choice and the constraints that may prevent this. Social science involves moving on from initial observations and descriptions of the street to questions about how the different aspects of consumption impact on how people live their social lives on the street. Concepts such as 'choice' and 'constraint', and how these are linked to consumption, help to shape the questions social scientists are interested in posing about the links between individuals and society, and how some of these change over time while others remain constant.

References

The Open University (2014a) 'Making lives' [Video], *DD102 Introducing the social sciences*. Available at https://learn2.open.ac.uk/mod/oucontent/view.php?id=443987&section=3 (Accessed 10 March 2014).

The Open University (2014b) 'The Life and Times of the Street: Part 1' [Video], *DD102 Introducing the social sciences*. Available at https://learn2.open.ac.uk/mod/oucontent/view.php?id=443760&section=2.3 (Accessed 10 March 2014).

Chapter 3
Connecting lives

Catriona Havard

Contents

Introduction

Imagine that you are wandering down a street on your own. Yet, are you really alone? Who and what are you connected to? Perhaps you are meeting a friend for a coffee or you are going to buy some food to cook for your family that evening. You might be talking on your mobile phone to somebody or listening to music on headphones. You could be on your way to work or on your way home. You might be on a street that you use regularly or you might be on an unfamiliar street that you are visiting for the first time.

Although streets might appear to be a collection of isolated individuals, people are connected to each other, to places and to things in various ways. People are also connected to each other through relationships and the activities they engage in, for example to family, friends, work colleagues, clients, customers and patients. People are even connected to others whom they don't know at all. For example, there are rules to follow when walking down the street and following these rules provides connections – and disconnections if someone doesn't follow the rules. People can be connected through the street itself and to places and buildings, for example connections are made through shopping, working and socialising in different locations. Things such as cars, work tools, mobile phones and other technological devices also connect people.

Figure 3.1 shows a mind map with descriptions of some of the connections that I have with people, places and things. As you can see from Figure 3.1, there are connections with *people*, such as family (son, husband, parents), work colleagues and friends. Yet, these connections are also linked to places such as my son's school, my workplace and, more geographically, Scotland, where I am originally from. The connections with my family, friends and work are the strongest connections in my life – through emotional ties as well as everyday familiarity, life experience and frequent contact, even if, with my parents, this is more often conducted at a distance.

There are also other connections with *places* such as the gym, the local pub, the allotment and the library, and connections to the people who use these places for a range of activities. The connections with people and places link to connections that I have with things and specific objects: when I visit my family in Scotland, I use my car to get there; when I go to the gym, I always like to go on the cross-trainer; and when I go to work, I use my computer. Some of the connections change over time: for example, I did not always have an allotment and, prior to having my son, I may have had stronger connections to the local pub than I do now! Disconnections can result as former connections change over time.

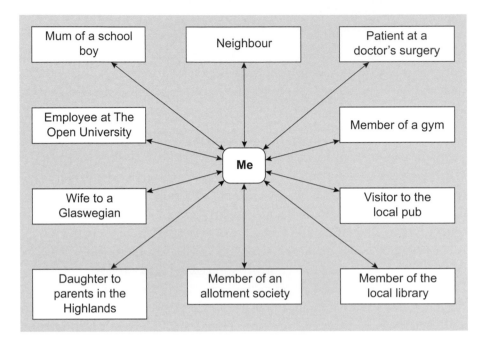

Figure 3.1   Mind map of connections

Activity 1

Draw your own mind map of connections to places, people and things. Which connections are the strongest? Which are the weakest? Have any of the connections changed over time?

You might wish to post your 'connections map' or provide a few examples of some of the connections you have on your tutor group forum.

City Road, like any other street, is a good example of connecting lives. It provides examples of the ways in which people are connected to, and disconnected from, each other, places and things. Social scientists try to look beyond the individual stories and examples of connections and disconnections to try to understand the patterns beneath these individual experiences. Although the film *Connecting Lives* (The Open

University, 2014a) focuses on one road, City Road in Cardiff, and on the individuals and the connections and disconnections they experience, any street in the contemporary UK would offer a similar sense of the ways in which society is made and remade through connections and disconnections. The different ways in which people relate to each other and the places where they live and work, and how they are sometimes disconnected, are also part of the way in which people's identities, as well as the **identity** of places, are made through connections and disconnections. This forms the subject matter of the second strand of the module – 'Connecting lives'.

Identity
Combines a person's sense of self (sometimes described as 'personal identity') – who you think you are – and how society perceives you.

1   Change and continuity

Society is made and remade through the connections and disconnections that people experience, and these are often influenced by change and continuity. Connections can be durable even if they are made and remade in the face of change. In *Connecting Lives* (The Open University, 2014a), Mark Hocking has worked on City Road for over 30 years and has long-standing connections with the area, although the nature of these connections has changed over time in response to economic changes. Mark notes with satisfaction that he has been able to maintain his connections to City Road even if he had to reinvent himself and his business to do so. He describes his former connections to the village of Roath and the long-established community there, whose cars he used to repair. He also notes that economic change meant the closure of his original business and disrupted his own connections, as well as creating a vacuum on City Road. Mark successfully reinvented himself and made connections to new clients by becoming an industrial designer, yet he remains connected to City Road.

Figure 3.2   Mark Hocking

In *Connecting Lives* (The Open University, 2014a), the restaurant owner, Nof Al-Kelaby, also has a long history of connections to City Road, which have changed as his restaurant businesses were forced to adapt in response to socio-economic change. Like Mark, Nof has successfully reinvented himself and his business, which keeps him connected to City Road. He previously owned a Hawaiian-themed restaurant, which used to be very popular for celebrations such as hen parties. However, as competition from large restaurants in the newly redeveloped Cardiff Bay area increased, business at The Hawaiian restaurant slowed down and Nof eventually closed this restaurant. He now has an Arabic restaurant called La Shish, which has allowed him to build a new set of connections to different groups on City Road and to reconnect to the Iraqi culture of his past. The new theme of the restaurant caters for the rising number of people from certain minority ethnic groups on City Road, especially the Arab community. By closing the original restaurant and then reopening with a different theme, Nof has formed new connections with a different set of clientele and revitalised his business and connections to City Road. Disconnections, therefore, can be productive and can make for new connections, and new or renewed identities.

Connections and disconnections are not just made and remade at the level of the individual. City Road, and the wider society of which it is a part, is also made and remade through these changing connections and disconnections. City Road has never existed in a bubble, but has always been linked to other places. Historically, City Road grew from a small country lane to a busy thoroughfare as a result of the growing coal industry in Wales. When Cardiff boomed as a port, exporting coal around the world, City Road was shaped by these new global connections and economic developments. Traces of some of these connections and disconnections can be seen in the buildings on and around City Road – from the terraced housing for the dock and factory workers to the north and east, to the much larger houses for the wealthy Victorian entrepreneurs to the west and south. Migrants have settled on City Road throughout its history – migrants from other places in the UK, and migrants from around the world who came to work in the port and in the coal mines of South Wales. In this way, City Road is made and remade through these connections to people and places. Today, it seems like the world is on City Road: in the people who settle there from all over the world; in the products sold there from all over the globe; and in the connections to other places that are made possible and speeded up by technology.

The development of new technologies in particular can make and remake connections and disconnections among people, places and things. The internet has meant that people and places can now be quickly connected to one another without being in physical proximity.

Figure 3.3   Sheri Hall who writes an online blog about City Road

Sheri Hall has tried to foster social and business connections on City Road by creating a blog that helps to promote business on City Road, where people can follow links to individual websites (Hall, 2013). Sheri's blog has fostered connections not only for businesses in the local community and Cardiff, but also across the world, where anyone with internet access can look at the businesses on City Road that have an online presence on Sheri's blog. For example, Turkish food sold on City Road becomes the connecting point linking people in a virtual community all around the world. Yet, connections can only be made through the use of technology and the internet if people have access to the internet and the skills to use it. Businesses that did not want to take part in the blog are disconnected from a possible wider clientele. In *Connecting Lives* (The Open University, 2014a), Sheri describes people's anxieties and suspicions when they are faced with this new way of connecting lives, and it is interesting that many businesses wanted to see her in person before becoming involved.

Activity 2

List some of the ways in which technology (perhaps a mobile phone, Skype or FaceTime) has changed the ways in which you make and remake connections.

You might want to share your ideas on the tutor group forum with others in your tutor group.

Not all connections can be sustained in the face of change. Change can bring disconnections, where existing connections are undone or changed. Both Mark and Nof have been able to maintain their connections to City Road through making new connections in response to the economic changes that affected their original businesses. Some changes, however, can occur very quickly or can be so dramatic in their nature that people can feel profoundly disconnected, and rebuilding connections can take time.

In *Connecting Lives* (The Open University, 2014a), the people at the food bank show just how precarious individual lives, and the connections that make up these lives, can be. One person relates how, in the space of a few days, he has gone from being somebody who had a wife, family and job, to somebody who has split up from his wife and is now unemployed and homeless. This illustrates how quickly disconnections can develop from a couple of incidents, such as the break-up of a relationship or an accident at work, which can lead to homelessness and unemployment. Events such as these show how fragile connections can be and how easily they can be broken, leading to dramatic changes in life circumstances. Not everyone is able to make new connections from disconnections.

Figure 3.4   John Arthur and his dog

John Arthur's story in *Connecting Lives* (The Open University, 2014a) shows how disconnections can spiral and how they can be long-lasting. On the one hand, a series of factors such as alcoholism, being taken into care, unemployed, in prison and/or homeless have led to a deep disconnection from society. All these aspects of John's life are linked. Homeless people like John who have to sleep rough on the street appear not to be connected at all, but excluded or disconnected from society. On the other hand, John is not completely disconnected and he tells of some of the connections he has been able to make. He describes how he likes Cardiff because it is a port city and he likes the diversity of people, which tends to characterise port cities. He feels that he is as much a migrant as those who come to City Road from abroad. John also has some connections with the students in the area who make him cups of tea and the Salvation Army who distributes blankets.

Stephen Sweetman's story in *Connecting Lives* (The Open University, 2014a) provides a different take on how a person can come to feel a deep sense of disconnection from society. Although Stephen has long-standing connections with City Road, these come from a past when he was able-bodied. His story thus illustrates how important people's bodies can be in the connections people make with the places they live and how these can be disrupted when people's bodies change. When his accident first occurred, Stephen describes how disconnected his disability and lack of mobility made him feel – to the extent that he didn't leave the house for almost two years. Having a disability can disconnect people from places, particularly when the physical environment is not adapted for people with mobility problems. Many places do not cater for wheelchair users, for example some shop doors are not wide enough or have a step or edge that does not allow the wheelchair user access. Stephen describes how difficult getting around in a wheelchair can be even though he is able to afford a more lightweight wheelchair than those usually available through the National Health Service.

Even buildings and events that have been designed to cater for wheelchair access can still make wheelchair users feel disconnected. Stephen describes how a family outing was spoiled when he went to a concert, as he was unable to sit next to his family. In this instance, having a disability disconnected Stephen from his family both physically, by making him sit two rows behind his family, and emotionally, by not being able to enjoy the concert together. However, with time and the support of his family, and by working for change in the environment in which he lives, Stephen has been able to make new connections and feel reconnected to his own body. In particular, he describes how he feels connected to other disabled people – both to those who have campaigned before him to improve the lives of disabled people and to future generations of disabled people for whom Stephen is striving to make things better.

Figure 3.5   Stephen Sweetman with his wheelchair

Summary

- The connections and disconnections that people experience make and remake social lives on the street and in wider society.

- Connections and disconnections are subject to both change and continuity, but not everyone is equally placed to maintain connections or to make new connections in the face of change.

- New technologies can make and remake connections and disconnections among people, places and things.

2   Personal and social worlds

Personal and social worlds are not separate. The personal – what is going on inside each person's head, how individuals feel about the connections and disconnections that make up personal lives – is linked to the social – the societies in which people live and the various factors that shape people's connections and disconnections.

The personal world is where people experience things on an individual level and their sense of **self**. The 'self' is everything that makes up a person and makes them distinctive in relation to other people. A sense of self, however, is shaped by the particular connections and disconnections that a person has to the places, people and things around them, and this can change, for example when any of these relations alter or new connections are made.

Self
Everything that makes a person and distinguishes them from other people.

Not all connections are possible and not all connections can be maintained in the face of social change or in changes in personal circumstances, such as having a baby, ill health, accidents or just getting older, as well as getting a new job, moving house or new relationships. Change makes for new connections and disconnections. Connections are not fixed for all times. The lives of the people on City Road in *Connecting Lives* (The Open University, 2014a) show that connecting and disconnecting are processes, as people change in relation to the social world they live in.

Migration, moving from one place to another, perhaps as a result of a new job in a new location or moving to another place to begin study, can result in disconnections from places. Moving can also mean disconnections with people who were once associated with a place, such as friends and family who no longer live nearby. The experience of migration can be disruptive: there may be partial disconnections from one place and new connections (and disconnections) to another.

In *Connecting Lives* (The Open University, 2014a), Bushra Fleih provides a sense of the connections that are important to her and her sense of self, and how they have been altered by the process of migration. Bushra mentions that in Iraq she used to work as a micro-biologist, but she is not sure how to go about finding work in the UK. Her work connections have thus been disrupted by migration to Cardiff. She is also a new mother and describes how the experience of becoming a mother strengthened the importance of her existing connections to her family, as 'everything changed' when her daughter was born.

Many women feel their sense of self alters once they become a mother and have to care for another person, and this changing sense of self can be particularly acute when the process of becoming a mother coincides with another major change like migration. It is clearly important for Bushra that she is able to maintain her existing family connections through Skype, as she is now far from her family and home in Iraq, and therefore physically disconnected from her family, friends and place of origin. This illustrates another way in which connections can be maintained through the use of different technologies.

Figure 3.6   Bushra Fleih using Skype to talk to family in Iraq

Stephen's experience in becoming disabled also profoundly changed his personal world and the ways in which he felt connected to the wider social world. Initially, his sense of self was altered to the extent that he felt deeply disconnected from society. He describes how he resisted using a wheelchair because that was for 'older people' and 'disabled people', and he didn't feel that he was one of them. Stephen later talks about how he made new connections to other disabled people and identified with those activists who had campaigned before him to improve the lives of disabled people. He relates how he now wants to campaign to make things better for future generations of disabled people. Becoming disabled changed how Stephen saw himself, resulting in his disconnection from society. Yet, now Stephen sees himself as a disability activist, an identity he is proud to claim, and he has made new connections to the wider social world.

Migration or other life-changing events such as becoming a mother or becoming disabled are not the only factors that can change a person's sense of self: sometimes making new connections in the same place or trying something new can change a person's sense of self. Nof, for example, appears to have changed his sense of self in opening the La Shish restaurant, as he feels more in touch with his former Iraqi roots and with the Arab clientele who now frequent his business. This illustrates how his personal, inner world – how he feels about the connections and disconnections that make up his personal life – has been changed by the connections he has remade to his former Iraqi culture. His new business, and the connections he has established through it, has changed the way he now feels about himself.

Figure 3.7   Nof Al-Kelaby in his La Shish restaurant

Personal and social lives are also connected by things. Although Stephen initially rejected using a wheelchair, this object is now very much part of his sense of self and his identity as a disability activist. The wheelchair, and particularly the lightweight model he was able to buy, allows him to connect with the social world through facilitating everyday activities such as shopping and going out. Other objects, such as gifts from loved ones or photographs of past events with family and friends, make and remake connections. Some objects, particularly new technologies, provide links between people and to distant places.

Some social scientists suggest that the objects people own can be perceived as an extension of the self. For example, owning a particular mobile phone or wearing certain brands of clothing can be a statement of a person's sense of self. Similarly, through owning certain objects, people can also try to change their sense of self and be someone they aspire to be: perhaps somebody who is more attractive or more affluent. Yet, not everybody can afford the objects they aspire to own and this can lead to a sense of disconnection. Similarly, the loss of an object can lead to a sense of disconnection because people are often emotionally attached to the objects they own. It is not uncommon today to hear people saying that they have their lives stored on their mobile phones, so losing a mobile phone can indeed feel like losing a rich set of connections. This can vary from the practical and mundane sense of being disconnected as a result of losing people's phone numbers, to a more emotional sense of feeling disconnected after losing photos or messages from loved ones.

Activity 3

Choose one object you own and jot down brief answers to the following questions:

- What meaning does the object have for you?
- How does it connect you to other people and places?
- How would you manage if it was taken away?
- Does it remind you of a person/people or a place?

My mobile phone doesn't have particular meaning for me, but it is extremely useful and I would be lost without it. It connects me to all my family and friends. I also have photos stored on it, which I would hate to lose as they remind me of happy occasions. I would manage quite badly if it was taken away, as I would feel unable to connect with people if I needed to.

Summary

- The personal, how individuals feel about the connections and disconnections that make up their personal lives, is linked to the social – the societies in which people live and the various factors that shape people's connections and disconnections.

- Society makes and remakes people, but society is also made and remade by the multiple connections and disconnections between people, and between people, places and things.

- Not all connections are possible and not all connections can be maintained in the face of personal and social change.

3   Identity

Connections and disconnections make and remake society and people's lives, but society also makes and remakes people and their sense of who they are – their identities. Identity, as John Clarke claims in *Connecting Lives* (The Open University, 2014a), is a powerful point of connection between the personal and the social because it is about who a person thinks s/he is and who other people think s/he is. Who people are is determined by their connections to other people and how they are seen by the people around them. A person's identity is attributed to them by other people and it is not always chosen.

Taking some of the people in *Connecting Lives* (The Open University, 2014a) as examples, Bushra might be described as a woman, a migrant from Iraq and a mother. John Arthur might be described as male, white and homeless. In each case, these are **social identities**, which are given to these two individuals on the basis of how they look, the activities they are engaged in and the information given about them in the film. These social identities connect them to other people and other situations, and highlight both what they have in common with people who share the same identity and what differentiates them from people who do not share this identity. Identities refer to difference as well as similarity. In each case, however, these descriptions might not be how either Bushra or John would choose to describe themselves.

Social identities
An identity given by connections to other people and social situations (often contrasted with personal identity).

A person's sense of self – their personal world – can be at odds with the social identities given to them by their connections to other people and social situations. This tension can be clearly seen in Stephen's story in *Connecting Lives* (The Open University, 2014a) where he initially rejects the idea of using a wheelchair because that would clearly label him as 'disabled'. Stephen has not chosen to become a disabled person: this is an identity that has been thrust upon him. As time passes, however, Stephen is proud to adopt the identity of a disability activist and this identity connects him to a network of activists with disabilities who share this common identity.

Similarly, Nof in *Connecting Lives* (The Open University, 2014a) describes the tension between his national and cultural identity, as an Iraqi, and the British identity he now feels due to his connections over time to City Road and Cardiff. He questions if he is 'in between'. This illustrates the tension between who Nof feels he is and how he is seen by others because our identities are partly given by society – by how other people see us.

Tensions also arise because people have multiple and overlapping identities. Nof feels simultaneously, Iraqi, British and 'in between'. He has connections to both countries, but he says that to some extent he feels out of place in both. Yet, at the same time, he also has an identity as a result of his occupation. He is a local restaurant owner despite the fact that he originally trained as an engineer. In fact, he opened his first restaurant (The Hawaiian) because he could not get a job as an engineer despite the fact that he had made over 250 job applications. This is a common experience for migrants who are often unable to gain the employment they have been trained for.

In every society, some people are accepted as 'normal', others marked as 'odd': in other words, some identities are positively valued, while others have negatively valued identities. Nof is clearly successful, but many migrants have to take up jobs that have a relatively low social value because they are marked as 'different' – their identities are negatively valued. Nof may be a UK citizen and a resident who has lived and worked in Cardiff for many years, contributing to the economy and running popular restaurants that are visited by many people, but, for some, Nof's skin colour and accent continue to mark him as racially or ethnically different, as 'not British' and 'not Welsh'.

Activity 4

Think of ten possible answers to the question 'Who am I?'. Don't think too long about it! Spend a few minutes writing your answers down.

Then try to organise your answers into those identities that you think you have chosen and those that you think are imposed. Are any of your answers group identities (for example, related to gender, class, ethnicity and/or nationality)? How do you feel others see this group?

It is not only people who have identities: places also have their own identities as a result of the connections and disconnections that make and remake them. City Road has been shaped by connections to many other places and this has shaped its identity as a street of restaurants and takeaway outlets, which represent cultures from all over the world. There is a Lebanese restaurant, a Mexican restaurant, Nof's Arabic La Shish restaurant to name just a few. Each of these restaurants in turn also represents a particular national identity, which has become a commercial identity or brand for a particular kind of food and evening's entertainment.

The identity of Nof's first restaurant, The Hawaiian, is particularly complex. Although it is called The Hawaiian, Nof took the idea of the restaurant not from the place in the Pacific, but from an Elvis Presley film, *Blue Hawaii*. This film presented an image of Hawaii that had become widespread in the 1950s and 1960s, as a romantic island paradise of sunshine and beautiful beaches. Of course, the image was selective even then, and the place itself has changed since, so that a contemporary resident of Hawaii might be quite surprised at how it was depicted in Nof's restaurant. However, the image that attracted Nof has persisted as part of popular culture, and in particular, contemporary ideas of a perfect holiday. The identity of Nof's first restaurant, then, was connected less to an imagined place, Hawaii, than to an imagined experience of going on holiday.

Identities are not static: they change as people's lives and their circumstances change. Migration is one example that disrupts a person's sense of identity, but people can take up new identities through education and work. Identities can also change through the ageing process, as people move through different life stages and new relationships. The identities of people who continue to live in the same place all their lives will also be affected by the changing identity of the place itself, as the example of Mark Hocking in *Connecting Lives* (The Open University, 2014a) illustrated. In addition, sometimes people choose to change their identity as their own sense of self changes. For example, in *Connecting Lives* (The Open University, 2014a) Monique chose to change her identity when she changed her religious beliefs from Christianity to Islam.

Figure 3.8   Monique Waheed outside the Islamic Relief charity shop

Activity 5

Look at the list of identities you noted for Activity 4 in response to the question 'Who am I?'.

Now do a similar list for yourself when you were aged 8–10 and for yourself in the future (20 years from now). Which identities are the same and which might have changed?

Not all choices are possible. Psychologists use the term 'label' to refer to an identity that is negatively valued and generally imposed by one person on another, rather than chosen. In *Connecting Lives* (The Open University, 2014a) John Arthur talks about how people sometimes throw bottles at his head because he is labelled as a homeless person who is responsible for his own situation rather than an individual with his own history of misfortunes. This negative identity – a homeless person – is a label given to him by other people. Not all identities are equally valued and, in this way, some identities can form the basis of **stereotypes**. This is when beliefs are held about a group of individuals that do not necessarily reflect reality. Moreover, stereotypes, like labels, involve seeing groups of people as somehow the same and defined by a single exaggerated characteristic.

Stereotypes
A widely held, but fixed and oversimplified, image or idea of a particular type of person or thing.

Forming stereotypes can influence decisions about whether someone belongs to their social group or not and, by doing so, can create

in-groups and **out-groups**. This is illustrated by the young people in the Pool Hall whom you met in the film *Making Lives* (The Open University, 2014b). When the young woman from Nottingham, newly arrived in Cardiff, joined the group of friends, she made her initial contact to become friends with them by saying 'you kinda look like me'. This shows that when she saw this group she thought that they would be like her, perhaps because of the clothes they were wearing or what they were doing, and categorised them as part of an in-group. Stereotyping involves an oversimplified way of making connections and disconnections.

However, when people are categorised as being different, they are seen as being from an out-group. When individuals look at people from an in-group (for example, same race and age), they are often much better at recognising their faces, even if they are unfamiliar, and worse at recognising faces from an out-group (different race and age). This bias in recognition could be a result of a lack of contact between people from different groups: if individuals are not used to seeing people from different races or different ages, for example, they have not developed the skills to recognise their faces. An alternative explanation might be that, when looking at the faces of people from an out-group, people do not pay attention to those from an out-group in the same way they would to people from their in-group. At one time it was not uncommon to hear people say things such as 'well, they all look the same to me' when talking about people from a different race to themselves. Stereotypes and in-group bias therefore can lead to prejudice and **discrimination**. It has already been noted that John Arthur has been on the receiving end of prejudice and abuse because he is labelled as a homeless person by others. Migrants can also be discriminated against, particularly if their skin colour or accents mark them as racially or ethnically different.

In-groups
People who are categorised as belonging to the same social, ethnic or age group.

Out-groups
People who are categorised as not belonging to the same social, ethnic or age group.

Discrimination
The unequal treatment of groups identified on the basis of difference, for example race and ethnicity, class, gender, age and disability.

Summary

- Identity is a powerful point of connection between the personal and the social because it is about who a person thinks s/he is and who other people think s/he is.

- People's identities are given by their ordinary life activities, places in their lives (past and present), their relationships with others and also by how people see them.

- Places as well as people have identities, and these are formed by connections and disconnections.

4 Module questions

4.1 How is society made and remade?

Society might look like a collection of isolated individuals, but people are connected to each other, places and things in various ways. These connections and disconnections, and the ways they stay the same or change over time, make and remake society in particular ways. People are connected to each other through relationships and through the activities they engage in. People are also connected to places and things. Yet, even as people make society, society also makes people – some connections and disconnections are possible, and some are not.

4.2 How are differences and inequalities produced?

Connections and disconnections make and remake society and people's lives, but society also makes and remakes people and their sense of who they are – their identities. Identity is about what a person has in common with others like them as well as about what makes them different. Yet, what makes people different is not always positively valued. Certain identities are positively valued in society while others are negatively valued. Some people might be excluded and treated both differently and unequally if their identity is not valued by others.

4.3 How do social scientists know?

In the film *Connecting Lives* (The Open University, 2014a), a number of individuals described their connections and talked about how they feel about themselves – who they think they are. This kind of description helps social scientists to understand how people feel about themselves and what connects people's personal worlds to the wider social world. From these individual experiences, social scientists are interested in asking what patterns and regularities lie beneath these individual experiences. Social science inquiry involves asking how City Road and the people we have met there might resemble others in the contemporary UK and elsewhere, and how their experiences might fit into wider patterns, and be shaped by them.

References

Hall, S. (2013) *City Road* [Online]. Available at http://cardiffcityroad.wordpress.com/2012/11/20/194/ (Accessed 10 March 2014).

The Open University (2014a) 'Connecting Lives' [Video], *DD102 Introducing the social sciences*. Available at https://learn2.open.ac.uk/mod/oucontent/view.php?id=444007&section=2 (Accessed 10 March 2014).

The Open University (2014b) 'Making Lives' [Video], *DD102 Introducing the social sciences*. Available at https://learn2.open.ac.uk/mod/oucontent/view.php?id=443987&section=3 (Accessed 10 March 2014).

Chapter 4
Ordering lives

Georgina Blakeley

Contents

Introduction

Have you ever looked at a busy street and wondered why it is that it generally seems to work so smoothly? People don't usually tend to collide with the street furniture that crowds the pavements, from street lights to rubbish bins and skips; material objects like street lights and traffic lights, drains and sewers tend to function as intended; people don't normally bump into other people, no matter how busy the street might be; and people tend to know how to get along with each other in the public space of the street. All of this is a kind of social ordering which, because it generally works so well, goes unnoticed by the majority of people as they go about their daily lives. Indeed, it is often only when things go wrong – due to a traffic accident, an overflowing drain or someone jumping a queue, perhaps – that questions are raised about how social lives are ordered.

When this social order fails to work as expected, two things become apparent:

- the expectations of order and the efforts that go into its making and remaking suddenly become visible
- the relationship between order and disorder becomes evident. It is often only when disorder occurs and is examined that insight into how order works can be gained.

City Road, like any other street, provides a useful starting point to explore questions about how social lives are ordered because it presents a moving picture of different sorts of people, what they are doing, their relations to each other, and the connections between people and the vast array of material objects, technologies and waste that surrounds them. Social scientists are interested in describing and explaining this complex combination of people and their relationships to the world around them, and this is one way in which social scientists can begin to know about social order and disorder. What particularly interests us here is how social order is made and remade through this complex combination of people and their activities, their daily routines, expected and standardised behaviours, and the relations between people and material objects. This forms the subject matter of the third strand of the module – 'Ordering lives'.

1   Change and continuity

In the film *Ordering Lives* (The Open University, 2014), there are numerous examples of the making and remaking of social order that takes place through what people are doing. For example, the street-cleaner who cleans the pavement tries to keep the street usable and pleasant as a social environment in which people can go about their daily lives. The mother who teaches her children how to cross the road safely is also contributing to the smooth ordering of life on the street. There are also various examples of the ordering that takes place through people's relations to material objects: the street signs that direct people to behave in particular ways; the menus and price lists in shops; the CCTV cameras that watch over the street; the regulation of access to particular places such as pubs and nightclubs. This kind of ordering often goes unnoticed by the majority of people who take such ordering of their daily lives for granted.

Figure 4.1   Street-cleaner picking up litter on City Road

This taken-for-granted quality of social ordering sheds light on two aspects of social order and why it generally works. First, social order in the contemporary UK works (most of the time) because people live their lives within a society that is already made and ordered (to some extent at least). Individuals take their place – and indeed often 'know' their place – within a society in which lives are already ordered. This links to the second point, namely, that social order works (most of the time) because people have learnt both the official and the informal rules about how to behave in particular places, with specific sorts of people, in certain types of interaction.

Children usually learn how to cross the road safely and behave appropriately in the street. In the process, they come to recognise that the street is a particular location, a public space that requires routines and behaviours, which are different from those at home. Social scientists call these processes of learning **socialisation** – and people learn through formal processes (the training that is expected of families, schools and other social institutions). People also learn about expectations and rules of behaviour from many other sources – from peers, through the media and even by experimenting and discovering what happens when they break such rules. In this process, social order is made and remade through learnt routines or habits, and through behaviour that becomes standardised and expected.

Socialisation
The ways in which people become social beings by conforming to the beliefs, norms and values of their society.

Activity 1

'Rules' are often specific to a particular time and place. Can you think of an example where the accepted rules are in the process of change? Or where the 'rules' are different in another country?

Smoking is one example where the accepted rules have changed: all public transport in the UK now expressly forbids smoking, as do pubs and restaurants. How acceptable smoking is, however, can vary between places and times of the day.

The taken-for-granted quality of social ordering, which implies that individuals act within a society that is already made to a significant degree and that individuals know how to act in an orderly fashion, highlights continuity in social ordering. But change does occur. Although people tend to behave in orderly, rather than **disorderly**, ways not everyone will agree on what are desired forms of behaviour and interaction – on what is 'appropriate'.

Disorderly
Disturbing the public peace, or acting in an unruly manner, or behaviour that is labelled as contrary to a desired or imagined state of social order.

Small-scale – and more occasionally large-scale – social conflicts often centre on arguments about whose rules should define social order. Moreover, the ability to define the rules is not shared equally by everyone in society. Some individuals have more power than others to define what counts as social order and disorder, for example students entering a bar have little power to define acceptable behaviour and dress code, compared to the bouncers who enforce these rules. As some students on City Road describe in the film *Ordering Lives* (The Open University, 2014), trainers acceptable on one occasion might be deemed unacceptable on another.

People sometimes challenge 'accepted' ways of doing things and their allotted place within society. Such challenges can range from leaving a fridge on the street to the anarchists' illegal occupation of the Gaiety Cinema on City Road (The Open University, 2014). Sometimes such challenges will lead to changes in the existing social order; sometimes such challenges will provoke a strengthening of the existing social order. The anarchists were eventually evicted from the Gaiety Cinema through a court order enforced by the police.

Figure 4.2   Anarchist occupation of the Gaiety Cinema

Sometimes people get into trouble for challenging and trying to change social order, such that changing order can be equated with creating disorder. In this respect, 'the eyes of the beholder' are important in deciding what gets defined as social *order* and what gets defined as *dis*order. The anarchist squatters on City Road illustrate this point well. In the media, 'anarchism' is often a byword for disorderly behaviour, and squatting as an activity is considered illegal and against the grain of a social order in which home ownership is a key feature. For anarchists themselves, however, it is the current unequal social order in which some people can afford homes and others cannot, rather than squatting, that is the source of disorder. Anarchists might argue that their vision is an alternative form of social *order*ing, which is based on the ability of individuals to organise themselves to provide order without the need for **authority** in the form of the police or governments, not *dis*order.

Much of the work that people are doing on City Road involves making and remaking everyday social order in the face of real or perceived disruptions or disorder – bearing in mind that perceptions of disorder can be just as significant as the disorder that might actually occur.

In *Ordering Lives* (The Open University, 2014), June, the lollipop lady who is employed by the local authority to help people – especially children – cross a busy road that's near to schools, provides a good example of how social order can be remade when it is disrupted. June wears highly visible clothing, which signals that when she is working she has a particular role to play. She also has particular tools at her disposal to make social order, not the least her oversized sign that resembles a 'lollipop stick'. She contributes to maintaining social order by using her sign and uniform to order the flow and interaction of parents, children and the traffic. But she also smoothes over potential disruptions of social order when, for example, a car stops on the pedestrian crossing and she tells the car to reverse to the appropriate place. What is also interesting here is the extent to which an individual's own sense of what is orderly and disorderly comes into play. June refers to one parent whom she believes doesn't manage his child as he should and announces, metaphorically, to show the level of her irritation: 'I could hit him!' This illustrates how what is considered orderly and disorderly behaviour, or appropriate and inappropriate behaviour, is not simply pre-given, but actively negotiated by individuals in their interactions in specific social settings.

In *Ordering Lives* (The Open University, 2014), Jerome, who is stopped by the police for driving without a licence or insurance, also demonstrates how individuals are often aware of what is orderly or disorderly behaviour, even when consciously pushing at the boundaries of social order. In acknowledging his fault and by saying he will learn from the incident, Jerome shows an awareness of the rules that govern this field of social order and the extent to which he has broken them. But in a small way this reminds us that social order is made and remade in social interactions, rather than being a solid block of rules and norms. In such interactions, especially when people experiment or challenge the rules, social order may change. No social order is permanently fixed – it is susceptible to change, as people change their views, expectations and desires about how lives should be lived.

Authority
The power to enforce rules or give orders that are likely to be obeyed.

Figure 4.3   June Rogers, the lollipop lady, stops traffic on City Road

Activity 2

What do you think you personally do that contributes to order and disorder when you are in a public space such as a street? Try to provide at least one example each for order and disorder. Make a note of your responses. Why not post some examples on your tutor group forum?

Summary

- Social order is made in part by people acting and interacting according to shared rules or expectations about how to behave and relate to their social and material surroundings.

- Very often, these shared rules and expectations are taken for granted and it is only when they are broken or breached that people notice that something is out of order or disordered.

- The power to define what counts as social order and disorder is not shared equally by everyone in society.

2   The private and the public

The idea of social order implies a sense that there is a larger context in which people act, whether this is at the micro-level of a home, school, street or neighbourhood or at the macro-level of the nation state or even a global social order. The context within which social ordering takes place is important in providing a sense of expectation – of what might be acceptable in one context, but not another – and in providing a sense of predictability, of knowing how to act and how other people will act. When people step out of their homes and into the street, they step from a personal and private space into a public one and, in so doing, become public and subject to different rules and expectations of how to behave in the public space of the street compared to the personal and private space of the home.

Through the processes of socialisation, referred to in Section 1, individuals learn what kinds of behaviour and practice are acceptable in one space compared to another. Thus, when people 'go out in public' and have to get along with others in the public space of the street, social order is generally made and remade smoothly from the complex combinations of people and their activities, expected and standardised behaviours, and the relations between people and the normal functioning of material objects.

Conversely, disorder can arise from activities and behaviours that are unexpected in the public space of the street or from material objects, which stop functioning in expected ways or are in the 'wrong' place such as the fridge left in the street in *Ordering Lives* (The Open University, 2014), rather than in its 'usual' private space of the home. *When* something occurs is also important – people's perceptions about what counts as disorder can vary depending on whether it is day or night. People's anxieties about disorder can be greater at night-time.

The appearance of the private and personal in public can disrupt the smooth running of social order because it unsettles the sense of expectation – of what might be acceptable in one context, but not another – and the sense of predictability, of knowing how to act and how other people will act. Practices and behaviours that are unexpected in the public space of the street might include excessive displays of affection or emotion, as in the night-time scenes on City Road in *Ordering Lives* (The Open University, 2014) when expectations of what is acceptable can change after alcohol is consumed. Similarly, the sight of a homeless person bedding down for the night in a shop doorway or a bus shelter can unsettle notions of acceptability and predictability because going to bed is a personal act normally carried out in a private space, rather than the public space of the street.

Processes and practices of social ordering can also be unsettled because the line between the public and the private is not a clear and settled one – it is a boundary that shifts, can vary across cultures and time, and is subject to negotiation, as definitions of what is public and what is private are contested. New technology, such as the ubiquitous mobile phone, can give rise to changing notions of what counts as public, private and personal spaces, and thus what might be acceptable in one context but not another. The ability to engage in a 'private' conversation within the 'public' space of the street blurs the boundary between private and public and, in so doing, can disrupt existing modes of ordering by changing what behaviours and practices are appropriate. For example, it might be acceptable for some individuals to conduct a 'personal' conversation on a mobile phone in the public space of the street when details of this conversation can be overheard, while for others this behaviour is intrusive and inappropriate within a public space.

Figure 4.4   Using a mobile phone on City Road: private or public?

The use of a mobile phone within the public space of the street might also change people's ability to become 'public' or to remain 'private' while in the street. The ability to use a mobile phone to connect to others on a personal basis while in the public space of the street can alter people's perception of what is public and what is personal and private, and thus what is acceptable behaviour in each space. This can also be seen in the increasing number of ways in which people can choose to remain in their own private and personal space while being in the public space of the street through mobile-phone usage or listening to music through headphones.

Of course, another possibility might be that people are connecting themselves to others in a virtual public space, such as the internet, on their mobile phones while separating themselves from others within the physical, public space of the street. The use of social media via mobile phones and other devices also challenges distinctions between public and private spaces. Privacy settings can give the impression that your data and interactions on these devices are not shared, but concerns have been raised over who can access this 'personal' information.

Activity 3

Note down some of the rules surrounding the use of mobile phones and how these change depending on their use in a public or private space.

All of these rules are a good topic for discussion, so why not post your ideas on the tutor group forum?

It is difficult to describe the rules surrounding mobile phone usage, as they can vary according to who is using the phone (for example, the person's age or gender), where and for what purpose it is being used. It can be frowned upon to use a mobile phone in a restaurant, although this might also depend on, for example, who one is with, what kind of restaurant it is and the type of occasion. Quiet coaches on trains could be seen as an ambiguous public/private space where use of mobile phones is discouraged. Other rules concern the purpose of the text message or call, for example is it considered acceptable to 'dump' a boyfriend or girlfriend via a text message?

Spaces that are in between the 'public' space of the street and the personal and private spaces of the home often require different practices and processes of ordering. For example, the hair salon or the tattoo studio involve personal and often quite intimate practices carried out in a public space, which are often negotiated through accepted modes of conversation, generally about the weather or holidays! These are 'safe' topics that help to make and remake social order in these potentially tricky spaces in between personal and public spaces, which we might refer to as 'semi-public' spaces. Relationships in these kinds of semi-public spaces where the client and professional might be seated in a space apart from others, but still often with ample opportunity to overhear conversations, do vary depending on differences such as age, gender and whether or not these relationships have been created over time or are relatively new. Cafés and restaurants can also be spaces in between the public space of the street and the personal and private space of the home, not least because eating is often more of a personal and private activity than it is a public one, and because many cafés or restaurants provide a sense of community and belonging to a regular clientele.

Figure 4.5   Connor in the tattoo parlour

Summary

- The context within which social order takes place is important in providing a sense of expectation – of what might be acceptable in one context but not another – and in providing a sense of predictability, of knowing how to act and how other people will act.

- There are different sorts of ordering that vary according to context, time, culture and who gets to define what counts as social order and social disorder.

- Public, private and 'semi-public' spaces require different practices and processes of ordering, but these can be unsettled because definitions of what is public and what is private are sometimes unclear and contested.

3   Sorts of ordering

The sorts of ordering discussed so far have included much of the 'taken-for-granted' ordering seen in the daily activities of people on the street – whether they are working or living there, using the street for various purposes, simply passing through, interacting with each other or relating to material objects such as street signs and price lists. The differences between the sorts of ordering that take place in public, private or semi-public spaces have also been noted. Other examples of ordering have arisen from an examination of what happens when disorder occurs and needs to be smoothed over, such as that caused by a car parking on a pedestrian crossing, a fridge in the 'wrong' place, driving a car without a licence or illegally occupying a building.

There are other types of ordering, which tend to be much more visible and deliberately noticeable. This kind of ordering tends to be associated with people who hold specific types of jobs. Such jobs make them responsible for trying to preserve social order and smooth over disorder. The role of the police might be the obvious example here. Some police officers wear distinctive uniforms and their physical presence is seen as standing for the protection of social order. They are legally authorised by the **state** to enforce the official rules (the law) and maintain order. Indeed, their role is often talked about using the popular phrase about maintaining 'law and order'. Although the police are agents who have a particular role in making and remaking order on the street, they are just one part of making social order. The police interact with other people – residents, shopkeepers and other official agents, such as people employed by the local authority – in the making and remaking of social order.

State
The political organisation that rules over a given territory and its people.

The police and other official agents have a particular role to play in making and remaking social order, as a result of the authority and powers they possess. They have access to what can be called the 'tools' of legal ordering, such as the ability to serve notices, issue fines and prosecute individuals for disorderly behaviour. Access to such tools, and the power to use them, comes from the state which sits behind much of the social ordering already discussed. The state establishes who might legitimately claim to exercise authority over particular aspects of social life, for example the rules governing bouncers are laid down and enforced by the state, and it plays a crucial role in defining and making social order.

Monitoring is an important element of the state's attempts to define and make social order in particular ways. In *Ordering Lives* (The Open University, 2014), the police on City Road were involved in carrying out Operation Clean Sweep in which they were encouraging local citizens to report problems of **antisocial** behaviour such as litter and graffiti – what could be called disorder – by phoning a special helpline. In this example, the police enlist the public's help in monitoring each other's behaviour and this is a crucial element in making social order work. In contrast, CCTV is used to monitor people's behaviour, often without the public realising it is being 'watched over'.

Antisocial
A type of behaviour that lacks consideration for others and may cause harm to society *or* a label attached to the behaviour of some groups of young people.

Figure 4.6   Police talk with local people in Operation Clean Sweep

Other people on City Road have a role in making and remaking order even if their role is less visible at first glance. The bouncers who vet who can enter public spaces such as bars and nightclubs and provide security in these venues, or the waiters in takeaways, all generally wear uniforms, which signal that they are performing a particular role in terms of ordering while they are at work.

In *Ordering Lives* (The Open University, 2014), Naveed Akram, the waiter in the takeaway, wears a uniform and plays a particular role in trying to maintain order among his customers. He does not make use of legal tools or rules and regulations to make social order, except for insisting on adhering to the price list, but rather uses humour and friendship with some of his customers as a way of maintaining a sense of order. This is also an example of how at night-time, and particularly when alcohol is consumed, people's perceptions of order and disorder change, as do their perceptions of the most effective ways to make and maintain order.

Some bars use bouncers to make order. Bouncers use their ability to include some and exclude others as a means of making a particular kind of order in the bars. People may be included or excluded on the basis of their age, appearance and the clothes they are wearing, or their ability to pay to enter the bar or nightclub. Such practices of inclusion and exclusion are a way of imposing order based on classifying potential customers in terms of who is 'normal' or 'desirable' and who is 'undesirable'. In *Ordering Lives* (The Open University, 2014), the policy at The Varsity on City Road dictates 'no trainers, hoodies, tracksuits or caps' because staff claim that behaviour is better when people do not dress in this way. The Ernest Willows pub, however, with its informal door policy that does not rely on bouncers, contrasts sharply with The Varsity's use of male bouncers. Here the making and remaking of order is carried out by the clientele themselves who 'keep an eye on things' to ensure things are kept in order. The manager of The Ernest Willows pub, Victoria Milner, claims that rather than being the source of making social order, bouncers can actually make things worse by being intimidating (The Open University, 2014).

The contrasting door policies of these two establishments point to a wider disagreement within society over who should have the authority to make and remake order, what might count as order and disorder, and who gets to define the rules that govern behaviour in the street. As we saw earlier, there is a distinction between a reliance on individuals in authority (such as the police or bouncers) to make and remake social order in a certain context, and a reliance on individuals knowing how to behave in an orderly fashion without the need for authority figures.

The policy at The Varsity relies on authority figures in the form of bouncers to make social order, while The Ernest Willows pub relies on the ability of its clients to internalise acceptable modes of behaviour. This latter view would sit well with the anarchist squatters on City Road. Anarchists claim that individuals are capable of self-regulation without the need for the state or other official bodies to intervene. Indeed, they would claim that the state and its symbols of authority, whether in the form of police officers, bouncers or traffic wardens, is more often the source of disorder than it is the source of social order.

Activity 4

Can you think of any other spaces or situations where self-regulation occurs – such that social order is made without the need for individuals in authority?

One example of a situation where self-regulation occurs is the way in which people often readily form queues and enforce the rules associated with queuing (for example, not pushing in), without the need for individuals in authority to regulate this behaviour.

Summary

- There are various sorts of ordering, some of which are 'taken for granted' and are seen in the daily activities and behaviours of people on the street, and some of which are more visible and deliberately noticeable, such as the activities of the police and other official agents.
- The state plays a crucial role in defining and monitoring social order.
- There is disagreement within society over who should have the authority to make and remake order, what might count as order and disorder and who gets to define the rules that govern people's behaviour.

4   Module questions

4.1   How is society made and remade?

Social order in the contemporary UK works (most of the time) because people live their lives within a society that is already made and ordered to some extent. However, social order is not static or fixed and this chapter covered various ways in which people's activities, relationships and interactions with each other and material things contribute to the making and remaking of social order.

Social order generally works because people have learnt the official and informal rules about how to behave in particular places – such that social order is made and remade through learnt routines or habits that become routine and expected.

4.2   How are differences and inequalities produced?

There are different sorts of social ordering that can vary across time, place and context. The chapter looked at much of the 'taken-for-granted' ordering on the street and the different sorts of ordering that occur in public, private and semi-public spaces. There are also differences in ordering, and perceptions of order and disorder, depending on the time of day and night.

Different sorts of ordering can also arise from different expectations of what is orderly or disorderly behaviour and these are influenced by differences in age, sexuality, gender, race, ethnicity and class.

Not everybody is equally well placed to define social order and disorder. Some individuals or groups in authority are better placed to get their definitions of social order and disorder to stick than others.

4.3   How do social scientists know?

The street is a good point from which social scientists can begin to know about social order and disorder because, by observing the activities and behaviour of people on the street, social scientists can begin to describe how social order is made and remade. From this description, social scientists begin to ask questions about why social order works most of the time and how social order is remade in the face of disorder or by challenges to the existing order. Concepts – for example, socialisation, authority, the state – help social scientists to think about, describe and ask questions about social order and disorder.

References

The Open University (2014) 'Ordering Lives' [Video], *DD102 Introducing the social sciences*. Available at https://learn2.open.ac.uk/mod/oucontent/view.php?id=444610&section=2 (Accessed 10 March 2014).

Reflections on social science inquiry

Georgina Blakeley

Contents

Introduction

Your journey as a social scientist started out on a street – City Road in Cardiff. It began there because everyone is familiar with streets even if not everybody lives on one. Although streets provide a familiar and thus approachable starting point, it is interesting to start looking at this taken-for-granted aspect of the social world in a different way. Sometimes this can be achieved by going somewhere new where what is different stands out. Sometimes, however, this can be achieved by going back to the familiar and observing it in different ways.

You might already have begun to look at streets with which you are familiar in a new light. Streets and social lives more generally can be viewed in different ways, for example through the people, their activities, and what they say about what they think and experience; through the interactions and connections between people and the material things around them; through the connections between people and things in one place and time, and those in other places and times; and the different and competing uses of spaces and times as the people, activities and experiences change.

1 The elements of social science inquiry

1.1 Asking questions

Social scientists are often interested in exploring the taken for granted and asking how aspects of society come to be as they are. This can be done by asking questions, for example:

- How might the street appear if you are in a wheelchair compared to if you have no mobility problems?

- How might the street appear to an older person at night?

- How might the street appear if you have no money?

- Has the street always been like this?

- Why are things as they are and how did they come to be like that?

Questions like these, or others that you can think of, can be asked about what you can see happening on streets that you know and on streets with which you are less familiar. Although City Road is distinctive (as are all streets), the patterns you can discover or assemble from it are likely to have much in common with many other streets elsewhere in the UK and beyond. As a result of this process of inquiry, it is possible to begin to see how people live together on the street as social beings. In that sense, a street can represent, on a small scale, what is happening within society.

Yet, everyone asks questions, so what is different about what social scientists do? Certainly, people do 'everyday' social science in the sense of being curious about the world around them. However, there are differences between this 'everyday' social science, which Lloyd Robson was doing in both parts of the film *The Life and Times of the Street* (The Open University, 2014a, 2014b), and the social science you are engaged in on this module.

- To begin with, social scientists try to be systematic and explicit in the questions they ask.

- Social scientists look beyond the individual's story and experience, no matter how interesting or moving these might be, to try to find the patterns, regularities and trends beneath these individual lives. This helps to see the links between an individual experience and wider society.

- By going beyond the individual story, social scientists are looking for patterns, regularities and trends, and trying to develop explanations for why some change and others persist. This process of inquiry thus allows, for example, an explanation for homelessness that does not depend on the individual characteristics of one person's story, but which draws attention to the broader patterns in society that explain homelessness as a social, and not just a personal, issue.

This process of social science inquiry is what unites the various disciplines that make up the social sciences. Whether you are interested in social policy or criminology, or are hoping to become a psychologist, political scientist, sociologist, geographer or an economist, you will all engage in this process. You may ask different questions, be interested in different topics and look for different explanations, but the way in which you do this will be similar regardless of the discipline you are interested in.

Through the introductory chapters of this book and the films, you have begun to understand some of the elements of social science inquiry, which you take forward with you into the rest of the module. Questions are one such element, and as you are going through the module, your studies will continue to be organised around the three module questions:

- How is society made and remade?
- How are inequalities and differences produced?
- How do social scientists know?

You will already have begun to form some possible answers to these questions through your work on the street. For example, you have seen how society is made and remade through the relationships people have with each other, the activities people engage in and the material infrastructure of a street that is often hidden from view. Regardless of the specific examples that you have taken from your study of City Road in Cardiff, the important point to remember is the active nature of the process of making and remaking, which always hints at the possibility of change.

In terms of the second question, City Road in Cardiff provided many examples of the differences among people and the ways in which some differences can become inequalities, as the rewards and costs of social lives are not equally distributed. Here it is important to look not just at how and why some differences become inequalities, but at how and why some inequalities persist over time and become entrenched in society.

In terms of the third question, City Road offered various examples of how social scientists go about finding out about the world through describing and observing, asking questions, and looking for the trends, patterns and connections that underpin individual stories and experiences.

1.2   Concepts

Another element of social science inquiry that you have begun to use is concepts. Concepts, it has been argued, are terms that are in everyday use. Indeed, it is impossible to think or speak without them. Concepts are terms that act as a kind of shorthand, a simplification of what is a far more complex idea. What distinguishes the use of concepts by social scientists from their everyday use is the process of thinking about and reflecting upon the concepts that are being used. Concepts are not just picked out of the air randomly: some concepts are chosen deliberately; others are discarded intentionally. Concepts help social scientists to describe what is being observed and to ask questions. Concepts make a difference to the questions that social scientists are able to ask and the explanations they are able to construct.

The idea that concepts make a difference can be seen clearly in the module questions. For example, it would have been possible to have asked 'How is society made and repaired?' or 'How is society produced?', but these questions contain different concepts that change the emphasis of what is being asked. The module team deliberately chose to ask 'How is society made and remade?' because this focuses on the idea that society is not just given or fixed, but constantly in the process of being made. 'Produced', on the other hand, can suggest that once made, society is somehow a finished product. Similarly, 'How is society made and repaired?' could suggest, in its use of 'repaired', that when society is remade in the face of disruption, the change is always in a positive direction. To ask 'How society is made and remade?', however, contains no such assumptions about the positive or negative nature of change. These might appear to be very subtle differences, but they illustrate the ways in which social scientists try to reflect carefully upon the concepts being used because they make a difference to the questions being asked and the kinds of explanation being sought.

Two key concepts that you have already begun to work with are 'inequalities' and 'difference', and these will also provide a continuous thread throughout your studies. They draw attention to the ways in which people are different and the ways in which society in the contemporary UK is increasingly diverse. Yet, the focus is on how differences can become inequalities and the ways in which some inequalities can become persistent features of society – to the extent that they may be taken largely for granted.

2 Moving on

As you move forward through the module, the elements of social science inquiry, which you have already begun to use and think about, will help you to get the most out of your studies. You will acquire a deeper understanding of what it is to do social science throughout the module. In particular, the three module questions will help you to organise your learning by providing a common thread throughout your studies.

2.1 Making lives

You are now going to move beyond your initial social science journey on the street to look in more depth at some of the issues that you have already touched upon. The next strand of study materials you will encounter is 'Making lives'.

Think, first of all, about the two terms that have been chosen to describe the strand and remember that they have been chosen, not randomly, but deliberately, to convey one kind of meaning rather than another.

- 'Making' highlights the idea that society is not just fixed or given: it is actively made by individuals and groups through their relationships with each other, through the things they do and don't do, and through their relationship to the material world.

- 'Lives' highlights the idea that the focus of this strand is on how people live together as social beings.

The strand you are about to study looks at the central idea that lives are always in the making. People make and remake themselves, their lives and the society in which they live through trying to make the best of the opportunities that come their way, and through responding to change and challenges as best they can. Yet, people do not start with a blank sheet of paper – individuals have to make their lives within a society that is already made.

A key claim that you will encounter in this strand is that contemporary life in the UK takes place within a society in which much time and effort is spent on consuming – in other words, a consumer society in which people's ability and desire to consume is a key feature. This idea is not uncontested and you will encounter different ways of thinking about how today's society is thought about and made. The old and new combine, so that traces of an earlier industrial society, defined less by consumption and more by the work people did, are still visible and make a difference to the ways in which lives get made today.

Whatever the different ways in which social scientists characterise the dominant features of contemporary UK society, people today continue to face both choices and constraints in making and remaking their lives as they did in earlier times. This strand examines how and why some individuals and groups in society have greater opportunities to make their lives and the lives of those around them than others.

References

The Open University (2014a) 'The Life and Times of the Street: Part 1' [Video], *DD102 Introducing the social sciences.* Available at https://learn2.open.ac.uk/mod/oucontent/view.php?id=443760&section=2.3 (Accessed 10 March 2014).

The Open University (2014b) 'The Life and Times of the Street: Part 2' [Video], *DD102 Introducing the social sciences.* Available at https://learn2.open.ac.uk/mod/oucontent/view.php?id=443760&section=2.7 (Accessed 29 10 March 2014).

Making lives

Chapter 5
Consumer society? Identity and lifestyle

Kevin Hetherington and Catriona Havard

Contents

Introduction

This is the first chapter of the 'Making lives' strand. Its central concerns are identity, **lifestyle** and consumption – topics broadly familiar to you from the street scenes of City Road. Now, though, the focus of inquiry is wider in scope, taking in the contemporary UK society and the role that consumption plays in enabling people to make something of their lives, in a context of both choices and constraints.

The idea that people *make* their own lives, fashion themselves through what they buy and own, can hold a certain appeal. In what many regard as a market-driven, consumer society, *choice* – the invitation to choose between products and styles – is often highly valued. Although perhaps more by those who believe they actually exercise choice, rather than by those who feel they have little in the way of choice. The question of how much choice people have in their lives is core to this chapter. It is a question that, in an age of market expansion, has come to preoccupy a number of social scientists, not least over the extent to which our choices are our own.

Social scientists, however, often disagree about how much control people exercise over their lives. They argue and express their point of view, often forcefully, in this case about what is actually happening in society at large, the direction of social and economic change. So in this chapter, we will be looking at:

- The claims made about the nature of the contemporary UK as one driven by market-led consumerism.

- The evidence used to back up that claim and what it means for people's identities, their sense of self, to be fashioned through consumption.

Much of this chapter will be spent considering the nature of consumption, how far it defines lifestyles today, and the extent to which our choices are our own. In Section 1, we examine the broad patterns of consumption in the contemporary UK to get a sense of what people spend their money on and how consumer habits change over time. In Section 2, we address the question posed by a number of social scientists that the UK has shifted from an **industrial society** to a consumer society, one in which what is consumed is said to tell us more about people's sense of themselves than any job or career that they may have. In Section 3, we take a closer look at how consumption, and the images and brands associated with the products and services purchased,

You will read more about identity in Chapter 1 of *Understanding Social Lives, Part 2*.

Lifestyle
A shared set of activities and forms of identification that can be recognised as being part of a distinctive way of life (for example, luxury lifestyle, alternative lifestyle, retired lifestyle).

Industrial society
A society based on manufacturing, mass production and mass consumption.

are as much about the social messages that they convey as their actual usefulness. In Section 4, we look at how these social messages can help to shape an individual's personality and sense of self.

It is to the routine practices of consumption, however, to which we turn first.

1   Understanding consumption

For social scientists, what people spend their money on, the choices that they make about what to buy, can tell us a lot about the make-up of society. Consumption, in that sense, provides a window on society; it offers a way of looking into how people can make something of themselves through what they spend, and in turn, it throws light on how society shapes those very same consumption choices. As more and more of social life – from housing and education to pensions and health – becomes subject to market forces, distributed according to how much people can pay, so the nature of consumption holds out the possibility of revealing the changing character of society.

For some social scientists, the drive to consume has become all about individual lifestyle, about who we are and would like to be. Others stress that what we spend our money on is very much a social affair, where the pressures to conform, the expectations of others, as much as the quest for individual autonomy, shape our lives. Whether as individuals or as groups, though, what people buy and what they do with the things that they buy, can provide a sense of how people see themselves and their place in society. Equally, the inability to consume can also tell us much about the distribution of **life chances** in society: that is, who does and who does not have the means to consume.

Forty odd years ago, it was common among social scientists to talk about the UK as an industrial society, one based on manufacturing, where the majority of the workforce was involved in the making of things and working-class life was based largely on cash. Then, in the 1970s and 1980s, a number began talking about a **post-industrial society**, after many traditional manufacturing industries declined, working-class communities shrank and the bulk of jobs created were in the services sector. As society more generally became characterised by what it consumed, rather than what it produced, there was debate among social scientists about the arrival of a consumer society in response to how important a consumer culture and easy credit had seemed to become in remaking the fabric of society.

That did not mean, however, that as society changed, what went on before simply vanished without trace. It is still common to encounter the question 'what do you *do*?' when people first meet, and many people still think about the idea of work or a career as saying something very important about who they are. Yet, a quick browse through some of the

Life chances
People's ability to adopt a particular lifestyle, which depends on both choices and constraints, such as the unequal distribution of economic and social resources in society.

Post-industrial society
A society based on services, information technologies and consumer choice.

social networking internet sites or a flick through a lifestyle magazine at the newsagents tends to reveal a different question, namely, 'what are you *into*?' Issues of consumption, identity and lifestyle are inextricably linked to such a question, because those are the sorts of issues that also appear to matter to people when they think about who they are and how they present themselves to others.

So the things that people buy, and how they use them once they have bought them, can go some way towards helping us understand the nature of contemporary society, as indeed can the lack of ability to consume. The overall increase in private debt levels in the UK in recent years, especially among those who have not got the cash upfront to consume, also tells us something about the forces shaping today's society. Social science, in that sense, is as much interested in the actions of individuals as it is in broader social patterns, for example in the distribution of life chances and the changing pattern of inequality.

One way to start thinking about these issues is by looking at the practices associated with consumption.

1.1   'You spent how much?'

Take a look at Figure 5.1, which shows data collected by the Office for National Statistics (ONS) on what households in the UK spend their money on during a typical week. A household can be anything from one person to a group of people, related or unrelated, sharing a living space. Cast your eye over the amount spent each week on the different items and what people typically consume. Such statistical analysis gives you an idea of the kind of data that social scientists collect to get a sense of emerging trends and patterns.

There are 12 categories of expenditure in Figure 5.1, ranging from what could be seen as 'luxuries', such as recreation and culture, to essentials such as housing, fuel and power. If you read along from left to right along the horizontal axis at the bottom of Figure 5.1, you can get a sense of the average amount spent by households each week for each of the categories.

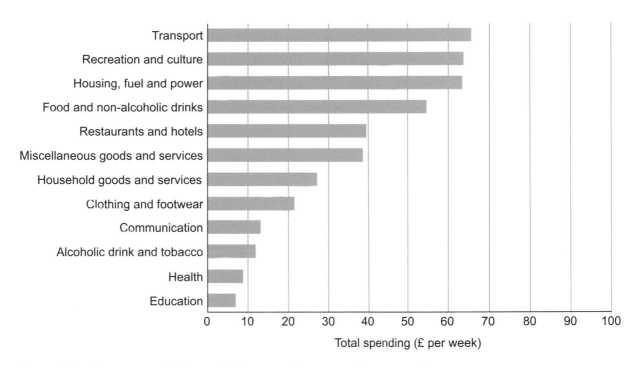

Figure 5.1   Average weekly household expenditure on main commodities and services, 2011 (Source: ONS, 2012)

Activity 1

The largest category at the top of Figure 5.1 is transport, which includes the cost of running a car, petrol and public transport, and may well divide into essential and leisure travel for a number of households. Below that, and not far behind, is recreation and culture, which covers things such as holidays, gardening, pets, as well as computer games, and beneath that is housing, fuel and power. Remember that the spending per week is an average amount for a household, so your particular household expenditure may be quite different.

Now look at the next two categories below those, which cover spending on food, non-alcoholic drinks, and restaurants and hotels.

• Do they fall into the category of essentials or luxuries?

• Is the amount spent on food about what you expected?

• Would you have guessed that restaurants and hotels would have come midway in the figure?

• Would it have made a difference if you knew that the figure for restaurants and hotels also includes takeaway meals consumed at home?

To be fair, the biggest weekly expenditure for a number of people is on their mortgage, although that is not included in the 'housing, fuel and power' category (rental payments *are* included). Rather, Figure 5.1 shows what people spend their money on after many of their major expenses have been paid, including council tax (rates in Northern Ireland), pension contributions and the like. It is concerned with what economists call 'disposable income'. Figure 5.1 tells us that people spend their money on a mix of consumer items, but that necessities are not always at the top of the list.

Of course, consumer habits change. Different things become important. Things once seen as a novelty for the wealthy few might come to be seen as an everyday essential for the majority a decade or so later. For example, in the 1980s very few people owned a mobile phone, which was a new and expensive novelty item then. Now, the vast majority of people do and it has become a major item of weekly expenditure – something that many people might say they could not be without, as it has become an integral part of their lives, allowing them to connect to others in an easy and convenient way. Smartphones are now the latest thing to have, as are plasma screen TVs, both it seems within the reach of the majority, even if for some that means using credit.

Figure 5.1 is helpful in that it provides some basic data, but it is limited. It is a form of numerical description based on a survey where a number of people have been asked to say what they consume on a regular basis. There is no breakdown of what people spend money on within those categories and the statistics do not tell us *why* people spend their money on the things they do, or whether they are funded out of income or debt. Nor do we get a sense of the significance of what people consume and what it means to them. The 'facts and figures' themselves cannot tell us this with any degree of certainty and require interpretation.

One such interpretation, which we turn to in Section 2, has been put forward by Zygmunt Bauman (1988; 2007), a leading commentator on contemporary social change.

Summary

- Consumption offers a window on the nature of contemporary society and how, in turn, people's lives are made through it.
- Facts and figures do not speak for themselves – they require interpretation.

2   Towards a consumer society?

According to Zygmunt Bauman (1988), people in contemporary Western societies can be broadly divided into two groups of consumers that he calls, in deliberately loaded terms, the 'seduced' and the 'repressed'. Bauman claims that we now live in a consumer society rather than an industrial society, but that it is not an equal society, just as the industrial society before it was not. But, he believes, the *forms* of inequality and freedom in a consumer society differ from what went before.

A consumer society promises choice and freedom to those who, because of their financial and social circumstances, are in a position to consume effectively. In industrial society it was really only the very wealthy – those whose wealth was based on land ownership, or rich merchants and factory owners (capitalists who profited from factory production), and a few well-paid professionals like bankers, doctors and lawyers – who could have defined themselves as consumers and lived lives defined by a luxury lifestyle. The idea that consumption should become available to the many rather than the few, for good economic, as much as social, reasons, began to develop in the latter years of the nineteenth century and has continued to develop up to the present time.

In contemporary society, there are still landed gentry, capitalists and professionals who can afford to consume to a greater degree than others, but they are now joined by many others who have access, in varying degrees, to the trappings of a consumer lifestyle. These others would include wealthy people, certainly, but also people with a good, steady income and a secure job who have enough money, or disposable income, and those who have access to relatively cheap credit to allow them to buy things beyond the basic necessities of life. Bauman calls these people the 'seduced' – the reason for his use of this term will become clear in Section 2.1.

For Bauman, the seduced group does not only include people with surplus income to spend on things that they want, but also people in a position to buy into the ideals of a consumer society which, he suggests, are based on a number of key features:

- The idea that markets offer people freedom of choice and that market freedom is the defining freedom in society.

- The idea that consumer activity can be a means to creative self-expression, a sense of self-worth and an identity that people wish to have.
- The idea that creating consumer lifestyles is the means to a sense of belonging, acceptance and membership within society.

In an industrial society, political freedoms such as the right to vote or the right to join a trade union might have been seen as the most important freedoms. A sense of self-worth and identity would typically have been made or created through having secure employment and skilled and satisfying work, or through citizenship rights. Not everyone had these qualities in their life, indeed few did, but a sense of social belonging and inclusion was often defined by following the forms of accepted behaviour appropriate to a person's class and **status**, which were often determined by the job that they did and the occupational community in which they lived. For Bauman, these forms of freedom, expression and membership have faded into the background as manufacturing and industry have become less dominant in Western societies. In their place, he claims that consumer freedoms have become more dominant today.

Status

A common, shared and recognised position that some people hold in society. Having a particular status is determined by a person's access to social resources that convey, in different degrees, recognition, honour and prestige on the status holder.

2.1 The 'seduced' and the 'repressed'

The seductive appeal of consumption, for Bauman, is that it offers not just goods and services that people want, but also a sense of both self-expression and social membership to those who are able to consume effectively. Buying something in a shop, taking it home and using it offers more than the satisfaction that that good or service can provide as something with a use. It offers entry into the social realm of shared meanings where one's identity can be established and displayed to others. It offers the promise of allowing people to make, through what they consume, a personality that they aspire to have, and that they can use to communicate to others their membership and position within society.

In the past, people might have done this through work and a limited range of leisure activities rather than activities like how one decorates one's home, the car one drives, the holidays one takes or the hobbies and pastimes that one has. It seems that a person is no longer limited to describing themselves as a mechanic, painter or domestic servant. Rather, they might use terms like 'classic car enthusiast', 'a punk', or someone who is 'into horse riding'. Certainly, it is clear that the patterns of our industrial work-dominated past have not altogether disappeared from society. The UK is still involved in manufacture and most people below retirement age have to find an income to support themselves based on a wage, state benefits and credits, or a combination of these. But those, like Bauman, who argue that we now live in a consumer society are making the claim that it is principally consumption that is the dominant feature in making identities, rather than production and work.

The 'seduced', then, in Bauman's terms, are those who can participate in this consumer society. They are included as members with a positive identity. The seduced include not only those with enough money to buy goods and services, but also those who are seen as valued members of a consumer society, both by other consumers and by those with something to sell to a lucrative market: the employed, the young, older people with good pensions and savings, and those in a position to achieve their aspirations through such things as talent, good looks or a particular skill that is valued and financially rewarded within society. In sum, the seduced, in Bauman's terms, are those in a position to be admitted to membership in society because they are able to consume effectively in the eyes of others.

The pressures to conform are strong because not doing so can easily lead to social exclusion and a devalued identity. Someone who does not have a car can be socially excluded in certain areas – notably ones where public transport is rather limited. An adolescent who does not have a smartphone might find themselves ridiculed and socially excluded from friendship networks. A person with mobility difficulties might find themselves physically excluded from some places. Increasingly, as many consumer services are provided online (or are cheaper online), not having ready access to the internet might lead to forms of social exclusion. All of these activities involve the ability, or not, to consume things like cars, smartphones or online internet services.

In this account, the seduced does not extend to everyone and neither is membership of the seduced necessarily a permanent characteristic, as a person's life circumstances can change. There is another group in Bauman's terms who are excluded from this consumer society or who are pushed to its margins – a group he calls the 'repressed'. This group would typically include those with limited life chances – the unemployed, the low paid, those in insecure or casual employment, recently arrived migrants, or those often not in a position to participate fully in a consumer society, for example some people with disabilities, the chronically sick and older people on basic state pensions. It might also include people from minority ethnic groups who experience other forms of social exclusion and discrimination.

Figure 5.2 The physical exclusion of people with disabilities by virtue of the design of the built environment is one means through which social divisions are made

Clearly, income matters a lot in defining whether a person belongs to the category of the seduced or the repressed, but it is not the only factor. For example, a young person with little money might find it much easier to participate in consumer activities than a person with a similar income who also has disabilities or is in a different age group. They might be in a better position to buy into the acceptance of others through having fashionable clothes, being able to go to the right clubs, listening to whatever music happens to be popular, being fit and healthy, or by having a large network of friends with whom they can share similar interests. They can often speak the lingo of consumption in a knowledgeable way and read its trends.

In contrast, an older person or a person with a disability might be excluded from this world, either because they have to spend what money they might have on basic foods, care, prescriptions, clothing and heating, or because they are more socially isolated, less mobile and less valued as target consumers with spending power by the companies that sell things. Their opportunities for self-expression and social membership in a consumer society are likely to be more restricted, unless, that is, they can compensate for a disadvantaged status by having some wealth or other skill. In this respect, they are more likely to be excluded from some aspects of this society and seen as somehow failed members of society, just as, to use the terms of the period, the slum-dwelling poor, debtors, criminals, the 'idle' (unemployed) or those confined to the workhouse were 100 years ago in a more industrial society.

2.2   Bauman's argument

It is perhaps easy to see why Bauman might call these people the 'repressed' and why he might suggest that society excludes them because of their inability to participate in consumer activity beyond its most basic forms – treating them as social outcasts. He has observed that there are different patterns of consumer activity within society and put forward an argument as to why things are how they are. In doing so, he has drawn upon specific concepts – terms that try to capture the key characteristics of consumer activity – to account for the evidence.

There are several points that Bauman is trying to get across in his argument:

- Consuming is the defining feature of present-day societies such as the UK.

- Membership and a valued identity within society are determined by the degree to which someone can participate in consumer activities.

- Society remains unequal and divided in terms of inclusion in and exclusion from the activities of consumption.

- Consumption is a key means for establishing and maintaining status within society.

It is important to note that he uses the more concise terms – seduced and repressed – to convey the main lines of his argument. These are intentionally simplified, rather abstract, terms, that set out the theoretical claims that frame his argument. They are not intended to convey the full complexity of social divisions within a consumer society, in much the same way that the division between capitalists and workers was a rather simplified picture of industrial society. No doubt there are more varied sets of positions that exist in society, with people able to move between these categories at different times and in different places. Bauman, however, is not seeking to provide an exhaustive classification of every position that might exist within contemporary society; rather, he is making an argument about consumer society in general.

His argument is a rather grand one, and as we have seen, rests upon the claim that the main lines of **social cleavage** today are no longer based on social class, but by access to consumption practices and the ability to use consumption to shape one's identity; that is, as someone who can act on the seductive appeal of consumerism to make something of themselves, or as someone effectively excluded from the process altogether.

However, that does not mean to say that Bauman's claims about contemporary society are wholly valid. While his concepts of the seduced and the repressed might have some broad explanatory value, they do not offer a particularly subtle picture. Like all social science explanations, it is open to question and scrutiny, perhaps by considering whether:

- there are other approaches that people can take to consumption
- those Bauman calls 'seduced' are able to see through that manipulation
- those Bauman calls 'repressed' might be able to create space to consume in ways that they find satisfying and inclusive.

While concepts like these are useful tools in social science, they are also open to challenge, adaptation or even rejection if they don't always appear to mesh with the evidence.

Bauman's argument, for instance, could be taken to present a partial view of the consumer, one solely as an individual with wants and desires who then goes out to consume. It might be argued that he downplays the importance of shopping for essentials, as a routine activity in which providing for others such as family members is just as important. It could also be argued that, for some consumers, the **seductions** of fantasy and luxury have little appeal, not because they do not have the money to shop, but because they are not taken in by the idea that they have no choice but to choose. For example, environmentally conscious people concerned with reducing their carbon footprint and recycling may have quite a different 'take' on

Social cleavage
The main lines of division and inequality that characterise a particular society.

You will learn more about social class in the 'Connecting lives' strand.

Seductions
Enticement and suggestion to direct people's choices along certain lines and not others, closing them down by degree.

consumption, one based on personal thrift and social responsibility, rather than luxury or excess. Equally, those who fund their consumption through credit and debt are not necessarily seduced by its trappings.

■ There are those who use high-end pawnbrokers, just as there are those who rely on payday lenders, but is it always clear whether this is down to temptation or necessity?

Activity 2

Reflect on the question above for a minute or two.

The number of pawnbrokers in the UK has risen four-fold since 2007 and payday lenders are now a familiar sight on many high streets, as increasingly are high interest stores selling sofas, TVs and the like, such as BrightHouse, which offers credit and payment by instalments to people who cannot afford upfront payment. Should they all be assumed to fall under the spell of seduction? How much of this debt is simply about 'getting by' and how much is down to temptation?

Bauman's point about the role of seduction is clearly about the power of seduction to control people's wants and desires, and all that that says in terms of how free people actually are from the lure of the marketplace. Seduction, though, is not a coercive force; it relies on suggestion and involves the encouragement of embryonic tastes already present by increasing their appeal to consumers. In that regard, seduction has a long history when it comes to consumption.

Summary

- Bauman's argument is that there has been a shift from an industrial to a consumer society, one based on new social divisions and forms of inequality.
- Bauman claims consumer freedoms dominate through the seductive appeal of consumerism, which controls people's wants and desires.
- That more and more of social life is shaped by the marketplace is not in contention. There is less agreement over the power of seduction, as not everyone agrees that they have no choice but to choose.

3   Consumer culture

When social scientists speak of consumption, they refer to a broad range of social issues which make and shape our way of life – or culture. The idea of society having a culture shaped by consumption is not new. Historians have argued that eighteenth-century British society could be described as being influenced by consumption. The landed gentry and a growing number of middle-class people of that time enjoyed buying fine things, for example luxuries such as porcelain, silver, tea and fine clothes. They did so not only to enjoy such things for what they were in terms of their use, but also because having luxury things was often seen as a mark of rank and status within society. This is arguably still true today. An expensive car, dress or watch can be desirable, not just because of its functionality, but because of how it is perceived by others as a mark of distinction and status. Some consumer items, therefore, are status symbols that convey a message to others about their owner.

In contemporary society, people sometimes measure a person, their status in particular, by the consumer trappings that they surround themselves with: where they live, the size of their house, the car they drive, the holidays they take, and so forth. The concept that a number of social scientists have used to try to capture this is 'conspicuous consumption'.

3.1   Conspicuous consumption

One of the first social scientists to write about the culture of consumption in this way was the American sociologist, Thorstein Veblen, in his book *The Theory of the Leisure Class*, which was first published in 1899. He studied the consuming habits of the new rich, the successful industrialists and their families, in the USA at the end of the nineteenth century. He found that they often bought things for a particular reason: they wanted the things they bought to make a positive impression and to demonstrate to others their newly acquired wealth and rising status within society.

A big house, quality furnishings, clothes in the latest fashion, expensive jewellery and antiques were the sort of high-status luxury items that the new rich often bought and put on display in their homes so that guests who came to visit for dinner parties, for example, would see the trappings of success on display. Those things became an extension of the people who owned them and Veblen coined the concept of 'conspicuous consumption' to try to capture this. He used this term to convey the process of visibly displaying status to others through what had been acquired – especially when a person had newly gained wealth and wanted to make an impression in wealthy circles. Buying luxury things and showing them off to others through display is what the concept is meant to capture. Conspicuous consumption is thus Veblen's shorthand way of isolating that social activity. These people, it turns out, were open to all manner of seduction in the nineteenth century.

Figure 5.3   Omega brand – an example of luxury, high-status goods

Luxury items and the trappings of wealth were an important means of displaying character and status at that time. For the wealthy, the conspicuous consumption of luxury goods is important to convey one's status as a prosperous person. Today, people most commonly associate conspicuous consumption with highly paid celebrities who have made their name in the music or entertainment industries, with sporting stars and city traders who could earn six-figure bonuses by being successful on the stock market, or with big lottery winners. But the likelihood is that, in more limited ways, many people today engage in acts of conspicuous consumption without fully realising it, even if they are not particularly wealthy or their lifestyles are not defined by luxury.

The reason why people do this is not simply because they want to show off, but because they want to 'fit in', to impress their friends and be accepted into social networks where they feel they ought to belong. Things like owning a top-of-the-range car or taking holidays in an exclusive resort can send such a message about status and inclusion. In fact, social acceptance can drive consumption at all levels of society, not just among the moneyed classes.

Figure 5.4   Conspicuous consumption then and now – the trappings of an ostentatious lifestyle in the nineteenth century and today

3.2   Consuming uses or conveying meaning?

What the concept of conspicuous consumption suggests is that people often consume things for social, as much as personal, reasons. But displaying status to others or the need for social acceptance are not the only reasons why people might want to own something. There is a whole range of social issues that social scientists might consider when looking at the practices of consumption. Clearly, people often consume things simply for their usefulness. A plain, mass-produced dishcloth is unlikely to be bought for any reason other than for its usefulness for cleaning purposes. But it is not impossible for people to find other uses for such mundane things. In the 1970s, for instance, punks became famous for using bin bags as clothing and safety pins as jewellery. This, of course, is an extreme example of using something for very different purposes from those typically associated with an item. But what about something like a pair of shoes? Shoes certainly have a useful purpose, but it is unlikely that people always buy them only for the use and comfort they provide, important though those qualities are. Other factors such as style and fashionability (or anti-fashion) might be important too, as might the brand or the name of the designer associated with them. Whether they are Jimmy Choo or Converse, the desired social messages associated with them may have little to do with purely practical footwear. Sometimes, the messages attached to an object or service – messages that are encoded into the **commodities** through design and logo – might be more important than consuming the thing itself.

Commodity
A good or service that is produced for exchange and sold in a market with the intention of generating a profit for the seller.

Activity 3

Even when the things consumed look more or less the same, the message associated with a particular brand can make a big difference. Figure 5.5 shows three images of burgers from:

- a fast food place on City Road

- a well-known high-street chain

- Byron, a gourmet burger restaurant chain owned by a private investment company.

The gourmet burgers from Byron are considerably more expensive than the other two – up to four times as much – so is the difference in price simply down to superior ingredients, or is it because of the image and message conveyed by tucking into such a brand? What kind of distinction is involved here? What lifestyle trait is being suggested?

Figure 5.5   Burgers from City Road in Cardiff, a well-known chain and Byron

The important point to take from the example of the burgers in Activity 3 is that signs and messages can have different meanings for people. They can suggest wealth or the lack of it, luxury or functionality, daring novelty or established tradition, sophisticated taste or trashy entertainment. Different people often want different things when they consume, although what they value, their tastes, are likely to vary considerably depending on factors such as income, education, exposure to different cultures. Issues of status and image – the impression that someone might want to give about themselves to others – are important aspects of a consumer society, which are expressed through the ways in which people read the messages associated with goods and services.

Someone buying their weekly shopping, purchasing organic produce at a local farm shop or farmers' market, is saying something different from someone buying the less expensive, basic range at a supermarket like Tesco or Asda. Each of these outlets conveys a different social message because of their associations with things like who typically shops there, price, items available, the status of the items available, and so on. We can observe the patterns and describe the activity involved, but that doesn't tell us why it works the way that it does.

Figure 5.6   A farmers' market – a place to buy food products or to convey meanings?

This is where the idea of seduction comes in and why Bauman describes those who are able to engage effectively in consumption within society as the seduced. What he is suggesting is that people are seduced not so much by the use that a good or service can provide, but with what it means, the image conveyed through having it. They are enticed by the allure that it has, by the associations between that good or service and the type of lifestyle associated with it. It is this, the signs of consumption – image, brand and logo associated with particular goods and services and what they mean to sections of society – that provide the basis for the seductive character of a consumer culture.

The skill in being able to read these signs, often in a tacit rather than a knowing way, holds the key to being a successful consumer. Even young children can be skilled in knowing that certain items, certain brands, mean more, have a higher status, than others. Consuming may be about how people relate to things as useful objects, but it is also associated with how they relate to each other through what those things mean socially – and that involves understanding the messages that those things convey. This will become more apparent when you read Chapter 7. What is apparent here is that people consume products, services or experiences because they mean something to them and enable them to express a sense of themselves – their identity – to others through what they consume.

Summary

- Historically, the well-off in society have engaged in conspicuous consumption in order to present a positive image of themselves to others.
- Goods and services convey signs and meanings about the type of people who possess and use them.
- The reading of signs and messages is a skilled accomplishment, shared with others to convey individual style and taste.

4   Consuming life

Once consumption could be used as an expression of self-identity and individuality – not so much to reflect one's character and rank within society, as Veblen had first suggested, but to project one's personality and individual taste – it opened up all sorts of possibilities about how people could make and represent themselves to others.

4.1   Individuality and personality

The argument that consumption could be used to express individuality and personality was first put forward by Warren Susman in the 1970s (Susman, 2003[1973]). He developed the argument from an historical study of 'how to consume', which was derived from domestic economy and self-help manuals written during the nineteenth century. These books, aimed principally at the middle-class market, provided advice on how to set up home, what to put in it, how to entertain and host dinner parties, and so on. (Mrs Beeton's *Book of Household Management*, published in 1861, is the most famous example in the UK.) In effect, they gave advice on what and how to consume.

Based on a detailed reading of what they described, Susman suggested that prior to about 1880 these books were mainly concerned with providing advice to people on how best to present their good character, associated with their social position or class, through the consumption of appropriate and tasteful things for their home: through decoration and use of ornaments, management of the family finances, and entertaining. Around the 1880s, however, he claimed that the emphasis in such books shifted away from a concern with displaying character to that of displaying individuality and personality.

Susman argued that people were becoming less concerned with displaying their rank or class position through the goods in their home, and more concerned with displaying their individual taste and personality through the things that they had acquired. The concept of character was very much tied up with social rank and class, and prompted such questions as: 'What will people think of us as respectable middle-class people?'. In contrast, the concept of personality represented a more individual expression of identity, a concern with expressing oneself through what one consumed around the home, and prompted a different question: 'What will people think of me as an individual?'

At the end of the nineteenth century, the importance of leisure and consumption in ordinary people's lives, rather than just for the wealthy, was becoming significant: 'the new personality literature stressed items that could be best developed in leisure time and represented in themselves an emphasis on consumption. The social role demanded in the new culture of personality was that of a performer. Every ... [person] was to become a *performing self*' (Susman, 2003[1973], p. 280, emphasis added). It is in this sense that people make themselves up, not as a kind of fiction, but as one way of expressing who they are or want to be. At the heart of these changes were the new practices and sites of consumption of the time – most notably associated with the department store and the mail order catalogue.

This concern with personality is one that registers more fully today. In consumer society, as Bauman (1988) stressed, people are preoccupied not with class, but with personal taste and individuality. Today, people are less concerned with consuming things as a means to displaying their good character, than they are with using consumption as a way of expressing individual personalities, both for a person's own satisfaction and to say something about themselves to others. People no longer use objects that they own to convey simply social position, but as an expression of a particular lifestyle that they might aspire to – as an extension of the self.

4.2   An extension of the self

Indeed, the symbolic and self-expressive aspects of the objects that we consume are perhaps more in evidence in today's consumerist culture than in the period described by Susman. Material goods, as we have seen, can help to promote social standing and economic status, but according to Helga Dittmar (2007) they can also promote a person's sense of uniqueness and symbolise close interpersonal relationships with loved ones, as well as be a record of memories for events. Possessions, she argues, can constitute a 'snapshot' of personal history and memories, providing a sense of continuity in people's lives.

The investment of so much emotional attachment to owned objects has led to what has become known as the 'ownership effect', whereby a person shows a greater liking for an object that they own compared to an identical object that is owned by another.

Activity 4

Think about some of your favourite possessions. Choose one of these items, which means a great deal to you – preferably something that you have bought rather than been given. Think about the following questions and note down your answers.

- Why does this item mean so much to you? Why is it important?
- What does the item say about you?
- Can you imagine yourself without this item?
- What might the item say about you to someone else (perhaps you might ask someone that you know this question)?
- Would the item's loss also be a loss of part of you, part of yourself?

One of the reasons that people may show this ownership bias is because objects that are owned are often perceived as an *extension of the self*. The self is everything that we are: it is our physical body, our personality and all our memories – it is what makes us different from other people. It has been claimed that when we acquire a new object it can become a part of our self, or become an extension of our self (Belk, 1988). Material possessions illustrate that identity and the self have boundaries beyond the physical body. Perhaps the more obvious examples of objects seen as an extension of the self are tools, musical instruments, jewellery and clothes, but if objects in general are perceived as being a part of the self and part of identity, then it may be possible to change or enhance a person's identity by acquiring new objects.

According to this interpretation, people sometimes gain possessions to provide themselves with a characteristic that they feel they are lacking. People may buy objects in the hope that they will be closer to their ideal self: that is, the person they aspire to be, or the person they aspire to be viewed as by others (Dittmar, 2007). As such, these objects may differ depending on a person's social characteristics, on grounds of gender, for instance. For example, according to one study, men tended to buy instrumental and leisure items (such as electronic devices and music) that promote their feelings of independence and activity, while women were more likely to buy body care items, clothing and jewellery that could enhance their appearance and emotional aspects of the self (Dittmar et al., 1995).

For Dittmar (2007), possessions as an extension of the self often symbolise positive aspects of identity, where a more ideal sense of self may be gained through the possessions owned, or a more positive image gained by their association with a particular social group. Her argument, overall, is that contemporary consumerist culture has had a significant impact on people's sense of self and how they represent themselves to others.

4.3   A devalued self?

Not everyone, though, is in a position to freely use objects as an extension of their sense of self. If Bauman is to be believed, there is a gap between those who have been seduced and are able to satisfy their desires for the ownership of objects, and those who also embrace the consumerist model, but are unable to satisfy their desires through a lack of resources. The latter group, as we have seen, would be those who are typically excluded because of their social circumstances: the unemployed and the poor, those trapped in poorly paid jobs, some older members of society with limited means and, more generally, those who do not have the money to participate in the consumer culture. Being excluded or marginalised within a consumer culture, however, does not just mean that you are restricted in your ability to consume; it means something more significant for Bauman: that your identity becomes *devalued*; that you come to be seen as a non-participant in a society where membership and belonging are defined by the ability to consume effectively.

If those who are enticed and able to participate in consumerist practices are seen to possess a valued, positive identity, then those who are deemed ineligible for membership, that is, the 'flawed consumers' whose resources do not measure up to their desires, occupy a negative identity. For those who are seduced by the trappings of modern-day consumption, yet cannot afford to participate, this negative identity, for Bauman, is compounded by the 'pain of hopelessness' (Bauman, 1988, p. 141), brought about by the unattainable nature of the goods and services on offer. Credit only goes so far and is not obtainable by all. Confronted on a daily basis by the range of possible choices, the inability to consume is thought to erode the self-confidence of such individuals, melting their self-esteem in the process. In that respect, the temptations of the consumer market only serve to reinforce this hopelessness.

Whether valid as a claim or not, what is perhaps interesting about Bauman's argument is that he considers flawed consumers as 'collateral casualties' of consumerism (Bauman, 2007): that is, casualties that are more or less a side-effect, an unintended consequence of the arrival of consumer society and its seductions. The language is drawn from military warfare, of civilian lives unintentionally damaged or lost because they just happened to be in the vicinity of a planned military attack. On the basis of this analogy, devalued identities are something that society has to put up with if the majority want to enjoy the attractions of a market-driven, consumer society. When the overall thrust of a more prosperous society is based upon the need to consume, where the possession of objects are a precondition of performing certain lifestyles, then some people are inevitably going to lose out in a society of consumers. Their marginalisation is not seen as intentional on the part of anyone, it is just the price to be paid for consumer progress.

Summary

- People today are less concerned with consuming things to display character and rank, and more concerned with displaying individuality and personality.

- Owned objects may be experienced as part of an individual's extended self and used to present a more ideal self to others.

- Not everyone is able to enjoy the attractions of a consumer culture, and those excluded may suffer a devalued identity in the eyes of others.

Conclusion

Throughout this chapter, a major concern has been to consider the role that consumption has played in enabling people to make something of their lives, whether that be through the ability to buy into a particular lifestyle or fashion an identity through the things that they use and own. The focus on choice has been central to the idea that it is possible for people to define themselves through what they consume. Before we move on to the next chapter, however, we need to be clear about what is involved in the making of choices.

The notions of freedom of choice, individual self-expression and market freedoms in general are a pervasive part of contemporary consumer culture. They hold up an ideal that few can oppose when the alternative is lack of choice and imposition of lifestyles. As individuals, we are often pressed to make tacit or explicit choices about ways of living, not only about what we buy at the shops, but what is best for us in terms of education, health or provision in old age. 'Life is what we make of it', many of us are often told. Consumption, in terms of this sentiment, speaks to individuals making something of themselves. But it is also important to recognise that consumerism can tell us much about how people's lifestyles are *made by society*. Whereas consumption is often about individual lifestyles, consumerism is a characteristic of society.

From Veblen onwards, as we have seen in this chapter, the promotion of needs and the projection of desires act as pressures for individuals and groups to conform to accepted ways of consuming. Individuals may seek autonomy, but they do so in ways that are acceptable to the consumer culture of which they are a part. People, in that sense, make their own lives in and through society, fashion themselves in relation to it and face marginalisation if they make the wrong choices.

This chapter has also shown that if we actively make our own lives in and through society, some people are better placed than others to make choices, right or wrong. Just as earlier industrial society was marked by social divisions and inequality, so too is a consumer-driven society. Much of this chapter has explored the lines of cleavage that have appeared to open up as a market-driven, consumer culture has embedded itself under the banner of freedom of choice – from those able to take advantage of it to those less able or unable to act. Bauman's argument in particular was considered at length and it is important to remember that it is an argument: that is, a set of claims about the nature of contemporary society and the extent to which our choices are our own. Social scientists have their point of view, ones which often revolve around a series of key claims and, if they are to amount to more than an assertion, are backed up by evidence.

In the following chapters, you will find out about a number of social science arguments in relation to a range of different topics. The next chapter maintains the focus on consumption and choice, but this time in the context of the big supermarkets and their use of power or, as some would argue, abuse of power on the UK high street.

References

Bauman, Z. (1988) *Freedom*, Milton Keynes, Open University Press.

Bauman, Z. (2007) *Consuming Life*, Cambridge, Polity Press.

Belk, R.W. (1988) 'Possessions of the extended self', *The Journal of Consumer Research*, vol. 15, pp. 139–68.

Dittmar, H. (2007) 'Consumer culture, identity, and well-being: the search for the "good life" and the "body perfect"', *European Monographs in Social Psychology Series*, New York, Psychology Press.

Dittmar, H., Beattie, J. and Friese, S. (1995) 'Gender identity and material symbols: objects and decision considerations in impulse purchases', *Journal of Economic Psychology*, vol. 16, pp. 491–511.

Office for National Statistics (ONS) (2012) *Family Spending, 2011 Edition* [Online]. Available at http://www.ons.gov.uk/ons/rel/family-spending/family-spending/family-spending-2011-edition/index.html (Accessed 11 April 2014).

Susman, W.I. (2003[1973]) *Culture as History: The Transformation of American Society in the Twentieth Century* (2nd edn), Washington, DC, Smithsonian Books.

Veblen, T. (1899) *The Theory of the Leisure Class: An Economic Study in the Evolution of Institutions*, New York, Macmillan.

Chapter 6
Supermarket power: winners and losers

John Allen

Contents

Introduction

Supermarkets are often seen as convenient places to shop. Open all hours in some places, relatively cheap by most standards, and offering a range of goods that was inconceivable just 30 or 40 years ago, supermarkets have transformed the way that people shop. Much of that can be traced to the growth of the big superstores, but nowadays, with online retail taking off and supermarkets moving back onto the high street in the convenience store format, the big supermarkets look set to build on that transformation.

In fact, one of the striking facts about shopping habits these days, at least those that involve the basics of everyday life, is that most of it is done through the big four supermarkets. It's worth keeping in mind that with the arrival of online shopping and convenience stores such as Tesco Express and Sainsbury's Local on the high street, the big four supermarket chains – Tesco, Sainsbury's, Asda and Morrisons – take just over three out of every four pounds that are spent on food and groceries in the UK (Kantar Worldwide, 2013). That is a lot of consumption, and indeed a lot of money, accounted for by just a handful of big retailers.

Figure 6.1   The big four supermarket chains: Tesco, Asda, Sainsbury's and Morrisons

And, for some, that is precisely what is wrong with how people shop for basics today. A major worry is that as the big four chains battle it out for control of the grocery market, consumers will have no choice over where they shop. Already in places where one or more of the big four supermarkets dominate, there are concerns that the lifeblood of the community has been drained by such developments. The presence of a new Tesco or Asda has often been linked directly to the closure of the old family butcher's, fishmonger's or greengrocer's shop further up the high street. The losers in this battle for high street domination are, it is claimed, not just the small independent shops, but anyone who prefers to buy their meat or vegetables at a nearby street market or traditional store. If we are in fact living in a consumer society, as Chapter 5 debated, then why all this talk about freedom of choice?

The issue becomes highly charged when the matter of choice turns on the size and power of the supermarkets. Have the big supermarket chains grown so big that they can now dictate food shopping habits? Do they have an overbearing grip on the nation's shopping basket? The growing dominance of supermarkets up and down the country raises such questions and, in particular:

- Does the power of supermarkets widen or narrow our shopping choices?

Activity 1

The matter of choice is, in fact, far from simple and the issue is one that divides opinion on supermarkets. Whether or not you are a regular shopper at one or more of the big four supermarket chains, what choice do you feel that you have over where you shop in your local area? Is choice about having a variety of local shops, independent shops and markets in your area? Or is choice more about price? Is it about the availability of a wide range of goods at affordable prices?

Take five or so minutes to consider why, if indeed you do, you shop at a supermarket – whether online or at a convenience or superstore. Jot down what role choice, in terms of price, say, or the range of goods on offer and the type of shop, plays in your decision.

- Do you, for example, shop at a supermarket because of its low prices and discount offers?
- Do you choose to shop with them because it offers a welcome addition to the independent stores on the high street, giving you a greater choice locally?

- Given the choice, would you rather not shop at a supermarket at all, but do so anyway? If you avoid shopping at supermarkets, then jot down your reasons for doing so.

Make a short list of the factors that influence where and how you or your household shop, and we shall return to it later in the chapter.

For those opposed to supermarkets on the grounds that they restrict choice, the issue, usually, comes down to one of domination, with the big four chains said to abuse their dominant position at the expense of just about everybody else – consumers, local communities and vulnerable workers here and abroad. In contrast, those who welcome the spread of supermarkets, on the high street and online, point to the benefits that can spring from supermarket power, not only from the sheer range of products and produce available, but also from the lower prices it brings. A win–win situation where everybody gains is thought possible, as opposed to a scenario in which there can only ever be 'winners' and 'losers'.

Much of this chapter will be taken up with exploring these two lines of argument, and whether those with more power, like the big supermarkets, make our lives less equal by always getting their way over those with fewer resources.

In Section 1, we look at the nature of supermarket power and map the lines of disagreement between those for and against the big supermarkets. Following that, in Section 2, we consider the impact that supermarket power has had over where we shop and the fate of the high street. Then, in Section 3, we explore whether the price of the cheap goods on supermarket shelves is the denial of a living wage to others, both in the UK and in low-cost countries such as Bangladesh. Throughout, we shall be looking at the respective *claims* made by the opposing sides to the debate over the significance of supermarket power and also at the *evidence* used by each side in support of their argument.

1   What makes supermarkets powerful?

Since their arrival in the UK in the 1960s, the growth and spread of supermarket chains has proved controversial, not least because of their size. By 'size', however, I am not referring to store size, but rather to the size of their commercial operation and ability to dominate the marketplace.

As the likes of Tesco and Sainbury's have increased their share of the UK grocery market and moved back onto the high street, as well as online, so it is often assumed that their power has grown in line with that. In other words, it is presumed that the bigger the supermarket chain, the greater is its ability to get its way over those with fewer resources. With online grocery sales predicted to double over the next five years and convenience chain stores set to outpace existing superstores, it seems fair to contend that the economic leverage of supermarkets will grow too. A retailer's size matters in this context because it is said to confer both **market power** and **buying power**.

Market power
The power to influence market conditions, including price, independently of competitors.

Buying power
The relative bargaining power between firms and their suppliers.

Figure 6.2   Tesco's delivery van – 'Freshly clicked'

Market power refers to the ability of supermarkets to act in the marketplace in ways that their rivals can do little or nothing about. Market share gives them certain advantages over independent retailers and smaller chains, for example over the ability to charge different prices for goods depending on whether the local competition is strong or not.

In itself, there is nothing wrong with some retailers having a greater share of the market than others. It is only when they abuse their dominant position that their power becomes a matter of concern, for example when supermarkets use their dominant position to trade unfairly by selling goods below cost or if they use their size and influence to, say, brush community opinion aside.

The buying power of the big supermarkets is somewhat different, although it, too, is directly related to the size of their market share. In this case, it is relative size that matters – that is, how big a supermarket is in relation to its suppliers. It comes down to the bargaining power that the supermarkets have in their dealings with food manufacturers, farmers and clothing subcontractors.

The larger chains are said to have an advantage over smaller suppliers in so far as they are often able to extract more favourable terms from them, over price, for instance, where their ability to buy in bulk enables them to demand discounts from a small dairy farmer or T-shirt manufacturer. Again, though, it matters most when the big retailers are seen to abuse their dominant position by unfairly squeezing suppliers' margins or colluding among themselves on the price of everyday products such as milk, butter and cheese.

If all this sounds terribly economic, there is a simpler point to hold onto here: size clearly matters when it comes down to the ability of supermarkets to flex their economic muscle, but the crux of the issue, as mentioned, is how retailers use the power that they have to hand.

Activity 2

Think about it for a moment. Are the likes of Asda, with all the resources of its big US parent company Wal-Mart behind it, so powerful that they can put others out of business or mould the face of communities to their advantage?

Can they impose their will on local neighbourhoods so that those who live there have no choice but to shop at their outlets? Do you feel that your local supermarket chain or indeed chains are overbearing in this way?

Figure 6.3   Wal-Mart's headquarters in Bentonville, Arkansas

Obviously, nobody can force us to shop at Asda or Tesco, so how you see the big supermarkets using their power is more likely to depend on whether you think they use their size as a force for widening choice or as a lever to restrict choice, so that only they gain. For the situation to resemble anything like **domination** the major supermarket chains would have to hold a firm grip on the market for groceries, almost to the extent that they had manoeuvred themselves into a commanding position across the country and online.

Domination
To impose upon or constrain the free choice of others so that they have no choice but to comply.

Before we go too far with this line of thought, however, we need to be clear about the two sides of the debate over supermarket power.

1.1   Checkout controversies

There is something a little contrived in setting up the argument over supermarket power as a stark opposition, given the various positions in between, but it is helpful sometimes to draw the contrast sharply so that the claims are clearly drawn.

Let's start with the *claims* of those who broadly oppose supermarket dominance, the *anti-supermarket* campaign groups and organisations. For them:

- The market power of the big supermarket chains has made it increasingly difficult for smaller shops to compete and prosper, with traditional stores closing down in their thousands across the UK. This has not only led to a 'hollowing out' of town centres, it has also restricted 'real choice' for consumers in the marketplace.

- The immense buying power of the supermarkets has given them a stranglehold over the food and clothing supply chain. Increasingly, costs and risks are borne by suppliers. While supermarkets may provide a good deal on price for shoppers, they do so at the expense of workers both in the UK and abroad – often women, sometimes children – who have to suffer poverty wages.

- The size and financial assets of the big supermarkets enable them to exert real pressure on local planners and politicians. Aggressive lobbying by the big retailers has enabled them to get their own way on store development, both on the high street and out of town, usually at the expense of what is best for local people.

On the basis of these claims, those who oppose the spread of supermarkets have done so on the grounds of their dominant position. Too much power is thought to be concentrated in too few hands, leaving the rest of us subject to supermarket domination. In short, there is more at stake here than cheap shopping.

In contrast, the *pro-supermarket* lobby, led quite naturally by the big four supermarkets, see supermarkets as a force for good. They *claim* that supermarkets use, not abuse, their economic size for the benefit of communities and consumers, suppliers and workers, alike. As they see it:

- The market power of supermarkets has brought about an explosion in diversity and choice for consumers at prices lower than ever before. Rather than posing a threat to local retailers, their high-street stores help ailing high streets by drawing specialist or 'boutique' stores to them, enabling small traders to thrive and prosper.

- The buying power of the supermarkets has enabled them to raise standards for their suppliers. In their dealings with factory owners and workers abroad, they have sought to raise wages to a level that, while far from wonderful, has lifted many out of poverty and hardship.

- In run-down areas of the UK, the economic leverage of the big supermarkets can act as a force for social and economic regeneration. Large superstore development, as well as convenience stores, bring tremendous benefits to local communities, in the shape of jobs for the unemployed, improved self-respect and skills development.

The claims provide different standpoints on what supermarkets do with their power and its consequences: whether our shopping choices are constrained or broadened. As you work through the rest of the chapter you should bear in mind that such claims are the elements of an *argument*, that they rest on assumptions about how, in this case, power in society is distributed between institutions like the supermarkets, groups of shopkeepers and individual consumers. Understanding how an argument is put together, the claims made and how the evidence is used to support such claims is a critical social science skill. As such, you will find it worthwhile to keep an eye on how the two arguments are constructed.

1.2   Two sides to an argument

So opinion is divided on the matter of supermarket power and, in practice, it largely turns on whether supermarkets are assumed to wield their power at the expense of others or for the benefit of others. Those opposed to the growing power of the big retail giants believe that the small, independent shops are struggling to survive the onslaught of the big four supermarket chains. As they see it, our shopping choices are now dictated by the big four chains, to the extent that the needs of supermarkets on the one hand, and shoppers and small high-street stores on the other, are now mutually exclusive. Or in the language of the sociologist Dennis Wrong (1997), power here is understood as a **zero-sum game**.

Zero-sum game
A situation in which one party's gain is balanced by another party's loss. If you subtract total losses from total gains, they sum to zero.

One way to grasp this is to think of a game in which there are only winners and losers, so that if one side gains the other side must lose. In a zero-sum game, there is only a fixed amount of resources in play so that the scores of the winner and the loser sum to zero. It is a little like the cutting of a cake where, if one person takes a large slice, there is less cake for everyone else.

So, if supermarkets increase their grip on where and how we shop, dominating the food chain to suit their own ends, there has to be some give in the system. That give is felt by shoppers in the high street whose choice is denied as local independent shops are ruined one by one and invariably replaced by convenience chain stores and lifeless retail parks. The big four's gain, in this case, is experienced by consumers and small shopkeepers as pain.

Needless to say, the pro-supermarket lobby do not see it this way. They argue that the nation's shopping basket, far from being a game whose pay-offs sum to zero, is more akin to what Wrong (1997) and other social scientists refer to as a **positive-sum game**, where all parties involved benefit to some extent.

Positive-sum game
A situation in which the sum of total gains and losses of all parties involved is positive; that is, they sum to more than zero.

Rather than a fixed amount of resources in play, the economic success of the big supermarkets has increased choice for everyone, for example by meeting the demand for fresh fruit and vegetables from around the world regardless of season. On this view, there is more to the 'cake' than first thought and everyone wins: from the consumer and supermarket shareholder to the supplier, and even the migrant worker who washes and packs mixed salad leaves for Tesco. It is all about gain, not pain.

The issue, then, is what are we to make of these competing claims, and about power and supermarket dominance? In social science terms, do the supermarkets operate a zero-sum or a positive-sum game of power on the high street and, more extensively, online and in the UK groceries market?

In the next section, we look first at the impact of supermarket power on where we shop and the fate of the high street. We then move on to Section 3 to consider whether the suppliers of goods to supermarkets are better or worse off by working with the big supermarket chains.

Summary

- The growing dominance of supermarkets in the UK rests upon their market power and their buying power. Both forms of power can be used by supermarket chains to dominate the food and groceries market.

- Pro- and anti-supermarket campaigners argue over what supermarkets do with the power at their disposal. One side claims that supermarkets widen our shopping choices; the other side claims that they restrict them.

- Both sets of claims rest upon assumptions about how power is distributed in society. A zero-sum game implies that it is impossible for both sides to win, whereas a positive-sum game suggests that both sides may gain to some extent.

2 From monopoly over the high street …

Picking up on your response to the issues raised in Activity 2, around the possibility of the major supermarket chains manoeuvring themselves into positions of domination or **monopoly** in local neighbourhoods and town centres, I wonder if you felt that the big supermarkets will always triumph over the small shopkeeper, or that the global retailer will inevitably win out against the local entrepreneur? It is obviously hard to say, but when the language is often in terms of supermarket 'giants' or corporate 'monoliths', the impression of power and reach can sometimes be almost tangible. Wal-Mart, the world's largest retailer, mentioned earlier as the US owner of Asda, is a classic case in point.

Monopoly
A position where a firm, or group of firms, has the power to prevent, restrict or distort competition in a particular market.

Wal-Mart and its UK offspring, Asda, are unquestionably big and it is hard not to see them as being able to get their own way despite opposition from others. The UK marketplace for food and groceries seems far from a level playing field and that, for some, is simply the end of the story. But for us, it is more of a starting point, where we need to be clear not only about the nature of supermarket power in the UK, but equally, as noted in Section 1, about what they *do* with that power in terms of shaping our choices over where and how we shop.

- So, what is the relevant *evidence* about supermarket power in the UK today?

2.1 Power in store

There is some evidence that appears to be beyond dispute (so much so it is often labelled as 'fact'). One such fact concerns the market power of the big four supermarkets and their ever-increasing share of the UK food and groceries market. Tesco became the front-runner in 1995 and, although it has dipped recently, it still holds a market share of just under one-third of all grocery shopping in the UK. This is nearly as much as the second and third largest supermarket chains, Asda and Sainsbury's, combined. Morrison, the fourth member of the supermarket quartet, now has nearly 12 per cent of the market, largely as the result of its acquisition of the Safeway supermarket chain in 2004. The Co-op, after buying its rival, Somerfield, in 2008, has just over 6 per cent. Waitrose and Marks & Spencer, as well as the German-owned Aldi and Lidl, make up the rest, each with 5 per cent or less of the market (Competition Commission, 2008; Kantar Worldwide, 2013). See Table 6.1 for additional information on UK supermarkets.

Table 6.1 Who are the supermarkets?

Name	Market share	Description
TESCO	30%	Sales in 13 countries worldwide. Operates over 2300 stores in the UK, two-thirds of which are convenience stores
ASDA	17%	Part of the US Wal-Mart chain. Operates around 500 stores in the UK – of which just under a third are convenience stores
Sainsbury's Try something new today	17%	Operates over 1110 stores in the UK – of which just over half are convenience stores
M MORRISONS	12%	Operates over 500 stores in the UK – of which around one-fifth are convenience stores
The **co-operative**	6%	Operates 2800 stores in the UK, mainly at the convenience end of the grocery market
Waitrose	5%	Part of the John Lewis Partnership. Operates over 300 stores in the UK
ALDI	4%	German-owned, with sales in 14 countries. Operates over 500 stores in the UK
YOUR M&S	4%	Operates over 750 stores in the UK, including its Simply Food groceries outlets, together with 430 stores overseas
LIDL	3%	German-owned, part of the Schwarz Group, with sales in 17 countries. Operates over 500 stores in the UK

Sources: Competition Commission, 2008; Kantar Worldwide, 2013

Online grocery sales, although set to expand, currently make up only 4 per cent of the market, so the big supermarket chains have moved back to the high street to gain a share of the 'top-up' market that local stores and small traders previously counted on as their own. All the big four have expanded on the high street by opening in the convenience store format, buying stores from independent chains to capture passing trade from local and busy working people. In the past, the out-of-town superstores are said to have driven retailing out of the high street, but now with the big multiples moving into online shopping and returning to the high street as Sainsbury's Local, M-Local and Tesco Express or Metro, small independents find themselves up against their market power once again, but this time as a direct competitor just along the road.

For food writers like Joanna Blythman (2007), the adoption of the convenience store format by the big chains has sharply accelerated the rate of closure among small independent shops that were just about holding their own. For her, places like Dundee in Scotland are typical of the changes that have taken place. Back in the 1960s, she points out, 'there were ten bakers; now there are two left. There were eight or nine butchers; now there is one. Of the five fishmongers, one has survived. Where there were half a dozen grocers, one remains' (Blythman, 2007, p. 12). Some 40 odd years on, the city of Dundee plays host to six Tescos, three of which are either Metro or Express stores, one Asda, one Morrisons, one Sainsbury's, one Marks & Spencer and a number of low-price outlets. In Blythman's mind, the demise of the independents and the march of the big supermarkets into Dundee are two sides of the same coin. The big multiples have benefited at the expense of the small independents.

Or to put it in social science terms: a zero-sum game of power appears to be at work here where growing supermarket power is matched by an equivalent decline in the abilities of small independent shops to compete. The end-result is a high street stripped of diversity and life, as the big four limit the possible range and type of shops available. In support of this view, a snapshot survey of small and medium-sized grocery retailers conducted in 2011 identified the main obstacle to their business as competition from the big supermarket chains (ResPublica, 2011). Every year, it seems, the UK is less and less a nation of shopkeepers, as the number of small traditional shops suffers long-term decline.

Now, of course, the two trends could simply be a coincidence, rather than one the cause of the other. For anti-supermarket campaigners, however, there is no mistaking the fact that the nationwide market and buying power of the big chains give them an unfair advantage over independents on the high street. It is, they argue, this retail power that enables supermarkets to dominate the marketplace and which gives consumers little choice over where to shop. Or rather, the choice that shoppers have is a choice between an Asda or a Sainsbury's store, or a Tesco or Morrisons, which in their eyes is tantamount to the big four approaching a monopoly stranglehold on the marketplace.

Supermarkets attract this kind of criticism from consumers too, even though they may end up doing most of their shopping there. However, the claim that supermarket domination amounts to a monopoly over the high street or local neighbourhood requires looking at more closely.

2.2 Tesco Towns

Activity 3

Figures 6.4 and 6.5 below, respectively, provided a snapshot in 2007 of which supermarkets enjoyed a dominant position across different parts of the UK, and the towns in which Tesco had its highest and lowest market share. The data comes from a Competition Commission set up at the time to explicitly explore levels of competition in the groceries marketplace.

Cast your eye down Figure 6.5 and stop at Dundee. With, as we have seen, its six Tescos and their 52 per cent market share of groceries in the city, do you think that this is sufficient to give Tesco a monopoly over the food business in the area? Remember, to exercise a monopoly position, Tesco would have to have sufficient power over its rivals to the extent that they cannot effectively compete.

Now go back to what Blythman (2007) had to say above about the changed profile of shops in Dundee and give the matter some thought. Make a note of what other kinds of store are in evidence in today's retail market in the city. How restricted, in terms of market competition, are Tesco's rivals?

To be honest, I would have thought it debatable how far one could say that Tesco has a monopoly over food shopping in Dundee, given the presence of the other big supermarkets as well as low-price outlets in the city. But that has not stopped the anti-supermarket lobby from dubbing towns in which Tesco takes more than 50 pence in the pound spent on groceries as 'Tesco Towns'. Places like Inverness, for example, because of the number of Tesco stores in the local area, are often cited by the lobby as areas where people have little choice but to shop at Tesco. Although again, that's not strictly true, as Inverness, despite its four Tescos, also plays host to an Asda and a Morrisons, as well as a Lidl and an Aldi. Nonetheless, the lobby has been quick to point out the suffocating effects of the mega-retailers, which are able to prosper at the expense of small shops.

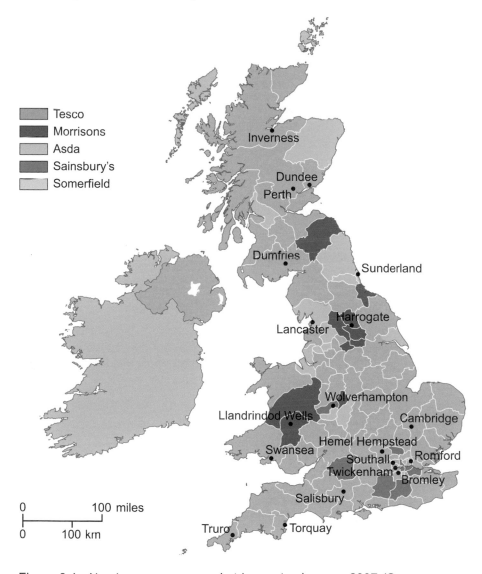

Figure 6.4 Number one supermarket by postcode area, 2007 (Source: adapted from *The Guardian*, 2007, based on Competition Commission data)

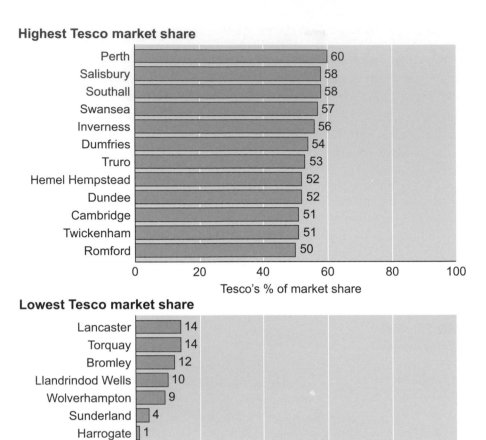

Figure 6.5   Towns in which Tesco has the highest and lowest market share (Source: adapted from *The Guardian*, 2007, based on Competition Commission data)

At the forefront of the anti-supermarket lobby is the Tescopoly Alliance. Launched in 2005, the Alliance acts as an umbrella grouping for a number of organisations and pressure groups, including Friends of the Earth and the New Economics Foundation (NEF), whose explicit political goal is to curb the market power of the major UK supermarkets. The Alliance draws attention to what it perceives as the negative impacts of supermarket behaviour in the marketplace and acts as a resource for local campaigns that share its aims. A book of the same name, *Tescopoly*, was published in 2007 by one of the leading campaigners in the NEF, Andrew Simms, and while he too directs attention to the excessive power and influence of the big supermarket chains, his prime target is what he sees as Tesco's monopoly power.

Figure 6.6   The Tescopoly Alliance logo (Source: Tescopoly Alliance, undated)

He points to the fact that, in the UK, the government sets the level at which a monopoly is said to operate at 25 per cent of the market. Above that level, a firm's control of the market is a signal that it not only enjoys a dominant position, but that it effectively has the power to distort competition and prevent others from doing business. Tesco's evident monopoly of the grocery market, he claims, is directly responsible for the ruination of local neighbourhood stores and corner shops, the 'hollowing out' of town centres, and the growth of out-of-town retail parks dominated by identikit chain stores (Simms, 2007).

At times, though, it is hard to know exactly what to make of this sweeping claim, apart from the fact that, on the basis of the 25 per cent mark, monopolies may be more common than you or I had supposed. That may well be so, but economists will tell you that it is not as straightforward as it looks to establish whether a firm enjoys a position of monopoly in a given market.

For one thing, it is not always immediately obvious what the size and scope of a relevant market is, especially in something like food and groceries. Is the market for the big weekly or fortnightly shop at the edge-of-town superstore different from just nipping out to shop at the small convenience store on the high street? Do shoppers switch between them or is there a clear break in their custom? Do Asda, Morrisons, Sainsbury's and Tesco compete with each other nationally or locally? And, if it is the latter, where do you draw the boundary of the local market?

This is just to scratch the surface of what is involved in trying to establish whether or not a firm enjoys a market share that all can agree constitutes a monopoly position. The government's cut-off point that could trigger a monopoly concern – 25 per cent of a market – does after all depend on how the market is defined. It comes down to 25 per cent of what exactly?

2.3   Local or national market?

So, if you wish to prove that a supermarket enjoys a monopoly position in the market for food and groceries, you would be inclined to define the market narrowly. If you want to resist that charge, however, you would opt for the widest market definition possible. The nef considers that, at the local level, no one supermarket should control more than one-third of the market (NEF, 2007), and the percentages in Figure 6.5 give it plenty of support for its case that at least one supermarket exercises 'monopoly powers'. In response, nevertheless, Tesco argues that the relevant geographic market for groceries is national, with everyone competing against everyone else (Tesco, 2007).

Why national? And why specifically Tesco? This is because, if you look at Figure 6.4 and the swathes of grey that signify Tesco's dominant position across the country, for Tesco there are no readily identifiable local or regional markets, each with their own profile of competitors, only a national market with national brands, a national pricing structure and a nationwide range of goods.

You read more about how life's shopping essentials have changed in Chapter 5.

More to the point, if the food and groceries market is national, then shoppers have a wide variety of retailers – the local organic butchers and the farmers' market as much as the countrywide multiple and smaller chains – to choose between. Besides, as the big retail chains are not slow to point out, the market in question is, strictly speaking, not limited to groceries. Life's essentials today include a range of household goods, from clothing to all manner of electrical goods, which are traded by supermarkets and other stores, and as people shop around for more things in more places, this too can be read as an absence of monopoly powers.

There is an important point about supermarket power at stake here. If the market for food and groceries is indeed national, then it is possible for the big supermarkets to claim that they use their not insignificant power for the 'common good', to deliver lower prices and more choice for shoppers over a wider range of products. The rapid growth of supermarkets in the UK over the past 50 or so years has, on this view, increased the resources in play, to the benefit of all parties concerned. Compared with the often overpriced corner shop, consumers now have access to a wide range of affordable goods. High streets too benefit from the new local convenience stores run by the supermarkets, which act as a magnet, enticing people to struggling high streets and draw in less traditional providers such as coffee shops and beauty salons. On this view, social scientists would argue that a positive-sum game, rather than a zero-sum game, of power is in play with an expanding national market delivering a 'win–win' situation.

So are supermarkets a force for good or do they abuse their dominant market position to suit their own purposes? Before you mull over the opposing claims and the evidence offered, there is a further set of claims to consider: whether the price of those cheap, affordable goods in supermarkets is paid for by others who, in this instance, are part of a wider global picture often far removed from the bustle of the high street.

Summary

- Between them, the big four supermarkets account for around three-quarters of the UK food and groceries market. This gives them significant market power.

- Anti-supermarket campaigners claim that supermarket domination amounts to a monopoly over the groceries market, with Tesco in particular distorting competition and profiting at the expense of small traditional shops on the high street.

- The establishment of a monopoly, in the case of supermarkets and Tesco in particular, turns on the definition of the relevant geographic market, whether the market for food and groceries is local or national. If the latter, then a monopoly situation is not proven.

3 ... to the domination of suppliers around the globe

Low prices at the checkouts can often be traced to the efforts of the big supermarkets to increase their market share by buying produce more cheaply and passing on the reduction to the shoppers. While this may sound like a good thing, not everybody thinks so. The crux of the matter, as before, is that the benefits passed on to consumers may be enjoyed at the expense of others. This time, though, those on the receiving end are the farmers and manufacturers who supply the supermarkets, together with their workforces.

Coercion
To compel by force or its threatened use.

Small suppliers regularly claim that the big supermarkets squeeze them up to the point that their economic livelihood is in doubt, by **coercing** them into price cuts. That may well be true at times, but their relationship with supermarkets is far from straightforward. What is easier and perhaps more obvious to talk about when it comes to being at the sharp end of supermarket power is the plight of those who work for the suppliers, great or small, without whom none of us would enjoy the benefit of cheap supermarket goods.

3.1 The real cost of low prices

Not so long ago, little was heard about the low-paid, often migrant, workers in the UK countryside who sort, cut and pack the salads and vegetables for the big supermarket chains, or indeed about their fellow low-paid agency workers in the fields picking and gathering them. Like the workforce in overseas factories who sew and stitch the clothes for Asda's George fashion range, for instance, often putting in what some claim are excessive hours for what seems like little return, this labour was, until recently, both distant and largely hidden.

Thanks in part to food journalists like Felicity Lawrence, those who pick the green beans and spring onions for Tesco or who sew the latest Asda garment in Bangladesh are now linked directly through their supply chains to the ability of supermarkets to sell goods at low cost (Lawrence, 2013). Without access to such pools of cheap labour, many of the products on supermarket shelves, she points out, would simply be unaffordable or at least expensive enough for us to think twice about buying them. In her book *Not on the Label* (2013), Lawrence has drawn attention to the plight of casualised agency workers employed by 'gangmasters' around the country.

Often paid hourly rates below the legal minimum, subjected to illegal deductions from their pay, and bussed from job to job at will, the many nationalities involved – Polish, Romanian, Hungarian, Bulgarian, Latvian and Slovakian workers among them – work in supermarket packhouses and food-processing plants that, for Lawrence, largely operate outside the restrictions of the law. More to the point, she claims that much of this abuse of migrant workers goes on with the knowledge of supermarkets, who turn a blind eye to the arrangement while benefiting from the low wages paid by gangmasters in the farming and food-processing sectors. At arm's length from the actual illegality of employment practices, supermarkets nonetheless gain directly from prices being kept low in the food supply chain.

But, Lawrence pointedly argues, you will not find any evidence of underpay or illegality on the label of the salad packets or boxes of chicken pieces that grace the big supermarkets' shelves (Lawrence, 2013).

Figure 6.7   Migrant workers harvesting cabbages in Lincolnshire

Connections (and disconnections) are the focus in the 'Connecting lives' strand.

For Lawrence, the connection between exploited migrant labour in the more remote parts of the countryside and the cost of what turns up on our plates is an elementary one; namely, that there is a high price to be

171

paid for cheap goods, and that cost is borne one-sidedly by the weakest and least powerful groups in the supply chain. To her way of thinking, consumers benefit directly from low supermarket prices at the expense of those employed by suppliers keen to give us salad and strawberries all year round. Suppliers, though, she acknowledges, are often themselves caught in the middle of all this, with their financial margins squeezed by supermarkets to the extent that they cannot actually afford to pay their workers a decent wage.

You might like to think of this as another claim about *domination*, where the big chains, by hiding behind their chain of subcontractors, in this instance, give the latter no choice but to pay their workers less, as supermarkets drive down prices at the factory and farm gates. On this view, those with more power are said to prevail over those with less, and a tally of who gains and who loses falls squarely, as we have seen, into a *zero-sum* game. The high cost of low prices at the checkout falls on both suppliers and their workforce, but disproportionately on the latter.

There is another twist to this argument, however, which is that the more distant the workforce, the greater is the assumed loss, for example with subcontracted garment factory workers in China, Thailand, Indonesia, Bangladesh and other low-cost locations bearing the brunt of the supermarket's buying power. Subcontracting through a **global supply chain** of the type illustrated in Figure 6.8 provides options for supermarkets over where to source particular products, as well as giving them control over price, turnaround times and the quality of the finished goods.

Global supply chain
A chain of suppliers that cuts across national borders, drawing firms and contractors into the process of making and delivering a single product.

The chains themselves, I should add, are often disconcertingly complex, with merchandise sometimes passing through the hands of buyers, suppliers, trading companies and sourcing agents before reaching the stores of an Asda or a Tesco in the UK. Even simple operations to do with clothing, say the cutting, trimming and sewing of garments for a supermarket, may involve more than one factory, and some steps may actually be completed by home-based workers. But this tangled set of arrangements rarely surfaces when the anti-supermarket lobby seeks to press home the political point that supermarkets are directly at fault for the poverty wages experienced by garment workers in faraway factories.

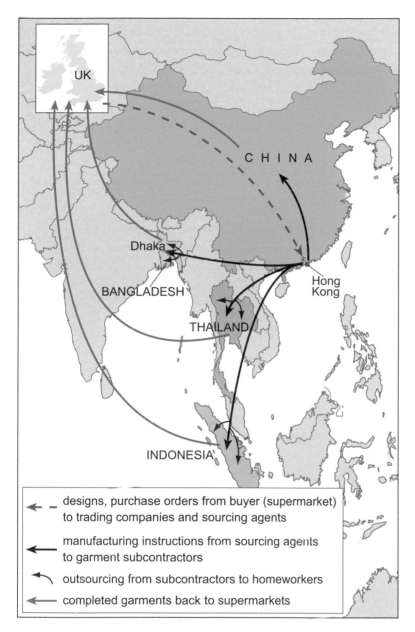

Figure 6.8 A typical global supply chain for garment production

3.2 Profiting from poverty wages abroad?

In 2006, War on Want, a large non-governmental organisation (NGO) based in the UK, targeted Asda and Tesco directly, accusing them of boosting profits at the expense of some of the most vulnerable workers in the world: sweatshop garment workers in Bangladesh. Based on a **sample** survey of six large factories, each employing between

Sample
A subset of a population that is used to represent the entire group as a whole.

500 and 1200 workers, in Dhaka, the capital city of Bangladesh, War on Want found evidence that the mainly female workforce had been subjected to forced overtime, overcrowded and unhygienic working conditions, verbal intimidation and refused access to trade unions. Above all, those factories, all of which were known to be supplying low-cost clothing for Asda and Tesco in the UK market, were found to be paying wages to their workers well below that needed to provide for themselves and their families. The relentless pressure on the factory owners to keep costs down or risk losing the clothing contract was said to leave them no room for manoeuvre.

Thus, the true cost of the cheap jeans and trousers, as well as the bargain-priced shoes, which line Asda's and Tesco's aisles, War on Want claim, is the absence of a living wage for workers in their supply chains.

If you find it hard to grasp exactly what that experience amounts to, then War on Want can make the connection for you – by way of Lina's story in Activity 4.

Activity 4

Lina is one of many workers named in War on Want's 2006 survey of garment workers in Dhaka. It is not her real name, of course, which has been changed to protect her from victimisation. Read the 'How cheap is too cheap?' (War on Want, 2006) extract below. Give yourself some time to consider the nature of the appeal.

- What is it about Lina's story that tries to involve you as part of it, not as someone to blame for her predicament, but as someone *connected* to her?

- What is the nature of that connection?

How cheap is too cheap?

Lina began working in a garment factory at the age of 13. The oldest of eight children, her parents became unable to pay for her education when her brother became sick. She moved from her village to the Bangladeshi capital Dhaka to get a job and help them make ends meet. Now 22, she works in a factory that supplies Primark, Asda and Tesco. She is one of the lucky ones to have learned how to operate a sewing machine, and so can command a wage of £17 per month. To earn this amount, she must work between 60 and 90 hours each week.

Lina earns far less than even the most conservative estimate of a living wage in Bangladesh, which is £22 per month. Her husband, whom she met in the factory and married three years ago, is now ill and unable to work. She must pay for his treatment as well as for her own living costs in Dhaka, and, despite her best efforts to economise, she is unable to send money to her family, who need it to get by. She says she is happy, though, to have 'done the best she could' for her family.

If you are wearing a piece of clothing bought from Primark, Asda or Tesco, it is quite possible that Lina sewed it. These high street retailers are able to sell their clothes at such an agreeable price because workers like Lina are forced to live on wages well below what they need in order to live a decent life.

Lina is one of 60 workers who were interviewed for this report, across six garment factories in Bangladesh. According to these workers, all six factories are producing 'significant amounts' of garments for Asda; four also produce for Tesco and three for Primark. The workers' testimonies in this report demonstrate the dismal life of a garment worker selling to Britain's bargain retailers.

Poor working conditions like those described in this report are systemic problems that exist across the whole clothing industry. But Asda, Tesco and Primark – like others at the budget end of the market – do raise more concerns than their rivals. The question is quite simply: 'How do they get their clothes so cheap?'

(War on Want, 2006)

The connection, for me, that Lina's story seems to be suggesting is that those who put on an inexpensive George suit from Asda or buy a pair of cheap jeans from Tesco are somehow caught up in a system that benefits them at the expense of workers like Lina. Because shoppers like a bargain, the pressure that sets up transmits itself directly to the factory floor in Bangladesh and requires others to make the clothes at a cost that fails to deliver a living wage.

There is, then, an obvious immediacy to the connection, one that ties those who wear the suits and jeans to those who stitch and sew them in far-off places. Consumers in the system merely go about their normal business of shopping at the supermarket, enjoying the low prices, but this, it appears, sets off a chain reaction that deprives others – that is, workers like Lina, in Bangladesh – from earning a living wage.

Figure 6.9   Garment workers, including children, in textile factories in and around Dhaka, Bangladesh

In 2008, War on Want returned to the same six factories and found that conditions for the garment workers showed no sign of improvement, with practices such as forced overtime and long working days still commonplace (War on Want, 2008). Then, in 2010, in response it appears to outside pressure, the minimum wage for garment workers in Bangladesh was raised by the government, taking the monthly pay for sewing operators like Lina to £32 (3861 taka), if production targets were met. But by this time, however, a living wage was estimated by War on Want to be more than twice that amount for a family household.

As you can see from the extract below, in a follow-up survey in 2010 of just under 1000 workers in 41 factories in Bangladesh, War on Want published evidence to show that wages were still falling below that required for a worker and their family to meet their basic needs.

Less than a living wage

As a result of sustained campaigning by women workers and other trade unionists in Bangladesh, the minimum wage for garment workers was raised in 2010 for the first time in four years. Receipt of wages in the garment industry depends on meeting an assigned production target. If production targets are met, a sewing operator's salary now starts at 3,861 taka (approximately £32) a month and a helper's wage at 3,000 taka (£25) a month.

Even with the new increases, however, these wages fall far short of the level which is considered to be a living wage – that is, enough to allow a worker to provide her family with basic human necessities such as food, shelter, clothing, water, health, education and transport. Trade unionists in Bangladesh calculate the living wage for a single worker to be at least 5,000 taka (£42) a month. According to the women workers interviewed for this research, the average monthly household expenditure for a family of four is higher still, and far in excess of the new minimum wage levels introduced in 2010:

Average monthy household expenditure in Bangladesh (in taka):

House rent …	1,825
Food …	3,973
Transport …	300
Education …	950
Medical …	715
Clothing …	675
Refreshment …	458
Total …	8,896

(War on Want, 2011)

Workers like Lina, it seems, are thus still deprived of a living wage, caught up in a system in which the benefits are mutually exclusive: *either* prices rise for consumers and the supermarkets take a cut in profits *or* workers like Lina suffer pittance wages. There is no in- between, just a straightforward zero-sum game in which, according to War on Want (2006), consumers are part of a system of domination that works in their favour. Or in the words of political theorist, Iris Marion Young (2003), through no fault of their own, consumers are tied into a system that produces harm and injustice on the far side of the globe.

Supermarkets are not oblivious to the hardships involved and have made commitments to improve pay and conditions at the overseas factories that supply them (Labour Behind the Label, 2011). The extent of that commitment, however, was tested in 2013 when a building that housed three garment factories on the outskirts of Dhaka collapsed after the owners apparently built two additional floors without government permission. Over 1100 workers lost their lives and many more were injured in what has become known as the Rana Plaza disaster.

The tragedy highlighted more than the unsafe working conditions still to be found in many of Bangladesh's many sweatshops; it also highlighted a gap in responsibility, as supermarkets and other clothing brands denied any direct blame for the disaster in a factory outside of their ownership and control. Besides, they argued, what would be worse for the workers is for them to move production elsewhere.

3.3   Bad jobs are better than no jobs

For the pro-supermarket lobby, the low price of goods on supermarket shelves in the UK has less to do with poor or unsafe working conditions in faraway places like Bangladesh, and more to do with the efficiency of their bulk buying practices and ability to reduce overheads. The working conditions in overseas garment factories may be awful at times and, of course, Bangladeshi factory owners should ensure that their workplaces are safe, but they have to follow the discipline of the marketplace and pay their workers the 'going rate' for the job. Any other course of action, the pro-supermarket lobby concludes, would simply distort the market and leave open the possibility of retailers shifting their business to another low-cost country. The real losers in that case, they argue, would be the Linas of this world. More importantly for what concerns us here, what underpins this claim is a *positive-sum view* of the power wielded by the big supermarkets.

Martin Wolf (2004), an economic journalist on the *Financial Times*, has put the more general argument that firms like Asda and Sainsbury's, which seek to source their clothing needs at ever cheaper locations abroad, do indeed exploit the poor by taking advantage of the profitable opportunities that a pool of cheap labour represents. But because outside companies in places like Bangladesh almost invariably pay more than local companies to attract workers, the garment workers fortunate enough to be employed can be said to 'exploit' the outside companies by extracting higher pay from them. The work and the wages may not look much by UK standards, but in Bangladesh they represent an opportunity that previously was not on offer.

Seen in this light, Wolf argues that, as low as wages are in the offshore jeans business, both the big corporates and the workers in the overseas factories stand to gain from the global supply arrangement. Rather than a *mutually exclusive* set-up where one side gains at the expense of another, the kind of global arrangement that Wolf has in mind is all about **mutual exploitation** (Wolf, 2004). Leaving safety issues to one side, workers in places like Bangladesh benefit from the higher wages available that, while far from wonderful, are a measurable improvement on existing livelihoods, and supermarkets gain through their access to pools of cheap labour. As the pro-supermarket lobby would have it, this is a win–win situation, which works to the benefit of all parties.

Mutual exploitation
An economic situation that both firms and workers are able to exploit to their advantage without either side losing out.

Since the mid 1990s, the garment industry in Bangladesh has expanded rapidly, with up to four million people working in the thousands of factories that have sprung up. In many respects, such factories represent a pathway out of poverty and, according to Wolf, the last thing a country like this wants is for the big retailers to stop sourcing their labour from them. That, he pointedly remarks, would threaten the steadily rising living standards of the garment workers. After all, if the factory jobs are so bad, why do Lina and others actively seek them out?

In much the same way that shoppers would go elsewhere if the big supermarkets in the UK failed to deliver choice and affordability, so workers in Dhaka would seek work elsewhere if the jobs on offer in the garment industry failed to pay above the local rate. No matter how bad such jobs are perceived to be by shoppers on the high street in London and Birmingham, despite War on Want's protestations, they are comparably better than most other jobs locally available in and around Bangladesh's capital city. Or so the pro-supermarket lobby insists.

The pro-supermarket lobby would also claim that the efforts of big retailers to source labour globally is yet another example of the use of supermarket power as a force for good, one that enables such retailers, through their global size and reach, to direct resources and materially affect people's lives in different parts of the world. As successful businesses that bring employment to thousands of people in the UK and overseas, the benefits add up to what we can now recognise as a positive-sum scenario where the amount of resources in play represents a net gain for all those involved: supermarkets and consumers at the UK end, and suppliers and their workers at the other, somewhat poorer, end. On this view of power, there are no losers, only winners.

Summary

- The large market share enjoyed by the big supermarket chains also gives them significant buying power. Suppliers claim that this is used to bargain down prices to a level that is often economically devastating.

- Anti-supermarket campaigners claim that through low prices consumers benefit at the expense of vulnerable workers, both in the UK and in factories abroad.

- In response, big supermarkets and the pro-supermarket lobby point to the mutual exploitation of cheap labour that takes place, which benefits overseas workers and retail corporations alike, and materially changes people's lives around the globe for the better.

Conclusion

So, the argument over whether supermarkets use their power to bring unprecedented choice at low prices is far from clear-cut. The two sides – the pro-supermarket lobby and those pitted against it – disagree as to the consequences of supermarket power. As I hope is now evident, where and how we shop are not as straightforward as may first appear, especially when the issue broadens out to encompass the plight of vulnerable workforces and the future of the high street.

Activity 5

At this point, I would like you to revisit your answers to Activity 1, more as a means of pulling together the range of issues discussed in the chapter than anything evaluative.

Run down the list of factors that influenced your or your household's shopping choices. If you shop at supermarkets and you jotted down, as I did, the choice of a wide range of goods at low prices, how would you square that with the anti-supermarket campaigners' claim that such a choice comes at a high price? For example, the price could be said to involve the denial of choice to others of a living wage or the narrowing of consumer choice along the high street.

You may find it helpful to think about the variety of claims expressed and the assumptions that they are based upon, as well as the evidence used to support them. To give you a broad idea, I have set out the two sides of the argument and their different components in Table 6.2.

Table 6.2   Does the power of supermarkets narrow or widen shopping choices?

Argument	Claims	Assumptions	Evidence
Anti-supermarket lobby	Supermarkets restrict choice over where we shop	A zero-sum game: supermarkets prosper at the expense of local high-street stores	Local market statistics and the falling number of independently owned shops
	The real cost of low prices is borne by suppliers and their workforces	A zero-sum game: cheap shopping is at the expense of vulnerable workers at home and abroad	Factory surveys and local case studies to highlight poverty and hardship
Pro-supermarket lobby	Supermarkets provide a wide choice of cheap goods at convenient locations	A positive-sum game: both consumers and local communities benefit from affordable goods and supermarket-led regeneration	National market statistics and local regeneration studies
	Exploiting workers to source cheap goods has led to an improvement in living standards	A positive-sum game: the mutual exploitation of cheap labour benefits all parties involved, even sweatshop labour	Factory visits and local wage-level comparisons to highlight improved living standards

By 'assumptions' in Table 6.2, I am referring to the underlying claims that social scientists draw upon when trying to make sense of the arguments expressed by the opposing lobbies. It is their way of explaining the nature of the arguments put forward. Understood through the eyes of social scientists, the argument of the anti-supermarket lobby effectively portrays the supermarkets as winners in a zero-sum game of power, where the big multiples use their power as a force to boost their profits. The alternative argument and underlying claim, expressed by those lobbying for supermarkets, as we have seen, points to a different kind of power play: that of a positive-sum game in which supermarkets as much as shoppers, suppliers as much as distant workforces, have much to gain from the big retailers exercising their power on the high street and beyond.

A social science argument, much like any argument, will set out its claims as some kind of provisional answer to a question, in this instance, the question that frames Table 6.2 about the power of supermarkets to shape choices. The relevance of the claims is something for you to judge, but you can only really do that by weighing up the evidence offered in support. When the question, claims and evidence are put together, you have, as mentioned earlier in Section 1.1, the elements of an argument.

In this case, the arguments of both sides tell us something about how institutions like supermarkets, the decisions that they make and the influence that they have, can shape the choices of others, either by constraining them or by enabling them. Depending on which of the two arguments you find the more convincing, you will be in a position to draw up a tally of the winners and losers on the high street and further afield; that is, a tally that can tell us something about how much choice people have over their lives. Bear in mind, nonetheless, that what people may want as consumers may conflict with what they want as workers or members of a local community.

When such patterns of advantage and disadvantage are drawn, however, they do tell us something about the role that power has in *making* lives more or less equal. Institutional power, like that of the supermarkets, is one kind of power, based on size and economic muscle, but the power of campaign groups like the NEF or War on Want, for example, rests upon a different set of resources: the ability to mobilise consumers, to tap into matters of public concern, to improve the life chances, for instance, of others less well off on the other side of the globe. This is the power to make a difference, to change society in a way that recognises that choices are socially and politically made, not simply predetermined.

In the next chapter, we take a closer look at what actually influences the choices that consumers make.

References

Blythman, J. (2007) *Shopped: The Shocking Power of British Supermarkets*, London, Harper Perennial.

Competition Commission (2008) *Groceries Market Investigation: Final Report* [Online]. Available at www.competition-commission.org.uk (Accessed 20 January 2009).

Kantar Worldwide (2013) *Grocery Market Share UK* [Online]. Available at http://www.kantarworldpanel.com/global/News/Grocery-Market-Share-UK—Strong-performances (Accessed 8 April 2014).

Labour Behind the Label (2011) *Let's Clean Up Fashion 2011 Update*, London, Labour Behind the Label.

Lawrence, F. (2013) *Not on the Label*, London, Penguin.

New Economics Foundation (NEF) (2007) *Detrimental Effects: Defending Consumers from Distorted Markets – A Response to the Competition Commission* [Online]. Available at www.neweconomics.org (Accessed 11 June 2014).

ResPublica (2011) *The Right to Retail: Can Localism Save Britain's Small Retailers?*, London, Economy Unit, ResPublica.

Simms, A. (2007) *Tescopoly*, London, Constable.

Tesco (2007) *Main Submission to the Competition Commission Inquiry into the UK Grocery Retailing Market* [Online]. Available at www.competition-commission.org.uk (Accessed 12 January 2009).

Tescopoly Alliance (undated) *Tescopoly: Every Little Hurts* [Online]. Available at http://tescopoly.org (Accessed 9 April 2014).

War on Want (2006) *Fashion Victims: The True Cost of Cheap Clothes at Primark, Asda and Tesco*, London, War on Want.

War on Want (2008) *Fashion Victims II: How UK Clothing Retailers are Keeping Workers in Poverty*, London, War on Want.

War on Want (2011) *Stitched Up: Women Workers in the Bangladeshi Garment Sector*, London, War on Want.

Wolf, M. (2004) *Why Globalization Works*, New Haven, CT, Yale University Press.

Wrong, D. (1997) *Power: Its Forms, Bases and Uses*, New Brunswick, NJ, and London, Transaction Publishers.

Young, I.M. (2003) 'From guilt to solidarity: sweatshops and political responsibility', *Dissent*, Spring, pp. 39–44.

Chapter 7
Advertising and consumer choice: the powers of persuasion

Catriona Havard and George Revill

Contents

Introduction

The previous chapter looked at the power of supermarkets and raised the question over whether or not they can influence what people buy. That question is the focus of this chapter, although this time in the broader context of the influence exercised by advertising and marketing. When faced with decisions about what products people wish to buy, do consumers always have a free choice in what they decide? Put another way, to what extent are our choices our own? There are, indeed, many forces that can influence what consumers choose to buy, such as the advertising people may have seen about the product, the product's appearance or the fact that they may have bought this product before. But does this advertising really persuade consumers to choose certain products over other ones? Or are people able to ignore the adverts that they see all around them?

In everyday life, people are often surrounded by advertising – from television, newspapers, magazines, billboards and the internet – and as much as they may try to ignore it, or claim that they might not be influenced by it, advertising may still change the way people remember things or choose what to buy.

Activity 1

Look at the logos in Figure 7.1. Can you name the company that each logo is associated with?

Figure 7.1   Company logos

How many did you get right? Is there anything striking about them in terms of the way that they are projected?

The answers for Activity 1, if you haven't guessed them already, are: Shell, Starbucks, McDonalds, Apple, Amazon, Volkswagen, Nike, and Red Bull.

Even if you do not buy from any of these companies, were you still able to name the majority of the companies that are associated with these logos? The logos all use bright colours and/or simple, easily recognisable shapes that stand out. Companies use branding and logos to stand out from their competitors, and they become so recognisable that even if you don't buy that particular product, people can recognise what it is, even without seeing the name of the company. As consumers, people are more likely to remember a company that has an easily distinguishable image associated with it than the product from the 'what's its name' company that has no logo. When consumers see a logo or specific brand, it often comes with its own personality, assurance of quality or emotional appeal.

The idea of branding and using advertising to persuade consumers to buy things is, of course, not a new idea. Advertising and marketing professionals have long recognised that who people are and how they feel shapes consumer behaviour. The development of marketing and market research based in social science concepts, techniques and methods from the 1950s onwards has provided marketers and retailers with more and better information about customers' preferences and habits. At the time, however, it also provoked some social scientists into issuing dire warnings about the ways in which such knowledge-informing advertising and marketing invaded personal privacy, and threatened society by acting as a hidden form of persuasion, which shaped and controlled behaviour without people's knowledge or consent. More recently, though, social scientists investigating the taken-for-granted qualities of shopping, as we saw in Chapter 5, have been more concerned to show how consumers interact with, and interpret for themselves, marketing messages and retail environments, rather than simply accepting what advertisers and marketers tell them.

Much of this chapter will be taken up with exploring this apparent contradiction in shopping today – between more free choice, and increasingly carefully crafted and targeted marketing and retail environments. In particular, it will examine the claim that consumption is at one and the same time 'our most creative and controlled behaviour' (Zukin, 2004, p. 7). By using the term 'controlled', Sharon Zukin acknowledges the many different strategies and techniques that marketing, advertising and retailing have at their disposal to persuade people to buy particular products. However, by linking this with the term 'creative', Zukin is arguing that shoppers are not simple dupes who only do what they are told, but rather, self-aware individuals who are able to examine information and adapt the situations in which they find themselves for their own needs and purposes.

In Sections 1 and 2, we look at the evidence for how consumer behaviour is shaped online and in store by some of the more subtle strategies of retailers, marketers and advertisers. In doing so, we set out the evidence for how consumers react to and experience retail environments, and how social scientists have developed different techniques to study these and their effects on shopping behaviour. Section 1 looks at how people shop online and how techniques have been developed to make online advertising more responsive to individual behaviour. Section 2 examines the role of music in creating an atmosphere in retail spaces, shops and malls, which encourages people to buy.

Finally, Section 3 explores Zukin's claim in relation to the idea of advertising and marketing as 'seduction', a form of persuasion that requires active participation by both advertisers and consumers. As you work your way through the chapter, you should give some thought to the balance between the range of *choices* on offer and the *constraints* involved.

You read about Zygmunt Bauman's concept of the 'seduced' in Chapter 5.

1   Advertising and persuasion

The previous two chapters focused largely on shopping in stores, however, many consumers now purchase a lot of products online. Indeed, a recent Office of Communications (Ofcom) report found that 82 per cent of people in the UK with an internet connection shop online for some products (Ofcom, 2011). In this section, we link this development to Zukin's claim by considering the evidence for how web designers use the ways people habitually read and interpret web pages to control and direct consumers towards particular advertisements and pieces of information on key parts of the screen. The section then draws on the concept of seduction to show that, by developing and using brand identity, retailers and marketers actively encourage consumers to creatively imagine themselves in relation to particular products and services. In this way, advertising and marketing may seduce customers into connecting their practical requirements to the emotional needs and wants that stimulate the desire for products.

Shopping online, as many will know, is a very different experience to shopping on the high street or in a supermarket. Online shopping can be conducted from a variety of devices: from a computer at home or work, a tablet or mobile phone. Shopping websites, unlike actual supermarkets and shops, can tailor their appearance for each individual customer. Companies such as Amazon often have recommendations for purchases, which are unique to each customer and based on previous items that they have bought. Online supermarkets also tailor their website for each customer by offering a shopping list facility where certain items, such as milk and bread, are always present when the customer visits the site, so they don't need to select those items each time they visit. By tailoring the websites to the individual customer, this encourages people to come back and do their shopping with the same retailer. However, there are also other methods that retailers use to try to persuade us to buy things.

There are techniques that websites use to try to attract consumers' attention and some of these are based on the way in which people look at websites. Often, when people want to buy a product online, they use a search engine to look for the product and follow a link to a retailer from the results of this search. Companies such as Google have designed their search page so that companies that have paid advertising revenue to Google have their adverts placed in positions on a screen where people are more likely to look.

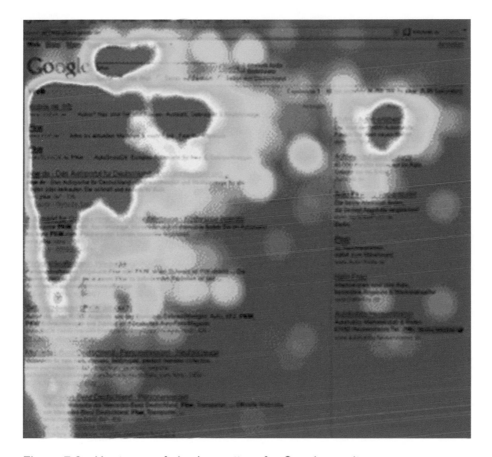

Figure 7.2   Heat map of viewing pattern for Google results

Figure 7.2 is a heat map that shows evidence of the length of time that a number of people look at the results from a Google search. This image was made using specialist eye-tracking equipment, which can monitor where people look on a screen and for how long. The image is called a 'heat map' because the redder or hotter parts of the image show areas that were viewed for longer, and the lighter blue/green areas are those that were viewed for less time. The areas of the website that are dark blue were not viewed at all. The image shows a triangle or 'f' shape pattern of where people were looking – the results on the left-hand side are viewed for longer and then there is another smaller area on the right-hand side that is viewed. What is also interesting is that only the first five to six answers in the search results appear to get looked at, and the results further down receive very little viewing.

Figure 7.2 shows that if you want customers to come and visit your website after searching for a product using Google, you really want your website to be one of the first six sites that appear on the left-hand side, or the first or second on the right-hand side.

Activity 2

Next time you go online, visit the Google website and type in something to search for. Look at the search results and where the product adverts are placed.

When you looked at your search results, did you notice any similarities with the heat map (Figure 7.2) above? Did you find that the first three results were adverts and that there were also adverts on the right-hand side?

1.1   Internet advertising

Social science research investigating the influence of adverts on the internet has tended to use two methods:

• surveys or questionnaires

• experiments.

In surveys, people are asked a series of questions about their internet usage and what they have seen and bought on the internet. This can obtain useful information about what type of things people are looking at on the internet, but may not answer the question of whether a specific advert is effective, as not all people may have seen the advert. Experiments can be useful to determine whether a specific advert or online marketing technique is effective. In experimental research, people can be shown websites with adverts and later asked about what they remember (recall) from what they have seen. Moreover, as you have seen in the image above, eye-tracking technology can now measure exactly where people look on a screen and for how long, so it can be determined whether an advert is viewed or what part of the advert is viewed.

Advances in eye-tracking technology have meant that advertisers can now place adverts on web pages in locations where they think people will look and that will attract attention. Many web pages now have what are called 'banner ads' which, if clicked on, will take you to the website of the advertised product. These adverts may be annoying when clicked on by mistake, as they take you away from the web page you were on, but banner ads are a good way for a web page to gain revenue, as the advertiser will send the website hosting the advert a small amount of money for each 'click through'. Interestingly, research on banner ads found that if they include videos and audios, people are more likely to click on them than if they just employ static images (Sathish et al., 2011).

Social media and networking sites are also subject to banner ads, and many of these can be tailored specifically to an individual user. This type of advertising is called 'profile based targeting'. These adverts use information from the social network site, such as the person's gender, age, location, marital status, whether they have children, and even likes and dislikes that may have been entered. Some social media and networking sites also gain information about the search terms people have used online, so that they can tailor adverts to specifically target a person. Moreover, when people click on an advert through their social media site, the product company can gain demographic information about that person, so they know what types of people are attracted to their adverts and products.

Social scientists are interested in how effective banner ads are at promoting products and influencing purchasing decisions. One of the ways in which banner ads can alter a person's perception about a product is due to the 'mere exposure effect': the more something is seen and becomes familiar, the more liable people are to have positive feelings towards it. This positive **affect** also appears to influence whether a consumer is likely to click on a banner ad, as the more positive the attitude towards a website, the more liable a person is to click on an advert (Cho, 1999). Furthermore, the more positive a consumer's attitude is towards a certain product, the more likely they are to buy that product when faced with a choice of which item to buy.

Affect
The seemingly intangible influences on how humans think, feel and behave, such as sound, touch, mood and atmosphere.

The reason someone is online in the first place can influence whether they remember seeing adverts or not. People are much more likely to remember adverts when they are aimlessly browsing and less likely if they are specifically looking for something (Pagendarm and Schaumburgh, 2001). One study suggested that, on average, people can remember seeing adverts on the internet around 50 per cent of the time (Dreze and Hussherr, 2003), although other research found that people surfing the internet actively avoided looking at banner ads (Dreze and Hussherr, 2003) or paid no attention to them (Chatterjee, 2008) and therefore had no memory of them. However, even though people may have no memory of looking at adverts on the internet, eye-tracking research has shown that most people look at the adverts at least once while viewing web pages (Hervet et al., 2011).

The evidence shows that it is possible to look at objects or, in this case, areas of a screen, without consciously paying attention and then have no memory of looking at them afterwards. Social scientists have called this inability to remember seeing adverts, even though they may have been looked at, 'banner blindness', and have suggested that it is similar to 'inattentional blindness'. Inattentional blindness is when there is no conscious memory of seeing something, even though the item may have been looked at directly. This failure to notice something is especially the case if:

- the item is unexpected

- there are lots of things going on that capture visual attention, or

- a person is focusing on a specific task.

This helps to explain why people who have a specific task in mind when they are browsing the internet fail to consciously notice adverts, as their attention is taken elsewhere. Moreover, if a web page has lots of information and images on it, conscious attention may be drawn away from the adverts.

■   However, could it be that adverts are unconsciously processed and influence purchasing decisions without the consumer even realising?

1.2   The seduction of advertising

Internet advertising research provides evidence that as web pages are viewed, consumers are often not consciously aware of all the things that they view. The issue of conscious awareness relates back to advertising in the 1950s, when psychologists such as Ernest Dichter (1947) were employed by advertising companies. Advertisers at that time specifically tried to tap into the unconscious desires and emotional needs of consumers. The aim was not to sell consumers products that met their practical needs, but to try and sell them products that fulfilled unconscious desires.

Dichter became famous for revolutionising the way that products were advertised, and transformed the fates of businesses such as Procter and Gamble, Exxon, Chrysler, General Mills and DuPont. He realised that people often felt guilty when they bought luxury items, so if a company wanted to market them successfully, the products should be advertised as items that a person can reward themselves with and thereby reduce guilt. This type of advertising still has links today with a certain cosmetics company suggesting that you 'are worth it'. Dichter also realised that the idea of obtaining power and being sexy could sell products and appeal to people's unconscious desires. Certain products could also give the illusion of reducing fear, with a classic example of a soap that claimed to 'wash the troubles away'.

Dichter understood, as was noted in Chapter 5, that people's possessions were an extension of themselves and their personalities, and could reflect an image to other people. He also believed that products had their own personality, and if advertisers could figure out that personality, then they could market it to people that it would appeal to. He was also aware that buying products could produce not only feelings of guilt, but positive emotions, such as boosting self-esteem, increasing feelings of individuality or independence. This type of advertising was an early form of *brand building*: that is, creating a product that has a personality and emotional associations that can then be sold to consumers.

One of the most widely used approaches adopted to explain how advertising persuades consumers to buy certain products is the Elaboration Likelihood Model (ELM) of persuasion (Petty et al., 1981). It was developed in the 1980s and is still used today by social scientists to explain how advertising influences people by changing their attitudes towards a certain product. When consumers have a positive attitude towards a product, they are much more likely to buy that product over other similar products.

The ELM of persuasion claims that there are two different ways in which people can respond to the information presented in an advert:

- the central route
- the peripheral route.

Which route is used will depend on whether the person thinks the product is relevant to them. For example, if a person is interested in getting a new mobile phone and sees an advert for a mobile phone, then the *central route* is taken. That person will pay close attention to the advert and information telling them about the particular advantages of that specific mobile phone, and depending on the quality of the advert's argument and their thinking about it afterwards (cognitive elaboration), they may have a more positive attitude towards that particular phone and be persuaded to buy it.

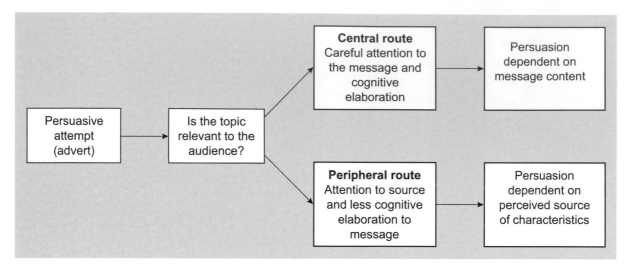

Figure 7.3   The Elaboration Likelihood Model (ELM) of persuasion

(Source: Petty et al., 1981)

On the contrary, if the product being advertised is not relevant to them, such as a new type of shampoo, they may not pay attention to the argument presented about why they should buy that shampoo and the *peripheral route* is used. Instead of listening to the advantages of that type of shampoo, they may pay more attention to the quality of the source: that is, the person in the advert. This could result in a more favourable attitude towards a product, if it has been endorsed by a certain celebrity such as a footballer or actor. However, it may not always convince them to buy that product, especially if they do not admire the celebrity endorsing the product or they are not credible to endorse that product.

According to the ELM, the central route uses controlled and deeper thought processes by consciously thinking about the specifications of a product, for example if a person has been persuaded to buy a specific phone because it has the latest software, best camera and battery life. As deeper thought processes are involved in the central route, once an attitude has been changed in favour of a certain product, it can be persistent and resistant to change. Although the change in attitude may be difficult to change in the short term, the shift in attitudes may not necessarily be long term. So, if a person forms a favourable attitude towards a certain type of phone, they are unlikely to change their mind about buying another type of phone in this instance. Nevertheless, when they go to buy their next phone, or are offered an upgrade in the future, they may consider looking at other makes of phone.

In contrast, the peripheral route is more automatic, based on affective associations (emotional feelings) and peripheral details. For example, if a person likes a particular actor and she endorses a certain shampoo, they might be more likely to buy it, even though they haven't really paid attention to why they should buy that type of shampoo. The use of well-known figures to advertise products helps to create a bond of trust between the product and the purchaser. However, the peripheral route is weaker than the central route and does not result in as strong or lasting change in attitudes. For example, if the shampoo advert starts using another celebrity that the person does not admire, or the celebrity who endorses the product does something they do not agree with that is picked up by the media, they may change their attitude towards the shampoo and be less likely to buy it.

The ELM claims that the most important determinant in persuading people to buy things is to try to ensure that the message or product is presented in such a way that it appears to be personally relevant to them. If the product appears to be relevant, then the consumer is much more likely to pay close attention to the advert and use the central route and this, in turn, should lead to a stronger and longer lasting change in attitude, and an increased likelihood that the product will be purchased. This can be seen in the adverts that are used online, as they are often targeted to specific individuals with the hope that the adverts are personally relevant to that specific consumer.

Activity 3

- What do you think about the claims of the ELM?
- Do you only pay attention to adverts when they are selling something that you are interested in buying?
- Do you pay attention to adverts that are not relevant to you?
- Have you ever bought a product because a particular celebrity endorsed it?
- Or do you not pay attention to adverts at all?

You may be someone who switches television channels as soon as the adverts come on, but regardless of what you thought about the ELM, there are several techniques that advertisers use that may persuade people to buy products, which the ELM cannot readily explain. The ELM adopts the assumption that advertising explicitly shows the consumer what it is advertising, yet advertising can often be ambiguous in its message. For example, there are a number of adverts where it's impossible to tell what the advertised product actually is until the end of the advert. The advertisers' aim is to make consumers curious about what the product is and keep them watching until the end. Nonetheless, if people are not interested in the advert in the first place and don't think the product is relevant to them, this strategy is likely to backfire.

Moreover, the ELM does not account for how some people are influenced to buy products or certain brands when they have no memory of seeing the advert. At the beginning of this chapter, you were asked to guess the companies according to their brand logo and, even if you knew what they were, you may not have necessarily remembered seeing any specific advertising for them. This is often because consumers have 'bought into' the brand's personality and they have a positive attitude towards it, without consciously remembering that they have seen any advertising for the product (Heath, 2012). People often use brands in this way to help them make short cuts in decisions about which products to buy. As you saw earlier, brands use colourful and easily identifiable logos, and they deliberately target specific groups of people as well as have their own personalities, such as being fun, carefree or sophisticated. Consumers may choose a brand that they feel matches their own personality and life circumstances, or they may choose a brand that they feel can change them into the person they aspire to be.

Much of this is in line with Zukin's (2004) argument that consumption can be both *controlling* and creative. It is controlling in so far as advertisers know how to play on people's emotions and desires, such as fear, sexual desire and independence, when trying to create brands and are able to target people on an individual basis. But there is also an element of *creativity* involved, where consumers are able to research items online, compare products before making a purchase and get the best deal or best product, as well as using such products to shape their identities, desires and emotions.

Summary

- People browsing the internet are often not consciously aware of all the adverts they see online. Seeing an advert for a product a number of times can make a consumer's attitude more positive towards it – through the 'mere exposure effect'.

- Advertising companies can use consumers' emotions and desires to try and sell products and build brands. The ELM suggests that there are two routes to persuading consumers to buy products – the central and peripheral.

- When faced with a large choice of what to buy, consumers often use short cuts in their decision making by relying on product branding.

2   Atmosphere and ambience

This section continues to explore Zukin's claim that shopping is 'our most creative and controlled behaviour' (Zukin, 2004, p. 7) by looking at how the atmosphere and ambience of shopping environments might subtly guide and shape the ways that people shop. It starts by thinking about how goods and services are often sold as part of a package called the 'total product', which includes, in addition to the item itself, a variety of experiences and associations with particular styles, fashions and lifestyle. It then looks specifically at how sound and music influence behaviour in shopping environments.

2.1   Selling the total product

Retailers and marketing professionals have become increasingly aware of the subtle clues present in products and retailing environments, and how these shape behaviour in retail environments for shoppers and consumers. In the 1970s, Philip Kotler (1974), an American professor of marketing, argued that one of the most important advances in business thinking at that time was the recognition that people, in their purchase decision making, respond to more than simply the tangible product or service being offered. Kotler distinguished between what he called the *tangible product* – the specific item being sold, for example a pair of shoes, a refrigerator, haircut or meal – and the *total product*. By 'total product' he meant the services, warranties, packaging, advertising, financing, pleasantries, images and other features that accompany the product (Kotler, 1974, p. 48). There are clear parallels between Kotler's idea of the *total product* and Dichter's idea of *brand building*, which you met in the previous section, as there are with the signs of consumption discussed in Chapter 5. All are concerned with the wider, less tangible, associations and affects gathered around particular brands, products and services, which encourage people to buy.

Kotler looked to the future in ways that ring true with many experiences of shopping today:

> ... in many areas of marketing in the future, marketing planners will use *spatial aesthetics* as consciously and skilfully as they now use price, advertising, personal selling, public relations and other tools of marketing. We shall use the term *atmospherics* to describe the conscious designing of space to create certain effects in buyers.

> More specifically, *atmospherics* is the effort to design buying
> environments to produce specific emotional effects in the buyer
> that enhance his [sic] purchasing probability.
>
> (Kotler, 1974, p. 50)

Kotler recognised that retailers and advertisers had long used their
intuition, appealing to customers by inspiring confidence in the retailer
and their products, and by placing products in advertising and shop
displays, so customers could identify and desire them. However, his
most important contribution was to recognise that the emotional
dimensions of shopping behaviour need to be studied by social
scientists.

More recently, social scientists have become increasingly interested in
how seemingly intangible things, such as sound, touch and mood,
influence how people think, feel and behave in a wide range of social
situations. Social scientists often refer to those senses, moods and
feelings that influence people substantially without them being aware as
'affects'. Shopping and shopping environments have become important
locations in which to explore questions of atmosphere and affect.
Kotler described the designed atmospheres of shops and stores as
'affect creating mediums' (1974, p. 54), yet this aspect of his work was
not explicitly picked up until many years later.

The affects of shopping provide a way of understanding some of the
intangible and hard to pin down influences on how people act and
behave in complex social situations, such as the shopping mall and
supermarket. Research into affects and their influence on how people
behave has borrowed techniques from anthropology, which are
concerned with exploring the detailed stories of people's lives. This has
enabled social scientists to develop new techniques to observe and
record information, providing detailed evidence of individual experience,
moods and feelings in particular social and environmental situations.
Research into affects and atmospheres also asks social scientists to
rethink the ways in which they understand social behaviour and how
this relates to individual experience.

With their enclosed spaces, security control, artificial heating and
lighting, entertainment areas and, in some cases, themed design,
shopping malls are just the kind of location that Kotler predicted
retailers and marketers would be able to control in order to exploit the
affective role of retail atmospheres on shopping behaviour. Kotler

argued that along with sight, smell and touch, sound was one of the four key ways in which retailers could create and manipulate retail environments.

The role of music as a background ambience in retail and other commercial environments is familiar to many. Music was first made commercially available for use in shops in the USA in the 1920s through the invention of Major General George Owen Squier who devised a way of piping music into shops using a telephone system. Despite changing ownership, the company is still a global player in the market for background music. Recently known as Mood Music, the company is best known by its earlier name, the Muzak Corporation. Although it is simply the name of a private company, the term 'muzak' has become part of everyday vocabulary to the extent that it is now used for any background music in public spaces, such as lifts, shops and restaurants. Indeed, there is evidence to show that music can quicken and slow down the speed at which people walk around stores, and even eat and leave their tables in restaurants and cafés. Likewise, other research on the type of music played in shops found evidence that some types of music are more appropriate to different kinds of goods. For example, classical music is good at encouraging customers to buy wine, and may actually increase the amount of money they spend by influencing them to buy more expensive brands and products.

Activity 4

Think about some adverts that you may know (perhaps ones you have seen on TV or heard on radio). Consider what kind of sound or type of music might be appropriate to accompany the following:

- a product sold for its natural qualities (for example a food product)
- a product sold as well made (for example furniture, a motor car)
- a luxury item (for example perfume, jewellery)
- something up to date and fashionable (for example clothing, mobile phone).

You may have thought, for example, that music suitable for advertising a food product might reinforce associations with nature by suggesting images of the countryside and wholesome living. Perhaps a slow impressionistic piece of classical music might be appropriate for this. In contrast, music suitable for a luxury item might suggest romance and fantasy, for example a love song or something with a Latin rhythm. In each case, the power of music in advertising is to stimulate suggestive ideas in the mind of the listener so that they might imagine the qualities of the product for themselves.

2.2   Shopping to music

Jonathan Sterne's (1997) study of the soundscapes found in a large-scale shopping complex called the Mall of America in the USA (in Bloomington, Minnesota) provided evidence of just how complex the sound world of shopping can be. The Mall of America is one of the largest shopping centres in North America, with in excess of 520 stores, over 12,000 workers and 35 million plus visitors each year. The Mall includes stores, restaurants and entertainment venues, including a theme park called 'Camp Snoopy'. Sterne points out that:

> At the Mall of America beneath the crash of a roller coaster, the chatter of shoppers and the shuffle of feet, one hears music everywhere. Every space in the Mall is hardwired for sound. The apparatus to disseminate music is built into the Mall's infrastructure, and is managed as one of several major environmental factors.
>
> (Sterne, 1997, p. 22)

Sterne illustrates how music flows through channels parallel to those providing air, electricity and information to all areas of the Mall. 'Facilities Management', the department responsible for maintaining the Mall's power supplies, temperature and even grounds-keeping, also keeps the Mall's varied soundtracks running. The Mall of America has three main sound systems: a set of speakers in the hallways, which plays background music quietly; a set of speakers hidden beneath the foliage of Camp Snoopy (the amusement park built into the Mall's atrium), which broadcasts the steady singing of digital crickets; and each store is wired for sound so that it can play music of its own choice. Sterne claims that in places like the Mall of America, music becomes a form of architecture (Sterne, 1997, pp. 22–3).

By describing music in shopping malls and stores as a form of architecture, Sterne is suggesting that, in shopping malls, music has become an integral and taken-for-granted aspect of the built environment. But there is perhaps more at issue here. Tia De Nora and Sophie Belcher (2000) argue that to find out how music affects shopping behaviour it is necessary to move beyond thinking of music as background architecture to explore how shoppers engage with the ambience of shopping and experience music as part of the atmosphere of shopping.

De Nora and Belcher (2000) explored the ways in which music affected shopping behaviour in clothes shops, focusing on several cities in the UK. They were interested in collecting evidence on how stores selected music that they thought would encourage shoppers to buy, and how shoppers reacted to the music as individuals. Evidence was drawn from a variety of shops, ranging from budget retailers and casual wear, young fashion to mainstream department stores and high-end independent shops. Posing as shoppers, but discreetly wired for sound, they used personal recorders to capture both in-store sound and their own ongoing comments. In addition to interviewing shoppers just outside of the shops studied, they also asked four volunteer shoppers to 'think out loud' into a recorder as they roamed through the shops and shopping precinct. The researchers followed their volunteer shoppers at a discreet distance, occasionally breaking in with questions and recording the answers and ambient sounds.

The different types of clothes shop studied had rather diverse clienteles, matched by rather different musical selections. At an upmarket store catering to women and children, which sold clothes in natural materials using ethnic prints (known by the pseudonym Mistral), the music was almost inaudible and included Enya, Ella Fitzgerald, The Lighthouse Family, 'Brit Pop' selections and, more recently, classical numbers; while at an internationally managed chain selling casual wear (pseudonym Canyon), the music is bought in from the Muzak Corporation. A few doors further down the high street, in a UK chain selling 'trendy'

Affluence
A high level of prosperity.

clothes to **affluent** young women (pseudonym Babe), the music is more definitely centred around club and chart tracks, in particular 'girl band' music (De Nora and Belcher, 2000, p. 86). Each shop in turn imagined its music appealing to a different target audience. For example, Mistral said that its music appealed to more than 'one specific age group … up-market and classical'; Canyon said 'modern, yet fairly middle of the road …'; and Babe said 'young modern females … in tune with what's going on in the music industry' (De Nora and Belcher, 2000, p. 87).

De Nora and Belcher found evidence that music did in fact influence the way people felt in shops. In the case of the volunteer shopper speaking into her recorder in the extract below, the music forms just one small affective dimension, which enhances her mood in a shop she already knows and enjoys. As De Nora and Belcher say:

> One volunteer shopper enters Mistral. She tells the [voice recorder] that she is going in to have a look inside because of the butterflies in the window. She says how she loves hats. She could come out of the store with four or five hats that she will never wear. Her philosophy is that you buy them and take them back. She says music adds to the fun atmosphere in the store, especially if you're looking at hats … . From the tape she is clearly euphoric, her energy levels are commensurate with the up-beat, 'happy' music and the highly stimulating displays of multi-coloured, multi-textured hats, scarves, jewellery and hats (Shopper Shadowing Exercise May 6 1998).
>
> (De Nora and Belcher, 2000, p. 91)

Store managers described how they had seen customers singing and dancing to the music. De Nora and Belcher found that their observations of store behaviour confirmed that dancing, toe-tapping, moving about in front of the mirrors, even singing, were all common, albeit most common in stores catering to young people (De Nora and Belcher, 2000, p. 97). They concluded that younger women are more likely to view shopping as a leisure time pursuit, more likely to visit a shop with no specific objective in mind and to shop in friendship groups. Young women purchase things they believe to be 'cool' (this word was heard repeatedly during the research), or somehow expressive of how they 'feel', or reminded them of images to which they aspire. These are also the kinds of shoppers most likely to make 'impulse purchases', that is unplanned, on-the-spot purchase decisions, and hence, De Nora and Belcher suggest, 'those most susceptible to the emotional structures that music places on offer' (De Nora and Belcher, 2000, p. 92).

On the basis of the evidence, De Nora and Belcher claim that music is an important part of the atmospherics of clothes shopping. It heightens awareness of how people already feel, for example when they are happy and in a party mood at the weekend. Music also helps shoppers imagine themselves wearing the clothes they see on display in particular social settings at a club, at work or on holiday. They argue that:

> … music is a device of scenic placement, it provides contextual cues that can be used to shape up the meaning of character and situation. As the manager of Persuasion puts it, 'when you're trying something on, you picture yourself in a place where they are playing this kind of music'.
>
> (De Nora and Belcher, 2000, p. 96)

Latching
To latch onto or connect with some aspect of physical or social environment or personal feeling, desire or aspiration. By latching onto something familiar or appealing in music, shoppers make a personal connection with the products on sale.

De Nora and Belcher call this quality of music **'latching'** – meaning to latch onto or connect with some aspect of physical or social environment, or personal feeling, desire or aspiration. Yet, as Sterne says, the music programmed for shops and malls is often devised for ideal rather than actual customers who might have a range of tastes and interests rather different from the imagined ideal customer. Because of this, music in shops is always as likely to repel as to attract customers. De Nora and Belcher found this in relation to many of the older women to whom they spoke as part of their research. These women typically made fewer excursions to the shops and 'had in mind' aims and objectives when they did embark on shopping trips. They were less likely to appreciate or enjoy the aesthetic materials in stores, particularly music as a 'distraction'. One customer told them:

> I call that pollution … I don't like any music in shops or in lifts or anywhere (Exit interview).
>
> I don't like it when it's jumping because I've got a hearing aid, you see so it's pretty awful … [Besides] I've got other things on my mind you know. I'm not thinking about music. I'm thinking where am I going to get this skirt I'm looking for (Exit interview, elderly woman).
>
> (De Nora and Belcher, 2000, pp. 91–2)

Sterne (1997) says that the companies who supply background music aim to create programmes of sound that will not cause offence and will provide a largely familiar backdrop in which customers feel comfortable. However, the inevitably wide diversity of shoppers in terms of age, gender, interests, social and cultural background means that the system is always 'necessarily clumsy', and conflicts arise. He illustrates this with a popular urban legend where two adjacent stores in a shopping mall are quarrelling. One shop plays light classical music and sells upmarket clothing. The other sells the latest fashions and plays 'Top 40' music, which includes some rap. The first store fears that the latter's music will chase away its customers and petitions the mall management to have the latter keep its music at a lower level. The second pleads otherwise – that turning down its music would make its store design less effective for luring in potential customers. The moral of the story, Sterne says, is simple: 'programmed musics in malls do not form a seamless and totally coherent system, nor do they always work together as they're supposed to' (Sterne, 1997, p. 45).

Attempts by retailers to control shopping behaviour with carefully programmed background music can have unintended consequences, as shoppers react to music in highly individual and creative ways.

Activity 5

How appropriate is De Nora and Belcher's concept of 'latching' to music that's played in clothes shops? Do you think that De Nora and Belcher's idea of 'latching' might be applied to music played in other types of shop or retail space in addition to clothes shops?

Think about how 'latching' might encourage consumers to buy particular products in the following:

- food shop
- wine shop
- sports goods store
- furniture store.

How do you think 'latching' might explain why some shoppers avoid, rather than enter, particular retail spaces?

Latching does seem to reflect much common experience in shops. Latching onto in-store music is designed to have different affects in different types of shop: in food shops, cheerful music encourages people to busy themselves and pay attention to the offers; in a sports goods store, it might help make people feel positive and adventurous; while in a furniture store, music might suggest relaxation, tranquillity and order at home. Yet, musical taste is very personal and varied, and it is impossible to design a retail soundscape that pleases everyone, or even the same people on different days and in different moods. Although music can be a powerful way of affecting people emotionally and used to create a controlled environment in which to shop, the way it can affect us directly may also be a barrier to its effective use by retailers. Evidence shows that individual behaviour, taste and choice, the way shoppers creatively adopt and adapt the circumstances in which they find themselves to meet their own ends and needs, is often at odds with retailers' desire to control shopping behaviour.

Summary

- Retailers and marketing professionals have become increasingly aware of the ways subtle clues, which are present in products and retailing environments, shape the behaviour of shoppers and consumers.

- Music is an important means by which clothes retailers encourage shoppers to identify with and imagine themselves wearing the products for sale.

- De Nora and Belcher (2000) found that shoppers 'latch on' to music in shops and imagine themselves wearing the clothes on sale in a variety of social situations.

3 Shopping: creative and controlled behaviour?

The previous two sections of this chapter have set out a range of evidence to support Zukin's claim that shopping is both 'our most creative and controlled behaviour' (Zukin, 2004, p. 7). As you saw at the beginning of the chapter, by using the term 'controlled', Zukin recognises that marketing, advertising and retailing use a wide range of strategies and techniques to persuade people to buy particular products. However, by linking this with the term 'creative', Zukin also argues that advertising and marketing are not simply a matter of deception – shoppers are self-aware individuals who are able to examine information and adapt the situations in which they find themselves for their own needs and purposes.

Sections 1 and 2 introduced two different approaches to how shoppers react to attempts to persuade them through online advertising and the use of music to create ambience in retail environments. Each section looked at the evidence for the different ways in which retailers attempt to persuade consumers to buy through advertising and marketing strategies, online and in store. Each section also examined a distinctive approach relating to how shoppers react to retailers' attempts to persuade them:

- Section 1 looked at the ELM of persuasion (Petty et al., 1981)
- Section 2 looked at De Nora and Belcher's (2000) account of 'latching'.

These approaches and the supporting evidence drawn upon in this chapter are useful because they enable social scientists to examine the extent to which shopping decisions are, in Zukin's terms, either controlled or creative. That is, controlled and constrained by the way sellers structure and provide information, and set their products within particular retailing contexts; or creative to the extent that shoppers make their own choices based on who they are, and what they need, want and feel that they can afford.

In Section 1, the ELM illustrated how, faced with an advert attempting to persuade consumers to buy a product or service, people may adopt two different ways of attending the advertising message. If they are already in the market for a particular item, they are more likely to take the 'central route' and focus on the message of the advertisement itself and what this tells them about the product sold by a specific retailer. Nonetheless, if they had previously considered the product not relevant to themselves and their needs, then consumers are more likely to pay attention to a range of secondary characteristics supporting the message of the advertisement. This 'peripheral route' encourages consumers to focus, for example, on the person delivering the message as a celebrity or authority figure who can be believed, or with whom the consumer wishes to associate themselves, their lifestyle and identity.

In Section 2 you looked at how De Nora and Belcher's concept of 'latching' can be used to understand the way music in shops encourages consumers to buy. De Nora and Belcher use the concept of latching to explain how music enables shoppers to make connections between specific items for sale, in this case clothes, and a variety of imagined social situations, personal feelings and desires. As one store manager reported in an interview with De Nora and Belcher, music in stores helps shoppers imagine themselves in the sorts of situation where they might wear the clothes they are trying on. Although the ELM and the concept of latching were developed in very different contexts, and seem to explain shopping behaviour in rather different ways, a closer look suggests that they have important characteristics in common.

Both approaches recognise that decisions are made in a wider context informed by the shoppers' economic and social circumstances, and how they imagine themselves and their needs and desires. For example, in the ELM, shoppers will already have had to think about whether they want and can afford to buy a product as a precondition of being subject to either the 'central' or 'peripheral' messages embedded in the advert. While in the clothes store, shoppers latch onto music with which they can identify, and which already speaks to them about the kind of person they are and the sorts of situation in which they either expect or would like to find themselves. This is the reason why there is evidence to show that some shoppers find the music in some shops off-putting. It also explains why some shops use music to tacitly inform consumers that this may or may not be the right kind of clothes store for their needs.

Both approaches also understand that products are often sold within a wider context. In this wider context, products become associated with particular senses of quality, the endorsement of particular authority or celebrity figures, while also evoking a range of feelings and emotions such as fun, confidence and exclusivity. These wider qualities of service, ambience and the associations with lifestyle were expressed by Kotler

(1974) and discussed in Section 2 as aspects of the 'total product' marketing philosophy. This is also reflected in Dichter's idea of products building brand image, which you met in Section 1.

Branding, as you have seen, is an important way in which these secondary qualities become associated with products. If you look back to the brands introduced at the beginning of this chapter, you will see that each brand is attempting to conjure up particular images, thoughts and feelings – people routinely associate these with the products that these companies sell. For the ELM, this is captured in the peripheral route, which might encourage someone to buy a product they were not specifically considering; while latching, for De Nora and Belcher, is the means by which consumers make the wider connections between their lives and the styles and values associated with the product.

3.1   Shopping and seduction

These techniques can all be thought of as forms of 'seduction' – ways of encouraging consumers to buy something that they might otherwise not have bought. Yet seduction, as you know from Chapter 5, is never simply a matter of imposing power: it always requires active participation and cooperation. Advertisers ask people to use their imaginations in order to visualise themselves with the product and, by doing this, consumers play an active part in persuading themselves.

Seduction requires advertising and marketing to offer consumers something in the form of a temptation or enticement. Adverts may suggest that purchases will get something free, for instance a two for one offer, or that they might receive benefits beyond the physical qualities of the product itself – that new car or item of clothing might change the life of the purchaser, improve their image and status, make them feel more 'loved' or 'happier'. However, the power of seduction in advertising also relies on the consumer recognising something about the product that they at least think or believe they want. To this extent, advertising presents customers with prompts that spur the imagination, enabling them to admire some specific quality in the product, aspire to the promises made about its ability to fulfil and transform lives, while at the same time enabling consumers to identify themselves with the ideas and images on offer.

Zukin highlights the active role that the consumer's imagination plays around identity and lifestyle when she argues that shopping has 'come to define who we, as individuals are and what we, as a society, want to become' (Zukin, 2004, p. 8). For Zukin, brand names represent our search for a better life, while designer boutiques embody the promise of an ever-improving self, one which fulfils our own desire to create and reinforce self-image. By understanding advertising and marketing in terms of words such as 'search', 'promise' and 'desire', she is acknowledging that seduction requires both sellers and buyers to play the game. Yet, Zukin also understands shopping within a broader context than simply individual shoppers and retailers. In this way, shopping for Zukin is a fundamentally important means by which contemporary society is made and remade. This might be thought about in several ways.

First, she argues that people are immersed in a world of advertising and shopping from which there seems to be no escape in the contemporary world. According to Zukin:

> No matter where we go or who we are, shopping dominates our lives. Brightly lit stores give life to city streets, and asphalt and concrete malls mark the vast suburban landscape. Billboards and websites speak to us all day and night, while commercials are on continuous replay in our minds. Bargains, discounts, sales, and ratings taunt us with the eternal questions: does it fit? How much do I need? Can I find a better price? Am I making the right choice?
>
> (Zukin, 2004, p. 253)

Whether shopping dominates our lives or not, Zukin is arguing here that it is not only adverts, but a whole culture of consumption that encourages people to want and desire goods and services. If consumers are seduced by advertising, then it seems reasonable to assume that individuals are already predisposed to engaging with advertising before they become familiar with any particular advert. How else, you might ask, can they already be susceptible to the power of advertising and its urge to buy in the first place? If this line of reasoning is correct, then it is not enough to draw simple causal links between individual adverts or retail atmospheres and shopping behaviour. From this perspective, the power of advertising and marketing to control is based on the way that the sheer volume of advertising in modern developed societies seems to present people with no alternative means of satisfying their needs, wants and desires other than to buy. For people exposed to this consumer culture from childhood, it may be very difficult to think of any viable alternative other than to go to the shops.

Second, shopping for Zukin is an inherently social experience. She argues that although shopping is made through millions of individual decisions, it is the whole experience of shopping as a social activity that provides the basis on which to judge shopping as either controlled or creative. Shopping is not only what people do for themselves, but what they do in relation to other people. Zukin claims:

> Everyone knows that shopping is no longer a simple matter of buying a can of beans at the corner store. The activity of shopping keeps modern economies afloat, links the family looking for jeans at Wal-Mart in California to factories in China and Bangladesh and enables us – if we buy and sell on eBay – to turn our shopping into an entrepreneurial investment. But shopping is also a cultural activity. Because it is usually what we do when we go out, shopping is how we satisfy our need to socialize – to feel we are a part of public life.
>
> (Zukin, 2004, p. 7)

In this way, Zukin understands shopping as making social connections between people making and buying things across the world, in much the same way that the global supply chains explored in Chapter 6 outlined. At the same time, it is an important way in which people share in, or distinguish themselves from, the social values and culturally accepted habits and behaviour of those who live around them. This might be in terms of how someone shopping for clothes wants to be seen by others at work or on an evening out, or it might be how a household member buys necessities and possibly a few treats for other household members during the weekly food shop.

Rather than simply emphasising the way in which retailers and marketers shape and control shopping habits, thinking about shopping in the ways suggested by Zukin highlights the broader social, cultural and emotional relations of which shopping and the things people buy form an integral part. Framed as a social rather than individual act, following Zukin, it is possible to argue that people do exercise some control in their shopping behaviour, turning it into a fun weekend activity or a way of demonstrating household care. Yet, they do so within the context of a broader range of social values, controls and constraints that shape behaviour. These are perhaps evident in the expectations people feel, as fashion-conscious teenagers, parents, partners or buyers and vendors, and which individuals carry with them when they go shopping.

Summary

- In different ways, the ELM and De Nora and Belcher's account of 'latching' support Zukin's claim that shopping is both 'our most creative and controlled behaviour'. That is, controlled and constrained by the way sellers structure and provide information, and creative to the extent that shoppers make their own choices based on who they are and what they need, want and feel that they can afford.

- Product branding, Kotler's total product marketing philosophy, Dichter's idea of brand building, and De Nora and Belcher's idea of latching can all be thought of as exploiting techniques of seduction to encourage consumers to buy.

Conclusion

This chapter has examined the claim that shopping is both 'our most controlled and creative behaviour', as claimed by Zukin (2004, p. 7). In Zukin's discussion of shopping, it is possible to see how shopping choices might be understood within a broader set of controls and creative responses than those simply presented by an individual's engagement with a particular advertisement. These situate the individual shopper within a range of contexts, including:

- a consumer culture, which shapes expectations about what alternatives people might have

- a set of economic relationships linking producers, wholesalers and retailers to consumers

- the ideas people have of themselves in relation to others in a wide range of circumstances – from work and leisure to intimate and household relationships.

Each of these contexts, as you saw from the preceding chapters, provides its own set of constraints, expectations and opportunities, which together help shape the ways in which people respond to advertising and retail environments. In turn, as Zukin argues, responding to this range of circumstances through shopping has become an important way through which society and lifestyles are made.

What links seemingly very different shopping strategies, at the mall and on the internet, is that both appear to offer a greater range of choice and freedoms in how and where shopping takes place than was available previously. As you read in Chapter 5, the pervasive nature of contemporary consumer culture provides individuals with particular conceptions of freedom and choice, individual self-expression and market freedoms, yet does not provide any alternative ways of imagining how life might be lived. Simply labelling this experience as controlled, and the millions of people who live and have lived in these circumstances as passively dominated by forces beyond their control, is to ignore the ways in which people creatively adapt and learn to work with and through the circumstances in which they find themselves.

Moreover, these constraints, expectations and opportunities associated with the circumstances in which people find themselves are unequally distributed through society. Thus, how consumers respond to advertising and marketing is shaped by individual financial resources and household commitments, as well as by self-image and conceptions of identity. Despite the evidence to show how carefully shopping experiences are organised, presented and controlled by retailers, consumers are increasingly able to manage the practices and experiences of shopping to meet their own individual and household wants and expectations. Cast as a series of choices and constraints, controlled and creative behaviour, there seems no simple answer as to who is in charge – consumer or retailer.

References

Chatterjee, P. (2008) 'Are unclicked ads wasted? Enduring effects of banner and pop-up ad exposure on brand memory and attitudes', *Journal of Electronic Commerce Research*, vol. 1, pp. 51–61.

Cho, C. (1999) 'How advertising works on the WWW; modified Elaboration Likelihood Model', *Journal of Current Issues and Research in Advertising*, vol. 21, pp. 33–50.

De Nora, T. and Belcher, S. (2000) '"When you're trying something on you picture yourself in a place where they are playing this kind of music" – musically sponsored agency in the British clothing retail sector, *Sociological Review*, vol. 48, no. 1, pp. 80–101.

Dichter, E. (1947) *The Psychology of Everyday Living*, New York, Barnes and Noble.

Dreze, X. and Hussherr, F.X. (2003) 'Internet advertising: is anybody watching?', *Journal of Interactive Marketing*, vol. 17, pp. 8–23.

Heath, R. (2012) *Seducing the Unconscious: The Psychology of Emotional Influence in Advertising*, Oxford, Wiley-Blackwell.

Hervet, G., Guerard, K., Tremblay, S. and Chtourou, M.S. (2011) 'Is banner blindness genuine? Eye tracking internet text advertising', *Applied Cognitive Psychology*, vol. 25, pp. 708–16.

Kotler, P. (1974) 'Atmospherics as a marketing tool', *Journal of Retailing*, vol. 49, no. 4, pp. 48–64.

Office of Communications (Ofcom) (2011) *International Communications Market Report* [Online]. Available at http://stakeholders.ofcom.org.uk/binaries/research/cmr/cmr11/icmr/ICMR2011.pdf (Accessed 28 February 2014).

Pagendarm, M. and Schaumburgh, H. (2001) 'Why are users banner blind? The impact of navigation style on the perception of web banners', *Journal of Digital Information*, vol. 2 [Online]. Available at http://journals.tdl.org/jodi/index.php/jodi/article/view/36/38 (Accessed 27 March 2014).

Petty, R.E., Cacioppo, J.T. and Goldman, R. (1981) 'Personal involvement as a determinant of argument-base persuasion', *Journal of Personality and Social Psychology*, vol. 41, no. 5, pp. 847–55.

Sathish, M., Kumar, V.B., and Bharath, S. (2011) 'Impacts of online advertising on sales', *Journal of Marketing and Communication*, vol. 7, pp. 11–17.

Sterne, J. (1997) 'Sounds like the Mall of America: programmed music and the architectonics of commercial space', *Ethnomusicology*, vol. 41, no. 1, pp. 22–50.

Zukin, S. (2004) *Point of Purchase: How Shopping Changed American Culture*, London, Routledge.

Chapter 8
Throwaway society? Waste and recycling

Rajiv Prabhakar

Contents

Introduction

Imagine that you come home after a shopping trip to a supermarket. What things might you throw away? You might start by throwing away excess packaging such as plastic wrappers or plastic bags containing fruit or vegetables. Cardboard casings on packs of tins might be thrown away next. You might throw away food that is now out of date after the shopping trip. An old loaf might be discarded in favour of the brand new loaf that you have just bought. Even older food at the back of a fridge might now be discarded. Later on, more waste might be created as items are used up. This could mean empty cereal packets, finished tins of baked beans, empty milk cartons and sweet wrappers.

Supermarkets, as was noted in Chapter 6, now sell an increasing range of products besides food, such as electrical items or clothing. You may have just bought a new kettle or toaster to replace one that has broken down and is now thrown away. An old shirt might also be consigned to the waste bin. This only refers to the waste that you might throw away from supermarkets. However, waste might also be produced by the supermarkets themselves. You will read shortly about a report from Tesco about waste that is created in the production process, before things are even sold to consumers.

Waste might be thought to cover things of little or no value – they are literally rubbish. However, waste might also be a symptom of a 'throwaway' society. A throwaway society refers to the idea that people in society are used to throwing things away, with little or no thought about whether there is any value in waste. It might be that as people get richer, they care less about what things are thrown away. Alternatively, questions might be asked about whether a throwaway society actually exists. There may be growing interest among the population about recycling or reusing waste. There might be a growing interest in society, for instance, on the steps people might take to protect the environment.

The creation of waste may also impact directly on the way lives are made and remade. For example, waste that is not recycled or reused is sent to landfill and landfill can contribute to 'greenhouse gases' that harm the environment. Indeed, some studies suggest that food contributes to about a fifth of global greenhouse gases (Hertwich and Peters, 2009). The European Commission (2010), for instance, estimates that 1 kg of food waste creates about 1.9 kg of carbon dioxide emissions. Although there are commentators who are sceptical about changes in climate patterns, the bulk of scientific opinion is that human activity has contributed directly to changes in today's climate (IPCC, 2013). As such, climate changes will affect how the contemporary generation makes choices about their own lives. Perhaps more importantly, changes in the environment today will affect the opportunities available to future generations.

This chapter considers one possible way of encouraging people to create less waste, that is, how people might be 'nudged' to waste less and recycle more. As part of this, you will study the way in which social scientists put together an argument based upon various claims about human behaviour and the questions they raise. The example used in this chapter considers the approach adopted by behavioural economists and efforts to encourage less waste. Behavioural economists start by making various basic claims about how humans behave. This then leads them to suggest how people might be nudged to behave in particular ways. The chapter then goes on to consider the available evidence to support or reject the underlying claims. Some of the limitations of the behavioural economics theory are mentioned, such as the impact of constraints on people's choices, as well as how economic organisations might add to waste alongside human behaviour.

Section 1 briefly outlines the social meaning of waste before moving on to consider the relationship between waste and affluence in Section 2. This section discusses the growth in waste and links this growth to rising affluence. Section 3 looks at ways in which it might be possible to encourage people to change their behaviour to reduce waste. It does this by considering recent interest in behavioural economics as a way of encouraging people to change their behaviour. This section also considers the evidence of behavioural change and how this tallies with the approach of behavioural economics.

1   The social meaning of waste

The first issue to consider is what is meant by 'waste'. The example of a supermarket shopping trip in the introduction provides you with some suggestions as to what is meant by waste. This refers to anything not wanted or consumed, or is obsolete and replaced.

It may appear from this that it is fairly easy to identify waste and that its meaning is stable over time. However, waste is not some neutral or uncontroversial idea. Different societies may have different ideas of what forms waste. Even in the same society, the meaning of waste may shift over time. Evans et al. write that:

> An emerging body of work now recognizes waste as a dynamic category that needs to be understood in relation to the contexts (social, economic, historical) through which it has been put to work, and the relationships in which it is embedded, and the complexity of meanings attributed to it.
>
> (Evans et al., 2013, p. 8)

Things that were previously seen as waste might later be seen as being valuable, or things that were seen as important may later be seen as waste. For example, think of comics or long play (LP) records that might have originally been thrown away once they were used, but later become valuable collectors' items. Mary Douglas wrote a book called *Purity and Danger* in which she studies the social meaning of dirt. She notes that dirt is often seen as matter out of place, and that different societies understand dirt and impurity in different ways (Douglas, 1966). All of this points towards the social meaning of waste and the way in which what forms waste is the product of shared or social understandings.

The social meaning of waste can also lead into the politics of waste. Politics can shape waste in a number of ways. Towards the end of the chapter, in Section 3.4, you will read a section about who puts out the waste in a household. In households with more than one person, the way in which basic tasks are divided can highlight political issues. For example, imbalances of power between men and women in the household may mean that women are charged with doing the bulk of domestic tasks in the household, and this could involve taking more responsibility for dealing with rubbish. However, these political issues are not confined to the household, as they may also extend to nations if richer countries ship their waste to fill landfills in poorer countries.

To see how the meaning of waste may be a topic of discussion or debate, consider the following extract from the first chapter of Charles Dickens' novel *Our Mutual Friend* (Dickens, 2002 [1865]). Dickens is often taken to be one of the most acute observers and critics of nineteenth-century society, with novels that discuss factories, prisons, bureaucracy, education and workhouses. In one sense, Dickens was a writer about the street (and may perhaps have written for this module!). In *Our Mutual Friend*, Dickens considers a type of 'throwaway society':

> How can you be so thankless to your best friend [the Thames], Lizzie? The very fire that warmed you when you were a baby, was picked out of the river alongside the coal barges. The very basket you slept in, the tide washed ashore. The very rockers that I put it upon to make a cradle of it, I cut out of a piece of wood that drifted from some ship or other.
>
> (Gaffer Hexham to Lizzie Hexham, in Dickens, 2002 [1865], p. 4)

Gaffer Hexham's challenge to his daughter Lizzie here is about what is thrown away. Gaffer sees value in what others think of as rubbish: the basket for his daughter was a cast-off in the Thames; Gaffer uses driftwood to make a cradle; he scavenges coal to provide heat for the family.

One response to the above extract is that: 'This is history but it is not like that today'. However, even though the particular things that Dickens mentioned may no longer be viewed as waste today, the main point is that waste does not have a fixed meaning and its meaning often shifts over time. Indeed, even today there are people and organisations that try to make money from waste. This includes people engaged in 'rag and bone' to those who seek metals such as copper from skips or waste dumps. This highlights the adage: 'Where there's muck, there's brass'.

Activity 1

Can you think of an example of how the meaning of waste has changed over time? Try to think of an everyday example in your life.

There is a range of things that you might have thought about. When I thought about this activity, I considered a simple example of buying a sandwich from a sandwich chain. Previously, I used to discard all the waste in one general bin. However, there has now been a change. When I go to dispose of the waste now, I put the waste into different bins: there is a bin for food waste, another for liquids and a third for other waste. This shows how the sandwich chain is asking me to separate waste and so gives me a clue that waste is now seen in different ways.

Summary

- Waste has a social meaning and this social meaning is bound up with issues such as the value of waste.
- The social meaning of waste is not fixed. Changes can occur between different societies and in the same society at different points in time. Debates about recycling help highlight the shifting meaning of waste.

2   Waste and affluence

Leaving the question of value to one side, how much waste is produced in society? Data on waste can provide initial ideas about how large an issue this is likely to be for society, and whether this issue has been growing in importance, for example with the amount of waste increasing over time. There are lots of ways of trying to assess waste. This chapter concentrates mainly on household waste, although it is useful to remember that there are other types of waste, such as commercial waste. As part of the discussion, this chapter will also consider waste from supermarkets.

Figure 8.1 gives data for household waste per person in the UK between 1991 and 2010. Household waste refers to all the waste that is collected from household bins as well as civic amenity sites (such as recycling centres or the
local tip).

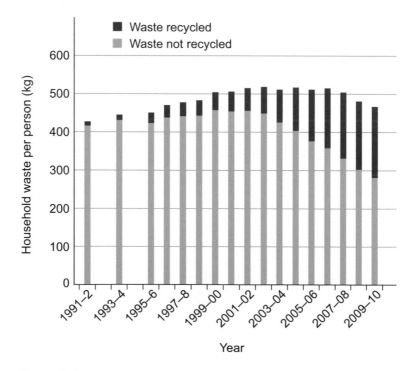

Figure 8.1   Household waste per person (kg) in the UK, 1991–2010 (Source: DEFRA, 2012)

Figure 8.1 presents the figures in units of kilogrammes of waste per person. For each year, the blue bar refers to the amount of waste that is not recycled. The red bar on top of this marks out the quantity of waste that is sent for recycling. The sum of the blue and the red bars for each year therefore refers to the total household waste produced per person for each year. The figure shows that between 1991 and 2010, each person created at least 400 kg of household waste. Moreover, between 1999–00 and 2007–08, each person created at least 500 kg of waste each year.

The available data is restricted to general household waste, but data also exists on specific types of waste, for example food waste. The Waste and Resources Action Programme (WRAP) provides data on food waste in the UK (2014). WRAP is a not-for-profit company aimed at encouraging people to cut waste and recycle more. It was set up in 2000 and is funded by the UK government as well as the European Union (EU). WRAP's (2013) report on household food and drink waste shows that seven million tonnes of this type of waste was thrown away in 2012. By weight, this is about a fifth of all household food and drink in the UK. However, WRAP (2013) says that 4.2 million tonnes of this waste is avoidable. This avoidable food and drink waste is therefore 60 per cent of the total food and drink waste, and worth £12.5 billion.

Tesco supermarket published figures for the first time in 2013 about the amount of food wasted from its stores in the UK. The report notes that customers threw away 35 per cent of bagged salad, 25 per cent of bakery items and 27 per cent of apples (Tesco, 2013). However, consumer waste is only part of the total food waste. Some waste might be created in fields or orchards. This occurs if supermarkets reject misshapen fruit or vegetables that they do not wish to sell to consumers, such as crooked carrots, broken broccoli or split swedes. Other food might be wasted through transportation, as it might be bruised or squashed. Unloading pallets or boxes in the store might result in further loss of food.

The Tesco report on food waste notes that for bagged salad, 17 per cent is lost in the field, 15 per cent is lost from general processing and 1 per cent is lost in retail. This means that 33 per cent of the waste in bagged salad comes from general production. Roughly, the same percentage of bagged salad is lost in production as through waste by consumers. This matters because it means that reducing waste in bagged salad cannot be tackled by focusing on individuals alone. Indeed, focusing only on consumer behaviour means that only half of the problem in waste in bagged salad is being addressed.

The growth of waste raises a number of questions. One of these is: why has there been a rise in waste in recent times? A variety of different factors might be outlined to explain the growth of waste. One explanation builds on the previous chapter and looks at whether growing affluence might also be associated with a 'throwaway society'. The previous chapter described how advertising and marketing can fuel excessive consumption. Rising levels of waste might be a flip side of this excessive consumption. In particular, rising waste might be associated with rising affluence. This means that as people get richer, they might be more inclined to throw more things away.

■   Why does the creation of waste matter? Even if waste is increasing, why does this matter for society?

Externality
The effect on society or the environment of economic activities that are not adequately reflected in the prices of goods and services.

The impact of waste on the environment provides one reason to be concerned about waste. This is an example of what economists call an **'externality'**. An individual's private decision to produce or consume has wider 'external' effects for society (although 'individual' here can refer to different things such as a person or an individual organisation). According to standard economic approaches, individuals are assumed to consume (or produce) up to the point where an extra unit of consumption (or production) equals its cost. For example, if the benefits from an extra bit of consumption are more than its cost, then people will consume more. If the cost exceeds the benefits from consumption, then people will not consume. People will stop consuming when an extra bit of consumption equals the cost of consumption.

For a 'negative externality', people consume or produce too much when compared to the optimal level for society. This is because the private cost from extra consumption (or production) is less than its social cost, and so people keep consuming or producing beyond the point at which the benefits to society are equal to the costs to society. Pollution is one of the classic examples of a negative externality. For example, consider a factory that discharges production waste into a river. If the river takes this waste downstream beyond the factory site, then the factory is able to get some benefits from discharging waste while not bearing all the costs of waste (as these are taken downstream). Thus, the factory does not bear all the costs of waste disposal and so will produce too much waste compared to what is best for society.

Waste might also raise concerns about the idea of environmental sustainability. Environmental sustainability refers to an idea that a pattern of behaviour adopted towards the environment is stable and can be continued indefinitely into the future. Unsustainability means that it is not possible to continue with present trends. This is because the trends are gradually destroying the environment.

There are different ways of trying to measure environmental sustainability. The Global Footprint Network is a non-profit organisation that campaigns in different countries over environmental sustainability. The Global Footprint Network provides one measure with its annual 'Earth Overshoot Day'. It has developed an 'ecological footprint', which refers to what humans consume from nature for their lives. This includes land and water areas used for buildings as well as ecosystems used to absorb waste. The Earth Overshoot Day refers to the date in each year when human consumption exceeds the capacity of nature to renew itself. As human consumption becomes more unsustainable, the earth overshoot date occurs earlier in the year. In 1993, the Earth Overshoot Day was October 21. In 2013, it was 20 August (Global Footprint Network, 2013).

2.1   Why did household waste increase?

There are signs then that waste has increased in recent times. What accounts for this rise in waste? Often in the social sciences there is no single explanation for a particular issue, but instead a range of possible explanations that may combine in different ways. A range of factors is likely to be important for explaining the growth in waste. A document published by the EU on waste management highlights a series of possible factors and draws particular attention to the role of rising affluence. It notes that:

> As European society has grown wealthier it has created more and more rubbish. Higher living standards mean that people are buying more products … Consumption has also changed dramatically. Today, consumers have much more choice and products are designed to have shorter lifespans … Advances in technology mean that people own and use many more personal devices, and update them more often. These lifestyle changes may have increased our quality of life, but they also mean we are generating more waste than ever before.

> (EU, 2010, p. 2)

It is possible to unpick a range of factors from this statement. The EU highlights the importance of a growth in consumption and you have seen the importance of this from previous chapters. Yiannis and Lang (2009) comment that: 'Consumerism has almost become a moral doctrine in many countries, unchallenged as the essence of the good life. According to this view, consumerism is the vehicle for freedom, power and happiness, with all of these things lying in the consumer's ability to choose, acquire, use and enjoy material objects and experiences' (Yiannis and Lang, 2009, p. 8). The growth of consumption creates more potential for waste, as people may be tempted to throw more things away.

Technology is also cited as a reason. Technological change allows updates of existing products to be made more frequently than in the past, for example with more regular upgrades of mobile phones. This means that products may be superseded more regularly, which shortens the lifespans of products and creates more potential for waste.

Higher living standards mean that households may be able to shift patterns of spending from 'necessities' to 'luxuries', and this spending can also fuel a throwaway society. For example, data from the Office for National Statistics (ONS) in the UK shows that in 1957, 42 per cent of UK household spending was on food, drink and tobacco (ONS, 2008). However, by 2011, 13 per cent of UK household spending was on food, drink or tobacco (ONS, 2012). (You came across the 2011 survey in Chapter 5, where the figures were presented in pounds per week rather than percentages.) It is difficult to make exact comparisons between different years as sometimes the categories for data changes over time and the definition of what counts as a household may change. Nevertheless, the figures suggest that for UK households the percentage of spending on food, drink and tobacco in 1957 was around triple the figures for 2011.

Food, drink and tobacco might generally be thought to refer to necessities rather than luxuries, or at least the food and non-alcoholic drinks that make up the majority of this category, and so the 2011 figures suggest that UK households were able to spend less money on necessities and more on luxuries. Rising affluence is another important explanation that is tied to this. Data on income, indicating rising affluence, is shown in Figure 8.2.

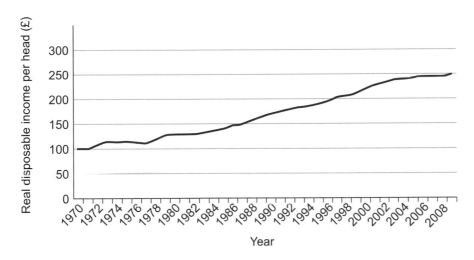

Figure 8.2   Real disposable income per head in the UK, 1970–2009
(Source: ONS, 2011)

Figure 8.2 shows a graph of real disposable income per head in the UK between 1970 and 2009. 'Real disposable income' means that income has been adjusted to take account of the effects of inflation. To assess changes in real income, it is usual to set a base year. In Figure 8.2, the starting year of 1970 is taken to be the base year. Real disposable income is the income that is available to be spent (or disposed of) after tax. Figure 8.2 shows an upward trend over the period. Thus in 2009, the real disposable income per head was roughly £250, almost two and a half times the level in 1970.

Figure 8.2 highlights that rising affluence occurred at the same time as the growth of consumer markets. This provides one explanation for the growth in waste. As people became richer, they were able to spend more money on products and also upgrade more regularly. This growth in consumption could create more waste, for example with the packaging that surrounds products as well as products becoming obsolete more regularly.

The effects of this shift in attitudes towards rubbish and wastefulness can be seen in the change in the levels of rubbish in the early years of the twenty-first century. Figure 8.3 presents information about the percentage of total household waste per person that is not recycled. The percentage of waste sent for recycling plus the percentage of waste that is not sent for recycling totals 100 per cent (since waste must be either recycled or not recycled).

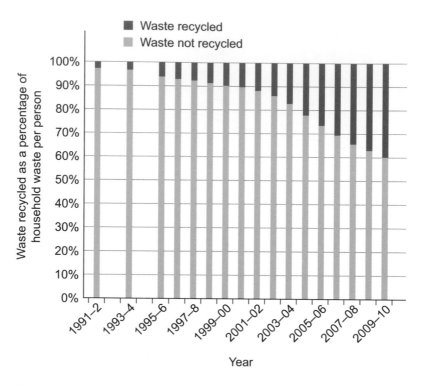

Figure 8.3   Waste that is recycled as a percentage of household waste per person in the UK (Source: DEFRA, 2012)

Figure 8.3 can be used to give a sense of the extent to which a growing percentage of waste is sent for recycling. It also gives a sense of the balance between waste that is recycled and waste that is not recycled. For each year, the blue bar refers to the percentage of household waste per person in the UK that is not recycled. The red bar shows the percentage of household waste per person in the UK that is recycled.

Activity 2

- What does Figure 8.3 show about the relative balance of waste that is recycled and waste that is not recycled?

- What does Figure 8.3 show about what has happened to the waste that is recycled over time?

For each year in Figure 8.3, the blue bar is larger than the red bar. In fact, the blue bar never falls below 60 per cent. This tells me that the majority of household waste that is created is not sent for recycling. I can see that the red bars in Figure 8.3 are getting larger over time. In

1991–2, 2 or 3 per cent of household waste was sent for recycling. In 2009–10, about 40 per cent of household waste was recycled. This suggests to me that household recycling has changed significantly over the past 20 years or so.

I want to make another observation: although rising affluence is associated with rising waste, it is also associated with greater recycling. This means that terms such as 'throwaway society' can mask a complex set of behaviours, with more things being thrown away combined with greater efforts at recycling.

Summary

- There has been a rise in waste across the world in recent times. This rise in waste can be tied to the idea of a 'throwaway society', where increasing consumption is also tied to the creation of more waste.

- A series of factors contribute to the growth of waste. One important factor is likely to be rising affluence. As people become richer, they can afford more things to consume, but also create more waste in the process.

- The creation of waste matters for a variety of reasons. Waste can have harmful effects on the environment and this influences the way that people make their lives.

3   Recycling and behavioural economics

Section 2 has described the growth in waste and how this might be linked to growing affluence. Reducing waste involves changes in the way that people make their lives. This section looks particularly at recent interest in behavioural economics as a way of prompting changes to individual behaviour. Behavioural economics tries to use personal psychological biases to 'nudge' people to make particular choices. In terms of recycling, behavioural economics asks: do people make the best choices on recycling waste?

Chapter 7 referred to the various techniques that advertisers use to influence people's buying habits.

Before doing this, it is important first to place the ideas of behavioural economics in context. To do this, I want to refer once again to the Tesco report (Tesco, 2013) on waste from its stores. If you recall, 68 per cent of bagged salad is wasted from Tesco and roughly the same amount of bagged salad is wasted through general production as through behaviour from consumers. This suggests that any effort to cut waste in bagged salad would mean changes in both general production as well as consumer behaviour. For example, supermarkets might change the way that they collect food. Instead of rejecting fruit or vegetables that are misshapen, supermarkets might sell them in store. Supermarkets may think that the consumer is only interested in the 'perfect apple', but consumers may also be willing to pay for misshapen produce (although possibly for a lower price). Supermarkets might also introduce changes in the way that they transport food or unpack it in store. Indeed, for some commentators, the most important issue in reducing waste and protecting the environment is to promote organisational change.

Alan Warde (2013), a sociologist who has published widely on consumption, explores topics such as food, waste and sustainable consumption. He argues that it:

... will take more time than climate science says we have available if we rely on nudging billions of individuals into minor beneficial modifications to their everyday habits to save the planet. It is the rich (rich countries as well as affluent individuals) who pose the greatest threat to sustainability; and it is agencies with substantial power (governments, corporations, institutions) which have the greatest capacity to make big differences to the environmental accounts. Focusing on changing individual behaviour seems to me like moving deckchairs around on the Titanic.

(Warde, 2013)

In organisational terms, the Tesco report on food waste highlights different ways that it says it will reduce waste in bagged salad:

- We will not offer multi-buys on larger packs and are developing an intelligent promotion strategy to allow customers to 'mix and match' products
- Introducing re-sealable bags across the range following a trial on shredded iceberg lettuce
- Twin packs offer 'eat me now, eat me later' opportunities for customers.

(Tesco, 2013, p. 9)

Activity 3

Consider each of the three main changes above that Tesco proposes. How might each of these suggestions reduce the waste in bagged salad?

First, the change Tesco proposes is not to offer any more multi-buys for salad on larger packs. This might mean stopping 'buy one get one free' ('BOGOF') offers on larger packs of salad. The aim of this is not to provide people with an incentive to buy more salad than they need or want. An 'intelligent promotion strategy' means allowing customers flexibility over what they buy. Allowing people a greater mix with their products might give people an incentive to combine a bagged salad with other items that complement the salad and so reduce waste, for example combining salad with pasta.

The second change, the provision of resealable bags, might encourage people to top- up existing large bags of salad with new bits of salad, rather than buying a whole new packet (which might contain bits of salad that people do not want). Using the example that Tesco mentions, this might mean people topping- up an existing bag with iceberg lettuce that they have shredded themselves.

Finally, the twin-pack idea might encourage people to think about what products they can eat immediately and those products that might last a bit longer, and so can be eaten later. This idea might fall into the category of supermarkets providing more information to customers about the products on sale.

3.1   Behavioural economics

The Tesco bagged salad example, however, shows that roughly the same amount of waste is created through the production process as by consumers. This means that even if changes to production are introduced, then it is just as important in this case to introduce changes to individual behaviour. Even if one believes that the critical issue is for organisations or other agencies such as government to change, it may still be important for people to change as well. The question is *how* to bring that change about and one answer is provided by behavioural economists.

Behavioural economics, as an approach, blends psychology and economics to shape individual decisions. The psychological aspect highlights the importance of psychological biases for understanding individual decision making. This has roots in a wider literature on the mental biases or limits on decision making. During the 1950s, Herbert Simon argued that people had mental limits in how much they were able to process information (Simon, 1955). Standard economics often suggested that people had almost unlimited capacity to absorb and process information when people made decisions. Simon argued that this view of humans was unrealistic, as people often struggle to compute a lot of information and so may suffer from 'information overload' (Simon, 1955).

In tandem, Daniel Kahneman and Amos Tversky won the Nobel Prize in Economics for their work in using psychology to understand how people make economic decisions. They found that if people were presented with different gambles, then people were often more concerned with avoiding losses than making gains. They called this 'loss aversion' and highlighted a psychological bias in people to avoid losses (Kahneman and Tversky, 1979).

Richard Thaler and Cass Sunstein (2008) popularised much of behavioural economics in their book *Nudge*. They build their argument in a series of steps, starting with a set of claims about human behaviour. When building their argument, Thaler and Sunstein contrast their claims about human behaviour with those used in mainstream economics. They write:

> Whether or not they have ever studied economics, many people seem at least implicitly committed to the idea of *homo economicus*, or economic man – the notion that each of us thinks and chooses unfailingly well, and thus fits within the textbook picture of human beings offered by economists ... Really. But the folks that we know are not like that ... They are not *homo economicus*; they are *homo sapiens*. To keep our Latin usage to a minimum we will hereafter refer to these imaginary and real species as Econs and Humans.
>
> (Thaler and Sunstein, 2008, pp. 6–7)

Thaler and Sunstein say that the Econs cover the claims made about human behaviour within standard economics. Econs only concentrate on their own wants or needs and maximising their personal happiness. They base their decisions on all the relevant information that is available at the time and only take action if the benefits of doing so exceed the costs. The Econ is almost a type of 'calculating machine'.

Thaler and Sunstein argue that the Econ is an imaginary term, which does not describe real people, and go on to make a series of claims about human behaviour, claims which are common also in the wider literature on behavioural economics (Thaler and Sunstein, 2008; De Meza et al., 2008; Dolan et al., 2010; Leicester et al., 2012). The following are some of the key claims that Thaler and Sunstein (2008) make about human behaviour:

- *Bounded rationality*: there are bounds or limits in the capacity of people to make rational calculations. One effect of this is that people rely on rules of thumb when making some decisions.

- *Overconfidence*: individuals tend to overestimate their capacity to filter and understand a mass of information. Also, people think that bad things are less likely to happen to them than to others.

- *Loss aversion*: people do not value potential losses and gains in the same way. They prefer to avoid losses rather than make gains and will take steps to avoid the prospect of losses.

- *Status quo bias*: this points towards a tendency that individuals have to fall back on existing patterns of behaviour and adopt the status quo.

- *Mental accounting*: this refers to a habit that people have of separating related areas of money matters. Instead of looking at the overall picture, they will prefer to place different parts of personal finance in different mental boxes.

The following activity asks you to consider some of the claims that Thaler and Sunstein (2008) make.

Figure 8.4   One way of thinking about behavioural economics is that people are like Homer Simpson!

Activity 4

Answer the following questions to find out if you are an Econ or a Human.

- Would you be more likely to become a kidney donor if you were automatically enrolled into a donor scheme but allowed to opt out, or if you had to sign up to be a donor?

- Imagine that you are shopping in a supermarket to buy jam. You look at a shelf with 20 different varieties. Do you look at each one of the jams or just pick one that is good enough to meet your needs?

- Would you be more likely to support a tax on fuel if it was called a 'greenhouse gas tax'?

According to behavioural economics, if automatic enrolment makes it more likely that you will be a donor, then you are a Human rather than Econ. This is because you resist change and just prefer the status quo. Thus, if you are automatically enrolled into a donor scheme, then you are not inclined to change anything and so will remain in the donor scheme.

Econs will weigh the merits of the different jams, while Humans will use short cuts such as one that is just good enough.

Brands act as a kind of short cut, as Chapter 7 explained.

Labels matter for Humans and so a 'greenhouse gas tax' would boost support among Humans rather than Econs.

Efforts like this to change individual behaviour can also be seen in debates on recycling. For example, Edinburgh Council produced a waste strategy plan for 2010–25 that aims to: 'Maximise participation in waste prevention, reuse and recycling through behavioural change' (Edinburgh Council, 2010, p. 2). It set a target of diverting at least 50 per cent of waste from landfill by 2015. To achieve this, the strategy says it will:

- increase the material that the Council collects for recycling
- take steps to improve the access people have to recycling
- encourage participation in recycling.

(Edinburgh Council, 2010)

A European Commission (EC) 'Waste Framework Directive' states that member states, including the UK, should have at least 50 per cent of household waste being recycled from 2020 (EC, 2012).

Organisations from both the private and public sectors can try to change the behaviour of people in a number of ways. Behavioural economics has recently attracted interest as a possible way of trying to tackle issues such as food waste. For example, Kallbekken and Sælen (2013) report results from a study of a chain of Norwegian hotels (52 in total) that looked at the impact of behavioural nudges on cutting food waste. One behavioural nudge was to give people smaller plates under the hypothesis that smaller plate sizes would reduce food consumption and so food waste. A second nudge was to put a sign up at the buffet, encouraging people to make repeat trips rather than trying to load their plates all at once. Some hotels did not receive either nudge for the purposes of comparison. Kallbekken and Sælen (2013) found that smaller plate sizes cut food waste by 19.5 per cent, and a sign providing a social cue at the buffet reduced food waste by 20.5 per cent.

In the UK, in a similar vein, the Conservative–Liberal Democrat government established in July 2010 a Behavioural Insights Team within the Cabinet Office to advise government on the different ways that policymakers might shape personal behaviour (Cabinet Office, 2013). The name 'Behavioural Insights Team' acknowledges that behavioural insights come from a wider range of theories than behavioural economics alone, even though the Behavioural Insights Team is often referred to as the 'nudge unit' in the media (BBC News, 2011; Glover, 2011; Cameron, 2012). A report from the House of Lords Science and Technology Committee on behaviour change remarks: 'Cabinet Office's Behavioural Insights Team (BIT) … is referred to in the media as the "nudge unit", and "nudge" has been used in Government policy documents, Ministerial statements and debates in the House of Commons' (House of Lords Science and Technology Committee, 2011, p. 11).

Significantly, behavioural economics suggests that by altering the context in which people make choices, policymakers can nudge people to make particular choices. The final choice rests with the individual. However, policymakers can affect these individual choices by altering the rules of the game. So, for recycling, this could mean councils altering the context within which people make decisions about recycling food, paper, plastics, and so on.

3.2   Choice architecture

Section 3.1 suggests that Thaler and Sunstein (2008) rely on a set of claims about human behaviour to build their argument. The next stage of their argument involves thinking about what these claims about individual behaviour mean for how policy should be designed. The key thing to hold onto is that the aim of behavioural economics is to effect large changes on the environment through lots of small changes in individual behaviour. This leads behavioural economists to a discussion of 'choice architecture'. The 'choice' part of this term refers to the idea of an individual choosing something or making a decision. However, Thaler and Sunstein (2008) suggest that choices are not made in a vacuum, but are shaped instead by outside factors such as institutions. They use 'architecture' to refer to the context in which choices are made and, as such, architecture refers to the idea of interlocking institutions.

Thaler and Sunstein (2008) develop a set of principles to shape choice architecture. They call these 'nudge principles', as the different principles are said to spell the term 'nudges'. It is important to note that each of these principles is linked to an underlying claim about human behaviour – this is how Thaler and Sunstein use their initial claims to build their argument:

- *Incentives*: although Thaler and Sunstein (2008) criticise standard economic approaches, they do not reject all of the claims. They accept that self-interest is important when designing institutions. This can be seen in the attention they pay to incentives. Self-interested agents compare the costs and benefits of an action, and may be interested in something as long as the benefits outweigh the costs. An emphasis on incentives appeals to this cost–benefit calculation.

  People might be provided with a financial reward for behaving in a particular way and this could be a stimulus to action. For example, supermarkets might give store card points if a person reuses plastic bags when shopping. Alternatively, people might face a penalty (financial or otherwise) that would prompt them away from particular types of behaviour. For instance, people could be fined for littering on the street.

- *Understanding mappings*: people have limits in their capacity to make rational decisions and so architecture should make it easier for people to pick options by understanding mappings. This could refer to the labelling on different products. For example, councils often use different coloured boxes for different types of recycling, with black boxes used for, say, newspapers and cardboard, and blue boxes for metal or plastic. Sandwich chains sometimes provide different bins also for different types of recycling (such as for packaging or liquids).

- *Defaults*: status quo bias suggests that people resist changes and prefer the status quo. This means that defaults are important when designing policy, as this defines the status quo. Defaults refer to what choices would be set or 'defaulted' to in the absence of any other choice made by people. For instance, a coffee chain might sell, in increasing order of price (and profitability), coffees in small, medium or large size. However, staff may be told to ask, by default, whether the customer wants a medium or large size to steer them away from the small size, and towards the more expensive options.

- *Give feedback*: people's choices are influenced by social norms and they might also develop rules of thumb when making choices. Feedback can help cultivate a norm or assist in fashioning a rule of thumb. For example, utility companies (such as gas, electricity or water) might give feedback to people when sending out bills on their energy use and whether they are using energy efficiently.

- *Expect error*: people are thought to have limits on their capacity to make choices. This means that designers of choice architecture should build in an expectation that people will make errors when making choices.

- *Structure complex choices*: mental accounting means that people often put things into different mental boxes rather than taking a comprehensive overview of a choice. To respond to this choice, designers should break down complicated choices into simpler choices. Recycling could cover a range of different materials, and choice designers could break this down into looking at how people recycle or dispose of particular materials. This may mean different nudges to get people to compost some of their perishable foods separate from how they dispose or recycle the food packaging.

These nudge principles do not prescribe a single course of action and there is a range of ways that these nudge principles may be combined. Some approaches might only use some of the principles. Approaches that use all of these principles might combine these ideas in different ways, for example by placing more weight on some of these principles than on others. This underlines that it is a mistake to see behavioural economics as pointing to one way of doing things. Rather, it maps a set of possibilities and this can vary in different areas.

Chapter 7 considered how advertising might be used to seduce people into buying things. This included providing mood music to create an environment that encourages people to consume. The use of music might be considered as one of the nudges that companies use to encourage people to buy their products. Overlaps therefore exist between nudges and advertising. However, not all advertising might be considered a nudge.

Thaler and Sunstein (2008) make a distinction between nudges and subliminal advertising. Subliminal advertising involves the use of hidden messages, such as messages about healthy eating being hidden in films or television programmes. They argue that a nudge is different, as it does not rely on hidden information. They say information about nudges is readily available to the public. Thus, although some adverts might qualify as nudges, other adverts (such as subliminal adverts) may not be nudges. Also, there are nudges that are not adverts at all. This implies that although nudges and advertising overlap, they are nevertheless different ways of trying to shape individual behaviour.

There is a variety of ways that people can be nudged to make choices. As an example of this, consider how choice architects might try to nudge decisions when people are doing something as simple as buying lunch. Look at Figure 8.5, which outlines the layout of a canteen.

The way the canteen is organised is an example of choice architecture. It shows how the design of the canteen is aimed at nudging people to make particular choices. The final choice of what to buy rests with the purchaser. The following are some of the ways that the layout of the canteen influences the purchaser's choice:

- *Incentives:* creating an express queue for healthy choices can provide customers with an incentive to pick healthy choices to get through the queue quicker. Allowing fewer payment options for dessert, so this is cash only compared to cash or lunch vouchers for other foods, gives people an incentive to pay for other foods rather than desserts, as it is easier for them to pay for this.

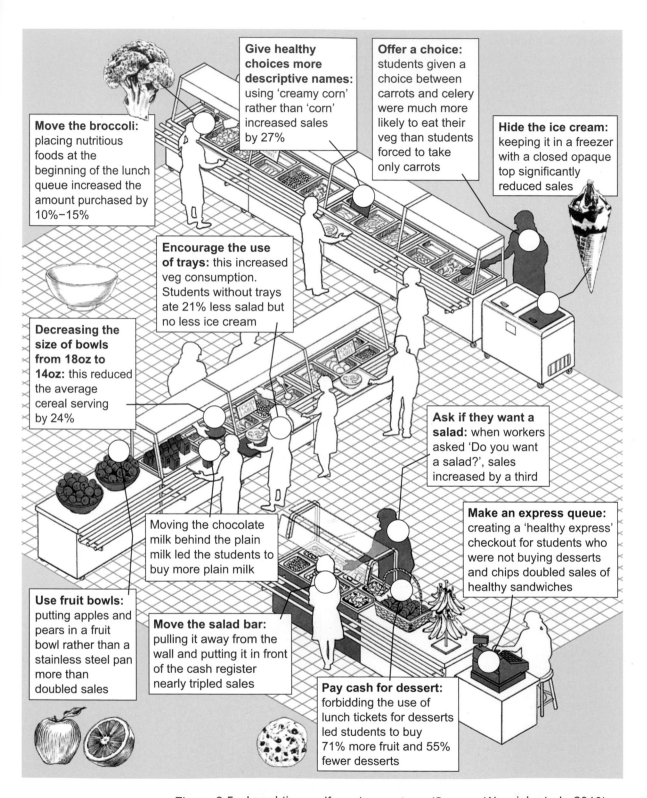

Figure 8.5   Lunchtime self-service canteen (Source: Wansink et al., 2010)

- *Understanding mappings:* this refers to how the way that options are presented or framed can affect decisions. Describing food in a more appetising way can affect choices. In the above, describing corn as 'creamy corn' can boost choices. Another example of this is how ice-cream is packaged. Putting ice-cream inside a freezer with an opaque lid does not present ice-cream in an attractive manner and reduces ice-cream consumption. Putting fruit in fruit bowls can make fruit seem more enticing.

- *Defaults:* questions asked by default can affect choices. For example, canteen staff asking people automatically, or by default, if they want salad is seen to boost the number of people who choose a salad to go with their meal. Defaults can be seen also in the size of the cereal bowls, where people are given smaller bowls by default. According to Figure 8.5, doing this reduces cereal consumption by about a quarter compared to those with larger bowls.

- *Structure complex choices:* although buying lunch may not be a complex task, choice designers can nevertheless try to structure or shape choices. In the canteen, this can be done by paying attention to where things are placed. For example, moving the salad bar away from a wall and closer to the cash register pays attention to how choices are structured. Similarly, putting broccoli at the start of the queue encourages people to pick some broccoli early on. The use of trays might also be seen as an example of how choices can be structured, as it seems that people make different choices when given a tray than when they do not use a tray. Giving people choices over carrot and celery rather than carrots alone structures choices in particular ways.

Activity 5

The list above provides an example of choice architecture being applied to buying lunch in a canteen. I would like you to conduct a similar task in another context: apply each of the nudge principles to consider how supermarkets might try to nudge people in particular ways.

There is a variety of ways that the nudge principles could be applied for the design of supermarkets, but compare yours to the examples below.

- *Incentives:* supermarkets give people an incentive to buy more goods through special offers such as 'BOGOFs' or other special discounts.

- *Understanding mappings*: supermarkets might influence choices through the labelling of foods, such as applying 'traffic light' systems to communicate information about fat and salt contents.

- *Defaults*: to reduce the use of plastic bags, supermarkets might instruct checkout staff only to provide a plastic bag if the customer asks for it.

- *Give feedback*: till receipts might be used to nudge people to make particular purchases, suggesting items that the consumer might like to complement what is already in their basket.

- *Expect error*: supermarkets may monitor and change the position of stock to accommodate any unexpected behaviour from consumers.

- *Structure complex choices*: shopping aisles could be arranged to group together complementary items (such as bread and cereals, tea and biscuits, strawberries and cream, and so on).

You might have the same examples or you might also have different ideas. This highlights that nudge principles can be applied in various ways.

3.3   Evidence on nudges

From the above, you can see how Thaler and Sunstein (2008) build their nudge argument. They set out the underlying claims about human behaviour and what those claims mean for choice architecture, and this framework, in turn, points towards the kind of evidence that would be needed to assess the likely effectiveness of nudge theory to change behaviour on recycling. One set of evidence, for instance, could explore the claims that they make about human behaviour. This would examine the evidence for and against each of the claims they make about human behaviour. Another set of evidence could explore the implications that they make on the basis of their claims about human behaviour.

Evidence on behavioural economics is still fairly small, although this is a growing area of research. There is evidence, however, from the USA and UK, on the effect of nudges on kerbside recycling (Schultz, 1999; Nomura et al., 2011). Nomura et al. (2011), for instance, have studied the effects of a feedback scheme on recycling in Oldham in the UK. This study looked at the role that feedback plays in shaping human behaviour. The feedback here is based on the idea that people are influenced by the behaviour of their peers. People are more likely to recycle if they think others are doing likewise. The study, as such, highlights the impact of social norms on behaviour.

Nomura et al. point to the fact that studies of recycling often focus at the level of the street. Possible reasons for this are that a street may often be the basis of a sense of community among people and so be useful for recycling schemes. Other advantages of streets include the tendency of streets to have a lower population turnover and so provide for a more stable community identity than larger areas. Streets also usually cover people living in similar conditions and so are useful for testing the effect of nudges on people living in similar circumstances.

They note that Oldham was the first council in Greater Manchester to introduce a food recycling scheme. Prior to its introduction in 2007, waste in 2006–07 was made up of: 85 per cent general waste; 6 per cent garden waste; 5 per cent paper and cardboard; 4 per cent glass, cans and plastics. After the introduction of the food recycling scheme in 2008–09, waste was made up of: 68 per cent general waste; 7 per cent garden waste; 8 per cent paper and cardboard; 14 per cent glass, cans and plastics; and 3 per cent food waste.

Nomura et al. then tested the effect of written feedback on recycling rates. This looked at 318 streets, covering 9082 households. Five thousand and nine households and 159 streets were the 'treatment group' that received the written feedback (the treatment), and 4073 households and 159 streets were assigned to be the 'control group', that is, did not receive the feedback. This is an example of a randomised control trial, which is a way of testing whether an action has an effect by comparing the results of those who receive the action (the treatment group) with those who do not (the control group). A leaflet was provided to those with the feedback, which contained either a smiley face ☺ or frown face ☹.

The study was conducted at three points in time. The first point was in August 2009, before the feedback leaflets were sent out. This was to assess how much food recycling occurred before the behavioural nudge was introduced. This would then help assess whether introducing the behavioural nudge would make a difference to levels of recycling in the treatment groups.

The second monitoring occurred in September 2009, just after the first feedback leaflets were sent out. The leaflets stated: 'Did you know: X per cent of homes in A Street recycle their food waste. The average for the area is Y per cent'. This was followed by a smiley face or frown face, depending on whether the street was better or worse than the average. The monitoring also looked at any changes in the control group at this time. This was to assess whether any changes that occurred in the treatment groups arose because of the behavioural cues rather than from wider changes that affected both treatment and control groups.

The third set of monitoring occurred in October 2009, after the second feedback leaflets were sent out. Nomura et al. (2011) found that feedback leaflets could help boost participation in food recycling by 2.8 per cent compared to the control group who did not receive the feedback leaflets. They noted that although this increase is modest, it may nonetheless provide cost savings for councils, which are likely to be useful in an era of tightening local finances.

3.4   Inequality and difference

I have discussed some of the ways that people might be nudged to make particular decisions. However, various constraints might still exist, which may stop people from behaving in particular ways. People might already be willing to behave in a specific way, but find that their actions are restricted by an outside constraint. The issue here is the constraint upon individual behaviour rather than the need to nudge people to behave in particular ways.

Poverty is an obvious constraint on individual behaviour. Poverty can take a number of forms. People might be 'time poor' if they do not have much time to do certain things. They may have a range of competing demands on their time and work long hours, either in paid employment or in the home. At home, people might have caring responsibilities for a young child or an older relative, or a lot of domestic tasks to do. There may be little time for these individuals to do anything else. Asking people to spend more time on recycling (such as separating waste into different boxes) may add another pressure on their time.

Lack of money, though, is perhaps the most obvious form of poverty. Lack of money can inhibit choices. Because of a lack of money, a person's wish to live a 'greener' lifestyle might flounder. Installing solar panels to have more efficient energy use is, initially, likely to be costly, for example because of having to pay for the solar panels and getting them installed. It may be some time before the benefits from reduced energy bills outweigh the costs of the panels and installation.

Mullainathan and Shafir (2013) argue that poverty literally impoverishes the mind. They use 'mental bandwidth' to refer to the range of things that a person is capable of thinking about. The greater the mental bandwidth, the greater the range of things that people are able to think about. Mullainathan and Shafir (2013) argue that poverty reduces mental bandwidth, as it forces people to cope with the effects of poverty and away from thinking about things more generally. They say that poverty then leads to the sort of psychological biases highlighted by behavioural economics, adding that behavioural nudges might be useful to cope with reduced mental bandwidth. In this way, behavioural economics is a response to poverty.

Behavioural economics here, though, is aimed at helping people cope with the effects of poverty. An alternative strategy is to tackle the roots of reduced bandwidth, that is, actually tackling poverty. Reducing poverty would reduce the constraints on the mind. Reducing poverty might involve a wider range of policies than behavioural nudges, such as redistribution through the tax and benefit system by the state. This suggests that other policies, besides behavioural nudges, may be important for tackling the constraints that exist on the mind.

Another issue is the relationship of inequality to differences among the population. Equality does not necessarily imply that everybody is the same or has the same outcomes. Equality allows differences to flourish with different life goals or plans. Nevertheless, some differences might be rooted in inequality. For example, inequality between men and women in households might mean that women have to do an unequal (and unfair) share of housework, and there is recent evidence of such inequality in a study of recycling behaviour.

■   Read the following newspaper extract about recycling behaviour between different households.

Why single men are rubbish at putting out the recycling bins

Men who live alone are the least likely to recycle in the UK, according to a study. As many homes come to terms with a backlog of discarded wrapping paper and empty packaging after Christmas, women will take on the most responsibility for disposing of it in an environmentally friendly way, according to new research.

> Results showed that single people living alone are less likely to recycle – only 65% did so, compared with 79% of mixed-sex couples. Of those living alone, 69% of women recycled some of their waste or unwanted items, whereas 58% of men were found to do the same.
>
> (Source: Fraser Thomas, 2012)

This report is based on a study by Pettifor (2012) on gender differences in recycling. Pettifor drew on the 2009–10 wave of an *Understanding Society* survey, which is a nationally representative survey of different UK households. She considered data for 2312 men and women living on their own as well as 3002 mixed-sex couples (either married or cohabiting). Pettifor found that there are gender differences in recycling. In households headed by a single person, women are more likely to recycle than men. For male–female couples, recycling is as likely if men or women do most of the household chores. Women do more recycling overall, although the marginal effect is greater for men – that is, if men and women each devote an extra hour of their time to doing more housework (for example by cutting back on leisure time) then men are likely to do more recycling than women.

This study suggests that differences exist among men and women in recycling. One implication of this research may be that if government wishes to develop behavioural nudges to prompt behaviour, then it may be useful to base this on different recycling behaviours among men and women. For example, if women recycle more than men, then any behavioural nudges might target men over women. This might inform efforts to develop a social norm among men to recycle or look at other ways that men could be encouraged to recycle. Of course, gender is only one of a series of factors that are important for **personal identity**. Gender meshes with other types of difference, such as those based on class, race, religion, and so on. People have a wide range of identities and so care should be taken not to put people in a single box. However, this example shows the way in which differences within society can interact with behavioural economics in a variety of complex and sometimes unpredictable ways.

Personal identity
A person's own idea of who she or he is: 'the real me'.

Figure 8.6 Empty glass bottles in the recycling tub

Summary

- Behavioural economics is one way of trying to get people to change their behaviour, for example to recycle more things. Behavioural economics makes a set of claims about human behaviour and then makes policy suggestions based on these claims.

- Outside constraints as well as individual behaviour are important for reducing waste. Organisations such as supermarkets, alongside consumers, play significant roles in the creation of waste.

- Inequality can limit the extent to which people can behave in particular ways. Differences over recycling also exist between particular groups, such as men and women.

Conclusion

This chapter has looked at the issue of waste and the ways in which people might be encouraged to create less waste through more recycling. Waste, as we have seen, is an important issue for how people live their lives, given the impact it can have on the environments they inhabit. The state of the environment shapes the possibilities that people have to make their lives today, as well as the way in which future generations may go about their lives. For example, if current generations undermine or damage the environment through their actions, then they will limit future generations from having the opportunity to make the best of their lives and thus restrict their life chances.

Case study
The study of a particular issue, place or event.

This chapter, more specifically, has looked at how people might be nudged into taking greater steps to recycle. Behavioural economics and recycling was chosen as a **case study** of the way in which social scientists build an argument. The chapter considered how behavioural economics is associated with a set of claims about human behaviour and how, in turn, these claims led to suggestions about how people might be nudged to behave in particular ways. The relevance of the claims was then considered in the light of the available evidence. It was acknowledged, though, that evidence on the impact of behavioural nudges is still fairly small and this highlights the need for further evidence to test the robustness of behavioural economics.

The discussion also outlined some of the limitations associated with behavioural economics. Data on supermarket waste shows that waste from consumer behaviour is only part of the problem and so tackling consumer behaviour is only part of the solution to cutting waste. Much depends on asking the right questions in the first place, including questions about the various constraints that are likely to shape the effectiveness of nudges to change behaviour.

Chapter 9, the final chapter of the 'Making lives' strand, explores further the relationship between questions, claims and evidence in the context of the choices and constraints that shape the lives of people in the UK today.

References

BBC News (2011) *Behind Closed Doors in the Downing Street Nudge Unit* [Online]. Available at http://www.bbc.co.uk/news/15343300 (Accessed 25 July 2012).

Cabinet Office (2013) *Behavioural Insights Team* [Online]. Available at http://www.cabinetoffice.gov.uk/behavioural-insights-team (Accessed 1 March 2014).

Cameron, S. (2012) *The Nudge, Nudge Unit has Ways to Make You Pay* [Online]. Available at http://www.telegraph.co.uk/news/politics/9392224/The-nudge-nudge-unit-has-ways-to-make-you-pay.html (Accessed 25 July 2012).

De Meza, D., Irlenbusch, B. and Reyniers, D. (2008) *Financial Capability: A Behavioural Economics Perspective* [Online]. Available at http://www.fsa.gov.uk/pubs/consumer-research/crpr69.pdf (Accessed 2 July 2012).

Department for Environment, Food and Rural Affairs (DEFRA) (2012) *Environmental Statistics – Key Facts* [Online]. Available at http://data.defra.gov.uk/env/doc/Environmental%20Statistics%20key%20facts%202012.pdf (Accessed 28 February 2014).

Dickens, C. (2002 [1865]) *Our Mutual Friend*, New York, The Modern Library.

Dolan, P., Hallsworth, M., Halpern, D., King, D. and Vlaev, I. (2010) *Mindspace: Influencing Behaviour through Public Policy* [Online]. Available at http://www.instituteforgovernment.org.uk/sites/default/files/publications/MINDSPACE.pdf (Accessed 6 July 2012).

Douglas, M. (1966) *Purity and Danger*, London, Routledge.

Edinburgh Council (2010) *Waste and Recycling Strategy* [Online]. Available at http://www.edinburgh.gov.uk/info/20239/waste_strategy_and_performance/1224/waste_and_recycling_strategy (Accessed 23 January 2013).

European Commission (EC) (2010) *Preparatory Study on Food Waste Across EU 27*, technical report 2010-054 [Online]. Available at http://ec.europa.eu/environment/eussd/pdf/bio_foodwaste_report.pdf (Accessed 3 May 2013).

European Commission (EC) (2012) *Waste Framework Directive* [Online]. Available at http://ec.europa.eu/environment/waste/framework/targets.htm (Accessed 27 March 2012).

European Union (2010) *Being Wise with Waste: The EU's Approach to Waste Management* [Online]. Available at http://ec.europa.eu/environment/waste/pdf/WASTE%20BROCHURE.pdf (Accessed 25 November 2013).

Evans, D., Campbell, H. and Murcott, A. (2013) 'A brief pre-history of food waste and the social sciences', *The Sociological Review*, vol. 60, no. S2, pp. 5–26.

Fraser Thomas, E. (2012) 'Why single men are rubbish at putting out the recycling bins', *The Observer*, 30 December.

Global Footprint Network (2013) *Earth Overshoot Day* [Online]. Available at http://www.footprintnetwork.org/en/index.php/GFN/page/earth_overshoot_day/ (Accessed 28 November 2013).

Glover, J. (2011) *What Is the Government's 'Nudge Unit'?* [Online]. Available at http://www.guardian.co.uk/commentisfree/2011/sep/19/government-nudge-unit-behavioural-insights-team (Accessed 25 July 2012).

Hertwich, E.G. and Peters, G.P. (2009) 'Carbon footprint of nations: a global, trade-linked analysis', *Environmental Science and Technology*, vol. 43, pp. 6414–20.

House of Lords Science and Technology Committee (2011) *Behaviour Change* [Online]. Available at http://www.publications.parliament.uk/pa/ld201012/ldselect/ldsctech/179/179.pdf (Accessed 24 July 2012).

Intergovernmental Panel on Climate Change (IPCC) (2013) *Climate Change 2013: The Physical Science Basis – Summary for Policymakers* [Online]. Available at https://www.ipcc.ch/report/ar5/wg1/docs/WGIAR5_SPM_brochure_en.pdf, (Accessed 19 March 2014).

Kahneman, D. and Tversky, A. (1979) 'Prospect theory: an analysis of decision under risk', *Econometrica*, vol. 47, pp. 263–91.

Kallbekken, S. and Sælen, H. (2013) '"Nudging" hotel guests to reduce food waste as a win-win environmental measure', *Economics Letters*, vol. 119, pp. 325–27.

Leicester, A., Levell, P. and Rasul, I. (2012) *Tax and Benefit Policy: Insights from Behavioural Economics* [Online]. Available at http://www.ifs.org.uk/comms/comm125.pdf (Accessed 24 July 2012).

Mullainathan, S. and Shafir, E. (2013) *Scarcity: Why Having Too Little Means So Much*, New York, Henry Holt and Company.

Nomura, H., John, P. and Cotterill, S. (2011) 'The use of feedback to enhance environmental outcomes: a randomised controlled trial of a food waste scheme', *Local Environment*, vol. 16, no. 7, pp. 637–53.

Office for National Statistics (ONS) (2008) *Family Spending, 2007 Edition*. Available at http://www.ons.gov.uk/ons/rel/family-spending/family-spending/2007-edition/index.html (Accessed 19 March 2014).

Office for National Statistics (ONS) (2011) *Social Trends 41* [Online]. Available at http://www.ons.gov.uk/ons/publications/re-reference-tables.html?edition=tcm%3A77-218733 (Accessed 21 March 2014).

Office for National Statistics (ONS) (2012) *Family Spending, 2011 Edition* [Online]. Available at http://www.ons.gov.uk/ons/rel/family-spending/family-spending/family-spending-2011-edition/index.html (Accessed 11 April 2014).

Pettifor, H. (2012) *Patterns of Household Practice: An Examination into the Relationship Between Housework and Waste Separation for Households in the United Kingdom*, Institute for Social and Economic Research [Online]. Available at https://www.iser.essex.ac.uk/publications/working-papers/iser/2012-14.pdf (Accessed 9 January 2013).

Schultz, P.W. (1999) 'Changing behaviour with normative feedback interventions: field experiment on kerbside recycling', *Basic and Applied Social Psychology*, vol. 21, no. 1, pp. 25–36.

Simon, H.A. (1955) 'A behavioural model of rational choice', *Quarterly Journal of Economics*, vol. 69, no. 1, pp. 99–118.

Tesco (2013) *Tesco and Society: Using our Scale for Good. 2013/14 Half Year Update* [Online]. Available at http://www.tescoplc.com/files/pdf/reports/ tesco_and_society_2013-14_halfyear_summary.pdf (Accessed 21 October 2013).

Thaler, R. and Sunstein, C. (2008) *Nudge: Improving Decisions about Health, Wealth and Happiness,* New Haven, CT, Yale University Press.

Wansink, B., Just, D.R. and McKendry, J. (2010) 'Lunch line redesign', *The New York Times* [Online]. Available at http://www.nytimes.com/interactive/2010/ 10/21/opinion/20101021_Oplunch.html (Accessed 4 February 2013).

Warde, A. (2013) *Sustainable Consumption and Behaviour Change* [Online]. Available at http://www.discoversociety.org/sustainable-consumption-and-behaviour- change/ (Accessed 7 November 2013).

Waste and Resources Action Programme (WRAP) (2013) *Final Report. Household Food and Drink Waste in the United Kingdom 2012.* Available at http://www.wrap. org.uk/sites/files/wrap/hhfdw-2012-main.pdf (Accessed 28 March 2014).

Waste and Resources Action Programme (WRAP) (2014) *Who We Are* [Online]. Available at http://www.wrap.org.uk/content/who-we-are (Accessed 2 April 2014).

Yiannis, G. and Lang, T. (2009) *The Unmanageable Consumer*, London, Sage.

Chapter 9
Reflections on 'Making lives'

John Allen

Contents

Introduction

This chapter acts as a conclusion to the first of the three module strands, 'Making lives', and provides an opportunity to reflect on how the preceding chapters can help tackle the core social science questions that underpin DD102:

- How is society made and remade?
- How are differences and inequalities produced?
- How do social scientists know?

It may not have escaped your attention that the first core question and the strand title 'Making lives' cover much the same ground. The making of society and the lives of each and every one of us that are made through it are perhaps best thought about as two sides of the same coin. On the one hand, life is what you make of it, yet, on the other, people have to live their lives in a society that for the most part has been handed down to them. I suppose you could say that, for want of a better expression, society has all the appearance of something that is 'ready made'.

Put another way, people make the best of their lives in and through society, or rather in and through a particular period of society that is already made up of any number of choices and constraints. People don't choose those choices and constraints, but they do inherit them. For example, joining the workforce for the first time in an economic recession is not something a young person would wish for, but it happens. And when it happens, people have to make their lives through the choices and constraints more or less laid down by previous generations.

Why does this matter to social scientists? It matters because, although individuals and groups *make* society, people's lives are, in turn, *made* by society. This is the conundrum that, in various ways, came into view in each of the chapters in the 'Making lives' strand. We will take a closer look at this conundrum here as it underpins your later studies of how society is connected and hangs together as a system of social order.

1   The story so far … making lives

There is a sentiment, one that I've already expressed, that many would find hard to disagree with. When someone insists that life is what you make of it, it usually implies that what you make of it is more or less down to you and your abilities. It's a sentiment that you can make a lot of or a little. Social scientists think about it a lot, considering it as more than just a sentiment and worthy of critical examination. But it works too in an everyday sense, where its meaning is obvious, although no less trivial because of that.

Mark Hocking, the garage proprietor on City Road who turned his business into a company that manufactures bespoke metal products, would, I think, have little trouble recognising the sentiment: namely, the value of taking any opportunity that comes your way to make the best of your life. Some of the other people who you met in both parts of *The Life and Times of the Street* (The Open University 2014a, 2014b), especially the café and restaurant owners, would very likely identify with its plain sentiment. Yet, and this is the reason for raising the example, just because some things about the way that people live their lives are plain to see, it does not mean to say that their *significance* is obvious.

Consider, for instance, the topics that, in different ways, ran through all of the chapters of the 'Making lives' strand, namely: shopping and consumption. Shopping is a familiar task to many – people buy things online, on the high street and, sometimes, on impulse. Consumers buy things for all sorts of reasons, many of which go beyond their mere usefulness. When the things purchased become the means through which people express themselves – their sense of self, their identity – when the objects bought become props that enable that identity to be performed, then the act of shopping takes on a significance beyond that of a routine practice. Defining ourselves by what we consume, as Chapter 5 showed, can be the means by which an identity is established and displayed to others who share similar tastes and lifestyles. It can literally buy, in all senses of that word, entry into a shared lifestyle by people *actively making* something of themselves through their desires and wants.

The social significance of all this does not simply end there, however. I stress *social* because, although people may actively make something of themselves through consumption, they do so together, with others. The creation of a consumer lifestyle, if Zygmunt Bauman (1988) is correct, is not something that is made without reference to what is valued and accepted by others who aspire to a particular lifestyle. Group membership is conferred only on those who conform to its accepted ways of consuming. The pressures to conform are not dictated by a higher authority but, as Chapter 7 pointed out through the examples of advertising and other pressures, work by stirring up particular wants and desires, and by channelling shopping choices along lines that reflect a quest for personality and individual autonomy. The ambition to be the kind of person reflected in our consumption choices may, in that respect, curb certain choices and close down possibilities that are considered inappropriate.

So the sense in which people fashion their lives through consumption suggests that it is not one without limits. The pressures to conform to a certain set of social expectations, to express yourself in a way that fits in with acceptable group behaviour, is one type of self-imposed constraint. But there are other types of constraint outlined in Chapter 5 that work on the basis of external constraint, rather than self-restraint, which place limits on what is possible in terms of achieving a valued identity and lifestyle.

Activity 1

To remind yourself of what those external constraints might be, take a look again at Section 2 of Chapter 5.

There is a range of reasons why certain individuals and groups might be excluded from participating in consumer activities to make something of themselves. Jot down two or three of the constraints mentioned in Section 2 of Chapter 5 before you read on.

The most obvious external constraint mentioned, I would have thought, is lack of money. Not everyone has the same ability to consume, with the unemployed and low paid, in particular, less able to buy into a consumer lifestyle, without, that is, going into debt. Even if the lack of income does not stop people from gaining acceptance by others on some level, it can make some consumer choices more difficult than others. The lack of job opportunities, the flattening of wages or dependency on basic state benefits may all, in one way or another, mean that those with little money have fewer chances to make something of themselves through consumption. Chronic poor health or a long-term disability may also act as a form of social exclusion, with physical access to shopping locations denied or made difficult. If infact people do make their lives in and through society, then clearly some are better placed than others to do precisely that.

Such thwarted life chances are sometimes attributed to personal shortcomings, where the lack of opportunities is seen as down to the particular individual, their lack of drive or ambition. Nothing is ever given to you, so this particular sentiment goes, and if you don't make the best of the opportunities that come your way then you only have yourself to blame. At times, though, it is hard to know exactly what to make of this belief, as is the opposite view that it is all down to chance and fortune. Coming of age at a time of high unemployment, for instance, can be seen as just plain bad luck, as is the running up of debt at a moment when financial economic collapse is just around the corner. With this set of beliefs, there always seem to be forces at large that people have little control over or can do nothing about, as if that is the way things were meant to be.

Indeed, individual shortcomings or the whims of fate can be convenient reasons for one's lot in this world, yet both sets of beliefs tend to overlook one important thing: that the choices that individuals make when confronted with external constraints, providential or otherwise, happen in circumstances not of their choosing.

After all, the society of which everyone is a part, in one way or another, is not an unmarked fabric when we start to weave our lives through it; it pre-exists us, it is *already made* and bears the imprint of a distinct social pattern of opportunity and privilege. More to the point, it has already been made by past generations who, collectively, have constructed the economic institutions, social norms and political conventions, which today place individuals and groups in varying positions of advantage and disadvantage in terms of their life chances. What this suggests is that all of the major relationships and institutions that constitute the fabric of contemporary society were, at one time, socially constructed; that is, previously made up by generations whose actions cannot be so easily reduced to the mere sum of individual choices (Hacking, 2001).

The sense in which society is 'already made' is yet another one of those instances where its significance is not altogether obvious, so let's take a more detailed look at what is involved.

1.1 An 'already made' society

An era's key social and economic shifts, when you are in the midst of them, are often hard to pin down. For example, the shifts some decades ago in the UK economy, from manufacturing to finance and services, and towards an ever more open and global economy, have had a profound impact on many people's lives, leaving some with fewer prospects of betterment while enriching others (Coe and Jones, 2010). Yet, such large changes are not necessarily experienced as seismic at the time, nor even as something actively made. So when the next generation is confronted with their existence, they can appear as less the result of a multitude of decisions, choices and opportunities (some taken, others missed) by those around at the time, and more the product of the brute force of history. For example, when some of the big UK manufacturers went abroad in search of cheap labour in the 1970s and 1980s, they took with them the jobs that left a gaping employment hole for subsequent generations. As one part of that shift, Bangladeshi garment workers may have benefited, as debated in Chapter 6, but deindustrialisation in the UK meant fewer job opportunities in the old industrial areas, especially in the north of England, for generations to come (Coe and Jones, 2010). It is not, I should stress, that the management of the big companies deliberately set out to hollow out parts of UK manufacturing or that the big banks set out to make themselves the engines of national growth, replacing a world of making things with a world of services, but that is what their actions helped to bring about. Or rather, I should say, that is the circumstances they helped to make, which confronts today's generation as if it were a force of history.

Looking back, with the benefit of hindsight, it is possible to chart the beginning of such shifts in the 1970s and 1980s, often gradual, largely diffuse, but no less significant because of that. Entering the jobs market in the 2010s, it may feel inevitable that the growth of the service sector would lead to a flattening of wages and greater consumer choice, but that leaves out of the picture the political choices that were made during and in the aftermath of such shifts. Market-driven consumerism did not arrive intact at the turn of the twentieth century; it was put together, patchily at first, through a variety of contested political acts driven by the centre-right against a backdrop of economic change (Rodgers, 2011).

In the words of the historian, Tony Judt:

> Much of what appears 'natural' today dates from the 1980s: the obsession with wealth creation, the cult of privatization and the private sector, the growing disparities of rich and poor. And above all, the rhetoric which accompanies these: uncritical admiration for unfettered markets, disdain for the public sector, the delusion of endless growth.
>
> (Judt, 2010, p. 2)

As Judt goes on to argue, the privatisation of public services and utilities, the outsourcing of all but non-essential jobs, together with the neoliberal belief that the market was the only institution capable of delivering economic efficiency, all helped to bring about a new order where it was more or less taken for granted that it was down to the individual to make their own choices about their lives. Collective provision, whether delivered through the state or employer, was broadly frowned upon and curbed, and individuals urged to make their own choices, not only about work and lifestyle, but also about financial provision in old age, in sickness and poor health, as well as in times of unemployment. In short, the political message of **market individualism**, as outlined by Judt and others, was that people owe it to themselves to make the best of what is on offer, not rely on government or employer handouts, as it were.

Market individualism
The organisation of markets to satisfy individual consumer choice.

Where have we heard echoes of that idea before? If it sounds familiar at all that is because it chimes with the routine sentiment expressed at the start of this chapter. Political beliefs and practices of the 1970s and 1980s, once firmly contested, have moved out beyond the formal political sphere to become the currency of everyday life. It's not that self-sufficiency is anything new – far from it – but rather the fact that freedom of choice has now firmly embedded itself in contemporary life as the hallmark of our times. What was once contested political terrain has become so routine and institutionalised that it is easy to forget the link back to the neoliberals, such as Margret Thatcher in the UK and Ronald Reagan in the USA, and the right-leaning political lobbies that first promoted it as an ideal. Choice and competition are now more or less taken for granted in many areas of social life, having spilled over from market economics into education, health and housing

(Rodgers, 2011) and, of course, shopping, supermarkets and the environment.

This is what social scientists mean by the term 'institutionalised'. It's a concept that tries to capture the sense in which a set of ideas and practices takes on a life of its own. This begins to feel like a natural part of so many different areas of social life, as if it had always been organised and arranged in that way. Market values, the freedom to choose, now seem for many an entirely reasonable way to allocate what were previously collective, public goods. Yet, 30 or 40 years ago in the UK, such an arrangement would have been, for the most part, unthinkable (Sandel, 2012). Society has changed. Large swathes of it have been made to work differently, but a full generation of such changes may be taken largely for granted. When that happens, it is this thing called 'society' that acts as a force on people's lives, something 'already made' that is, within the limits of which people have to make their own choices.

What is already made, however, can, of course, always be remade.

2   Making and remaking society

So far in this chapter, and indeed throughout this strand, the focus of attention has been on the making of people's lives and, in turn, how those lives are made by society. Talk of society as something made is important for social scientists because it draws attention to the *agency* of people: that is, their ability to actively construct, together with others, the society of which they are a part, given the limitations of past circumstances. But there is another reason for stressing that society is something that gets made and that is because anything that can be made, can, of course, be *remade*. It reminds us that things could be different, that even if we take existing circumstances for granted, they and society can change. Society can and does get remade, as the previous discussion in Section 1 of social and economic shifts illustrated.

What appears to one generation as an already made society, a set of institutionalised practices, was itself once the product of a wide array of individual and group choices, although some social and political groups, as already implied, are better placed than others to make the running. The demise of manufacturing and industrial production, and the rise of a market-based, consumer society outlined in Chapter 5, provided a large-scale account of a society remade, but you can find small-scale versions of the same transformation in what you have already studied:

- In the history of City Road in Cardiff where ironmongers, car showrooms and repair workshops, which once stood alongside one another, have given way to a street mainly of services – from takeaways, clubs and restaurants to convenience stores, hairdressers and nail bars (The Open University, 2014a, 2014b).

- In the transformation of lifestyles – from one organised around working lives and recognisable class identities, to one where people define themselves less by their job and more by what they consume (Chapter 5).

- In the use by the big supermarkets and high-street retailers of offshore subcontractors to source goods, which were once manufactured in the UK, on the other side of the globe (Chapter 6).

- In the adoption by marketing professionals of more subtle, targeted ways to shape and influence consumer behaviour (Chapter 7).

- In the growth of rubbish and wastefulness that has accompanied rising affluence and mass consumption, posing problems for environmental sustainability and disposal (Chapter 8).

Each of these changes, taken on its own, does not represent a societal shift, although taken together they all point in the same broad direction – towards a social order being remade as a market-based, consumer society. Although how far the contemporary UK is along the road to such a society is itself debatable and one that is of keen interest to social scientists.

It is useful to note that there is no suggestion here of a society being remade overnight. As Chapter 5 contends, the past does not simply slip away to be replaced by what is novel and new; rather, it combines with the new to form contemporary arrangements and alignments. For example, older shops on City Road are juxtaposed with the new service outlets, yet attract a wider variety of customers; UK factories continue to turn out heavy machinery and manufactured goods, albeit on a smaller scale, but with greater technological sophistication; identities for many are still tied to the workplace, yet fashioned through consumption too, and so on. So while social scientists are interested in how society changes, how it gets remade, they are also interested in continuity too, with what stays the same, and how the old and the new combine.

Behind all this, though, is a more pressing concern. Social scientists are not just curious about what stays the same; they are also interested in how some things and not others are *made* to stay the same.

Activity 2

You might like to stand back and think about the previous sentence for a moment.

- Why do some patterns of advantage and disadvantage persist over time?

- If class identities have really faded in a more affluent, post-industrial society, why has the gap between rich and poor actually widened?

These are not easy questions to answer, but there is a sense in which some patterns, like those of inequality or of social mobility, have actually been *reproduced* over time. If, as evidence suggests, life chances have remained more or less static over the past 30 years or so, is that perhaps because it is the inevitable outcome of the expansion of markets into everyday life, or because that is the way it has been made to be?

It's the notion of *reproduction* that I want you to focus on here, rather than any specific answer to the questions, and how positions of advantage are actually maintained.

There are disagreements among social scientists as to why such patterns of advantage and disadvantage persist, but one answer to how such patterns are reproduced is that it all comes down to *power and influence*. Or more accurately, it comes down to how power and influence are exercised by institutions, groups and decision makers over time. In Chapter 6, you met one group of powerful actors, the big supermarkets, and weighed up how their locational decisions and choices were made to 'stick', arguably by constraining the shopping choices of others on the high street. Power can be thought about in this way more generally, as something that shapes society by making certain ways of doing things 'stick'. That is, by constraining what people can do in such ways that leave them little choice but to fall into line with the interests of the dominant groupings in society. When such actions are reproduced and the interests successfully maintained over time, they come to resemble the institutional practices that I spoke about before. That is, they come to resemble the taken-for-granted arrangements of society, which remain largely unquestioned.

It is this type of power – institutional power – that for the most part lies behind why certain social arrangements get remade and others are made to stay the same. I say 'for the most part' because power comes in different shapes and sizes, as was evident from the more subtle forms of persuasion discussed in Chapters 7 and 8, and it is not only institutional power that is at work in making and remaking society.

Nor, too, should it be forgotten that what has been made can also be *unmade*; persistent patterns of advantage come under challenge too, with non-governmental organisations (NGOs) and political campaign groups taking it upon themselves to question existing social harms and unjust arrangements (Allen, 2012). Entrenched inequalities may be hard to shift, but that does not mean to say that they cannot be shifted. That is why it is useful to remember that things could be different, that there is nothing inevitable about the way things are, even though the 'already made' nature of society may leave us with that impression.

3   How are differences and inequalities produced?

Above, in Section 2, I spoke about patterns of advantage and disadvantage as something reproduced over time, albeit ones open to challenge. A key word here is *pattern*, because it suggests that although, for instance, the gap between rich and poor is still with us today and growing wider, the specific pattern of inequality may take a different *form* from, say, that of the pattern of inequality during industrial times. Indeed, Bauman (1988) says as much when he argues that the forms of inequality and freedom in a consumer society differ from what went on before. For that reason, it is worth considering what exactly he means by that.

Bauman's argument, outlined in Chapter 5, is that society remains unequal and divided today on the basis of whether or not you are in a position to consume effectively. Increased affluence means that there are greater numbers who now have access to the trappings of a consumer lifestyle. But not everyone, he points out, is in an equal position to consume. Some groups are better placed than others to join the consumer society; there are divisions based largely, but not solely, on income, which effectively exclude groups such as the unemployed and the low paid, those in casual employment, poor migrants, and many older and less able-bodied people of limited means. According to Bauman, this is the characteristic pattern of inequality in contemporary consumer society; one that contrasts with the lines of class and occupational status that characterised the major cleavages in industrial society. Not only is the pattern of inequality different, though, so too is its form.

By this, Bauman is referring to the fact that the new lines of division rest on a more recent set of economic, cultural and political drivers. There are at least three that come to mind:

- *Market* freedoms, rather than *political* freedoms, have become the benchmark of worth in society.

- *Individual* self-expression through consumption, the ability to buy into a certain lifestyle, has replaced *collective* class identities based on production and work.

- *Lifestyle*, more than *life chances*, provides a better indicator of membership and position within society.

Market freedoms
The freedom to choose based on the buying and selling of goods and services.

Political freedoms
The freedom to participate in society based on citizenship rights.

According to this view, market freedoms, individual self-expression, and the ability to create a lifestyle and identity through consumption have moved centre stage in society, intensifying the divisions between rich and poor. For political philosophers like Michael Sandel (2012), this movement of markets to centre stage matters because life becomes just that much harder for the poor and those of modest means. As he points out:

> If the only advantage of affluence were the ability to buy yachts, sports cars, and fancy vacations, inequalities of income and wealth would not matter very much. But as money comes to buy more and more – political influence, good medical care, a home in a safe neighbourhood rather than a crime-ridden one, access to elite schools rather than failing ones – the distribution of income and wealth looms larger and larger. Where all good things are bought and sold, having money makes all the difference in the world.
>
> This explains why the last few decades have been especially hard on poor and middle-class families. Not only has the gap between rich and poor widened, the commodification of everything has sharpened the sting of inequality by making money matter more.
>
> (Sandel, 2012, pp. 8–9)

Interestingly, for Bauman, the poor are conceived as 'collateral casualties' of the shift towards a more market-driven, consumerist society; an unintended side-effect, as it were, rather than any deliberate strategy of impoverishment. The poor are still present, but their exclusion is less a consequence of purported fecklessness or an unproductive, idle nature and more the result of their position as 'failed consumers'. As such, the intensification of the divide between rich and poor is seen as the direct outcome of the shift from an industrial society towards a post-industrial one. It is this shift, Bauman argues, which has *produced* a more unequal society; one *made* more divisive in terms of affluence and lifestyle as a market-driven society has taken hold (Bauman, 2007).

The new forms of inequality and freedom, then, are no accidents of history, some kind of aberration brought about by chance events. Yet, they can appear somewhat deterministic, as if they were bound to happen, rather than made to happen. As mentioned before, however, market freedoms, the ideals of choice and competition, did not move centre stage by themselves – they were actively promoted by political groupings and lobbies with a clear neoliberal mindset, as part of a broader agenda of social change. If they helped to intensify existing inequalities between rich and poor, they did so by taking advantage of the shifts taking place – from manufacturing to services, from the national to the global. The rise of global markets and global supply chains documented in Chapter 6 may have a certain inexorable feel about them, but there is nothing historically determined about the way that the advancement of individuality, personalisation and freedom of choice made, as Bauman claims, the less well-off in society feel marginalised and devalued.

This leads us back once again to the issue of power and influence, and how some ways of doing things are made to 'stick'. This time, though, it is not institutional power that I have in mind, but the more subtle ways in which behaviour can be shaped and influenced. Chapters 7 and 8 contain some examples of this type of influence at work, as indeed does Chapter 5.

Activity 3

As a way of familiarising yourself with the different ways in which power and influence can be exercised, consider the two pairings below. Each mode of power has taken into account one or more of the chapters of the 'Making lives' strand. Jot down your thoughts on the difference between the two types of power in each pairing.

- Coercion as opposed to domination
- Persuasion in contrast to seduction.

Coercion, you may recall, revolves around the use of force, whereas domination left people in positions where they had no choice but to comply. The latter is perhaps more prevalent where choice is more apparent than real for some individuals, for example those living in a market-driven society without the means to consume.

The promotion of choice and competition as ideals, though, suggests a more subtle influence is at work as well. That is where the ability to persuade comes in, as does seduction. The difference between the two can blur a little, as was noted in Chapter 7, but seduction is perhaps more akin to enticement and allure, whereas persuasion relies on the willingness of others to listen and communicate. Seduction, in that sense, brings into sharper definition the wants and aspirations that may already be present.

Bauman is adamant that people, or rather those who have money to spend, are open to the seductive appeal of consumerism, to the extent that they may fail to recognise that their choices are effectively made up for them. It is, he believes, seduction as a controlling influence that lies behind a more divisive society in terms of the contrast between poverty and affluence. Bauman's argument, however, is also about how *differences* are produced, in so far as consumer society exhorts individuals to make themselves up in particular ways, to invest in difference as a statement of personality. Social differences, on this view, are those that mark people off from one another on the basis of the things that they have acquired, the possession of which may act as an extension of their identity. The goods and services acquired send a message to others about themselves, about who they are and would like to be, fashioned out of the differences made available to them in the consumer marketplace.

Bauman, no doubt, has a point. However, if we put the detail to one side, he could also be describing how social differences in general are produced. The ability to buy into a certain lifestyle actively excludes others from it on the basis of lack of income. Money, the lack of it, is the prime characteristic that is *acted upon*; it is used to judge the worth of an individual and to portray them in a negative light, as marginal. Not having money, then, can turn 'the poor' into something more than simply failed consumers; it can separate them out as 'inadequate' or 'unworthy'. If such a stereotypical judgement is made to 'stick', then a social difference can turn into a social division. Much of the same set of processes can work for bodily differences, cultural differences or sexual differences, although not always with a negative outcome, as the next strand, 'Connecting lives', will illustrate.

For now, you need only hold on to the idea that differences, as much as inequalities, are socially produced – made, not given, for all times and places.

4   How do social scientists know?

In answering this question, it is useful to first notice that it has a rather open-ended quality to it, that is, compared to the other two module questions. It is one thing to talk about how inequalities and differences are produced, or how society is remade, and quite another to know whether what has been said is really little more than rhetoric on the part of myself and others. Social scientists often disagree, and an attitude of healthy scepticism to the ideas and claims expressed is one that is encouraged across all the disciplines. But that still leaves us with this question: how can one come to know that some claims are more valid than others?

For social scientists, one thing is certain, which is that the assertion of an opinion or belief about the make-up of society, on its own, is not sufficient to carry an argument. Any claim or point of view has to be backed up by supporting *evidence*.

Take the claim already discussed in this chapter, which formed the centrepiece of Chapter 5, namely that the contemporary UK is now a consumer society. Leaving to one side the issue of how the old and the new combine in such a society, Bauman (1988; 2007) and others support their claim by pointing to the evidence, which, as we have seen, includes a transformation in:

- lifestyles and the reach of markets
- the pattern of inequality
- the nature of personal relationships
- the means by which the majority of people earn their living, not from the production of goods, but from services.

Such evidence may or may not chime with your own views about how the contemporary UK has changed, but, at the very least, the evidence presented gives us something to judge, which takes us beyond mere assertion.

In a similar vein, the claim set out in Chapter 7 that advertising and the use of ambient music in shops shapes, but does not determine, what consumers buy, was not a simple assertion; it was backed up by a range of evidence. From the attention that consumers pay to adverts and how they are processed, to how sound and music influence behaviour in shopping environments, the evidence drawn upon highlighted the active engagement of consumers in whether or not they chose to be seduced.

As such, the evidence presented suggests that consumers are far from the stereotypical image of 'cultural dupes', that is, manipulated shoppers, which they are sometimes portrayed to be.

You may have noticed that in the examples given above, the evidence used to support such claims took a variety of forms. Statistical patterns and numerical trends are types of **quantitative evidence**, whereas case studies and sample surveys are of a more **qualitative** nature. In later strands, you will meet other types of evidence, but, for now, whatever type of evidence is drawn upon, what really matters is whether or not it holds up under interrogation. The temptation is to think about this in terms of the solidity of the evidence put forward; that is, how substantial it is in relation to the claims made. 'Hard' evidence, after all, sounds convincing. Oddly enough, though, for social scientists, 'hard' evidence can be misleading for two reasons:

1   It is possible for social scientists to support their argument by selecting only those bits of evidence that corroborate it, rather than those bits that may bring it into question. The evidence that best suits an argument may be chosen, while the facts that cast doubt upon its conclusions may be overlooked.

2   The same piece of evidence can be interpreted differently. Facts, as you will hear on more than one occasion in your studies, 'do not speak for themselves'.

As I write in 2013, it is a fact, for example, that there are more empty shops on the UK high street than ever before (BRC, 2013). Why that is the case, however, is more a matter of interpretation, with different retail lobby groups accounting for that fact in quite contrasting ways. The falling numbers on the high street only raise the question as to whether or not we are witnessing the death of traditional shops – they do not tell us *why* the numbers are falling.

The issue of supermarket power, discussed at length in Chapter 6, and whether it widens or narrows shopping choices is perhaps the clearest illustration of what is at stake over the selection and interpretation of evidence.

Quantitative evidence
Evidence that can be counted and turned into percentages or other numerical data, for example population numbers; the percentages of people who gave certain answers in a survey.

Qualitative evidence
Evidence that is not in numerical form (that is, not counted). There are many different types of qualitative evidence, for example text, images or the researcher's own observations.

In relation to the evidence presented, what caught my eye is that where
the anti-supermarket lobby draws attention to local market statistics and
the fall in the number of traditional shops to back up their claim that
supermarkets narrow shopping choices, the pro lobby point to national
market figures and regeneration case studies to support the opposite
conclusion, that supermarkets widen shopping choices. Both sides, then,
it appears are *selective* in their choice of evidence, highlighting what best
suits their argument, possibly at the expense of less supportive pieces
of evidence.

On the explanations of supermarket power put forward, what struck me
was the sharp contrast in *interpretation*. Where one side spoke about a
zero-sum game of power operating on the high street, with
supermarkets prospering at the expense of local, traditional stores, the
other side disputed that there is a fixed amount of resources in play and
argued for a positive-sum game, where all parties on the high street
benefit, shopkeepers and consumers alike. Surely, you would have
thought, both interpretations cannot be right. So how would they
account for the fact, mentioned above, that there are now more empty
shops on the UK high street than in living memory?

At a glance, this piece of evidence would suggest that supermarkets
have made it difficult for smaller, independent shops to compete and
prosper, hence the decline in the number of traditional outlets. This
would seem to support the interpretation of the anti-supermarket
campaigners, whereby if one side gains, the other must lose. On that
basis, a zero-sum game clearly seems to fit with the facts on the high

street. Those in the pro-supermarket lobby, however, would very likely have none of that. For them, empty shops on the high street are not an indication of the abuse of power by supermarket chains. They would be inclined to argue that other social and economic forces are at work, with high local property rates and the growth of online shopping, for example, leading to a fall in the number of traditional traders on the high street. Besides, the presence of a supermarket on the high street can act as a magnet for shoppers, drawing in numbers that benefit some of the newer service outlets – coffee shops, beauty salons, nail bars and mobile phone outlets – that have replaced some of the traditional shops.

So both sides would be able to offer an interpretation of the same piece of evidence, the very same fact. And, as we saw above, both sides are selective in their choice of evidence, choosing *different* pieces of evidence to support their argument. Where then, you might ask, does that leave us in terms of weighing up the claims made and the supporting evidence used to back up an argument? Should social scientists abandon the idea of obtaining reliable evidence altogether?

Not to my mind, because, as I see it, there is not really much of a choice. Evidence in support of an argument may sometimes be selective and open to more than one interpretation, but it still ranks as evidence. The crucial thing, I would have thought, is that we recognise these potential shortcomings and, as social scientists, work within these limitations to get to know which evidence base is the more reliable in the face of competing claims, or worse, in the face of mere opinion and plain assertion.

4.1   Making an argument

I'll repeat that previous line for effect: in the face of mere opinion and plain assertion. Earlier, I expressed the view that opinions and assertions, by themselves, are not sufficient to carry an argument. Arguments are made like anything else, put together to sway opinion, the elements of which may now be familiar to you from your reading thus far. They almost always start with a *question* around a particular topic, which in turn, generates *claims* as some kind of provisional answer to a question and, if they are to go beyond assertion, are backed up by *evidence*. In this section, I want to take a closer look at each of these elements to provide a sense of how a social science argument is built up, how it is constructed.

I say 'social science argument' because that is what concerns us here. No doubt, most of us, at one time or another, have argued our corner. You can fall out over an argument, you can even duck one, and social scientists are no different in that regard. They disagree much like everyone else, but the terms on which they disagree will very likely be over the relevance of the questions asked, the validity of the claims and the reliability of the evidence used to support them. The role of evidence in a social science argument is something that we have just touched upon and will consider at greater length in the following strand, so here we turn first to the role that questions play and then to the kinds of claim that you are likely to meet in the social sciences.

Believe it or not, social scientists can get quite animated over whether the right questions are being asked. It matters to them that the questions asked address *explicitly* the things that they wish to account for or explain. The question of supermarket power raised in Chapter 6, for instance, could have been just that: a general question about how much power supermarkets wield. But, as noted in the previous section, the issue of supermarket power is linked directly to a social concern: namely, the fortunes of traditional shops on the high street and whether the big four supermarkets limit or broaden consumer choice. In this instance, a general question was refined into a more specific one, precisely because of an explicit concern over competition and choice on the high street. Indeed, much the same can be said of Chapter 8, where the general question of living in a throwaway society was refined by behavioural economists into something more specific about why people do not always make the best choices over recycling and waste.

As is often the case, general questions may lead to more specific questions and it is helpful to think about the precise 'fit' of a question in terms of the issue that it is trying to address. That does not mean to say, however, that social science should shy away from the 'big' questions. After all, questions do not come much bigger than the one that asks whether we now live in a consumer society. It all comes down to the explicitness of a question, not its breadth or scope.

By 'explicit' here, I mean that the question itself is relatively clear and unambiguous, and in the case of the above 'big' question, that is largely so because there is broad agreement among social scientists over the meaning of the concept of consumption. If the same question about consumer society had been asked a century or so ago, however, it would very likely have made little sense, as the concept of consumption then referred as much, if not more, to the 'all-consuming' wasting disease of tuberculosis, rather than to anything to do with the economy. Health, the atrophy of the body, not shopping, would very likely have sprung to mind at the mention of consumption. Today, the concept of consumption tends to crystallise around a number of economic and social trends – around markets moving centre stage, around lifestyle and identity as ends in themselves, as well as the significance of brands and advertising – and this clear understanding makes it possible to ask the question about consumer society without fear of being misunderstood.

A social science argument, in that sense, can be less than convincing if the vocabulary used is vague or misleading. Moreover, if the questions asked are infact explicit, then it becomes easier to identify the *claims* made in relation to them.

Activity 5

Consider the questions raised by behavioural economists in Chapter 8, noted above, about whether people make the best choices over recycling household waste.

The question is explicit enough and Chapter 8 described how this led to the adoption of nudge approaches in an attempt to change behaviour on recycling. Such an approach, however, rests upon a series of *claims* about human behaviour, about how people make choices when left to their own devices. Turn to Section 3 of Chapter 8 and look at some of the claims listed. Jot down the ones that you think relate directly to recycling behaviour.

The most relevant claim is probably the assertion that people have limited ability to make the right decisions on recycling, even when it might be in their best interests. This is the point about bounded rationality. It is, I think, the broadest of the claims mentioned and ties in with other related claims:

- that people make errors when making choices
- that people do not always look at the overall picture – they cannot 'see the wood for the trees', so to speak
- that they are overly optimistic about their ability to recycle correctly.

At best, it seems that:

- people fall back on what they have done before
- they are cautious over adopting new recycling practices.

I may not have placed all the claims in the same order as you and may have unduly stressed some over others, but the overall claim, as I understand it, is that people are reluctant or too slow to change their behaviour, and when they do, they find it difficult to make the right choices. On those grounds, it is argued that people need to be nudged into doing what is best for them. Hence the importance placed on the design of choice architecture, which enables people to make what are effectively big social changes through small changes in their behaviour. As such, the emphasis is on positive reinforcement and how that can shift behaviour patterns.

So, this is a set of claims about the way people make decisions and, on that basis, what is required for them to act in their best interests. The nudge principles follow on directly from the claims made about human behaviour. The claims are explicit, in that they provide an answer to the question posed about recycling household waste and, in turn, evidence is sought to back up the approach. The search for *evidence* is the last element of the argument and, as has been suggested, without it the claims are little more than assertions.

A social science argument, then, rests broadly on such a reasoned sequence:

- it starts with a more or less explicit question
- this question, in turn, generates particular claims
- finally, evidence is drawn upon, often in a selective manner, to support such claims.

The sequence is not always so neat and clear-cut with, for example, claims sometimes more apparent than the questions they seek to answer. Nonetheless, once identified, the different elements of a social science argument enable debate to take place over the issues raised and the reliability of the evidence. Significantly, they enable social scientists to discuss, reflect and move on, as indeed you have done and are about to do.

5   Moving on

So that brings us to the end of the 'Making lives' strand. At the beginning of this chapter, I spoke about the conundrum that featured in different ways in each of the strand chapters: that while individuals and groups *make* society, people's lives are also *made* by society. In drawing attention to the latter, the aim was to show how society as a whole has a part to play in the making and remaking of people's lives. That sense of society as a *whole* is an intriguing one, more so because it hints at an idea at the heart of the social sciences: that society itself cannot be understood as the mere sum of people's individual actions. There is something over and above the collection of individual actions, a *social* element that acts as a force upon people's lives, something 'already made', as discussed in Section 1.1, which points towards the connected nature of our lives – the social relationships that shape our combined fortunes.

It is the social relationships between people that come strikingly into focus in the next strand, 'Connected lives', where the connections made to and through others are themselves the very fabric of society, and without which it would be difficult to fully understand how differences and inequalities are made and remade over time. Making connections, in that sense, is what binds us into society as a whole and which brings the rest of the world into our lives.

References

Allen, J. (2012) 'The power to make a difference', in Tyszczuk, R., Smith, J., Clark, N. and Butcher, M., (eds) *Atlas: Geography, Architecture and Change in an Interdependent World*, London, Black Dog Publishing.

Bauman, Z. (1988) *Freedom*, Milton Keynes, Open University Press.

Bauman, Z. (2007) *Consuming Life*, Cambridge, Polity Press.

British Retail Consortium (BRC) (2013) *British Retail Consortium* [Online]. Available at http://www.brc.org.uk/brc_home.asp (Accessed 8 April 2014).

Coe, N.M. and Jones, A. (eds) (2010) *The Economic Geography of the UK* , London, Sage.

Hacking, I. (2001) *The Social Construction of What?*, Cambridge, MA, Harvard University Press.

Judt, T. (2010) *Ill Fares the Land: A Treatise on our Present Discontents*, London, Penguin Books.

Rodgers, D.T. (2011) *Age of Fracture*, Cambridge, MA, Harvard University Press.

Sandel, M. (2012) *What Money Can't Buy: The Moral Limits of Markets*, London, Allen Lane.

The Open University (2014a) 'The Life and Times of the Street: Part 1' [Video], *DD102 Introducing the social sciences*. Available at https://learn2.open.ac.uk/mod/oucontent/view.php?id=443760&section=2.3 (Accessed 29 November 2013).

The Open University (2014b) 'The Life and Times of the Street: Part 2' [Video], *DD102 Introducing the social sciences*. Available at https://learn2.open.ac.uk/mod/oucontent/view.php?id=443760&section=2.7 (Accessed 29 November 2013).

Acknowledgements

Every effort has been made to contact copyright holders. If any have been inadvertently overlooked the publishers will be pleased to make the necessary arrangements at the first opportunity.

Grateful acknowledgement is made to the following sources:

Chapter 1: *Figure 1.2* (left): Copyright © Greg Balfour Evans/Alamy; *Figure 1.2* (right): Courtesy of Mivan; *Figure 1.3* (top left): Copyright © Radharc Images/Alamy; *Figure 1.3* (top right): Copyright © Keith Morris/Alamy; *Figure 1.3* (bottom left): Copyright © eye35.pix/Alamy; *Figure 1.3* (bottom right): Copyright © Wildscape/Alamy; *Figure 1.4:* Copyright © ITV Picture Archive; *Figures 1.5 and 1.6*: courtesy of the Library of the London School of Economics and Political Science, reference Booth/B/15.

Chapter 3: *Figure 3.*2: Copyright © Catriona Havard.

Chapter 5: *Figure 5.1:* Office for National Statistics (2012) *Expenditure and Food Survey*, Office for National Statistics. Crown copyright ©; *Figure 5.2:* Copyright © Rex Features/Image Source; *Figure 5.3:* Copyright © Sandro Campardo/epa/Corbis; *Figure 5.4* (left): Copyright © Time and Life Pictures/Getty Images; *Figure 5.4* (right): Copyright © Richard Bryant/Arcaid/Corbis; *Figure 5.5* (centre): Copyright © Robert Kadhim; *Figure 5.5* (right): Copyright ©iStockphoto.com/PeJo29; *Figure 5.6:* Copyright © Alex Segre/Alamy.

Chapter 6: *Figure 6.1*: Copyright © PA Archive/Press Association Images; *Figure 6.2*: Copyright © Paul Heinrich/Alamy; *Figure 6.3:* Copyright © Jay Fram/Corbis; *Figure 6.7*: Copyright © 67photo/Alamy; *Figure 6.9* (top and bottom right): Copyright © G M B Akash/Panos Pictures; *Figure 6.9* (bottom left): Copyright © Fernando Moleres/Panos Pictures.

Chapter 8: *Pages 253 and 254:* Fraser-Thomas, E. (2012) 'Single men found to be rubbish at putting out the recycling', *The Observer*, 29 December, Copyright © Guardian Media and News Ltd 2012; *Figure 8.4*: TM & Copyright 20th Century Fox/Rex Features; *Figure 8.5*: Wansink, B., Just, D.R. and McKendry, J. (2010) 'Lunch line redesign', *New York Times*, 21 October, Copyright © New York Times; *Figure 8.6:* Copyright © AKP Photos/Alamy.

Cover image: Copyright © iStockphoto.com/Meinzahn.

DD102 Module team

Academic team

John Allen, Professor of Economic Geography

Geoff Andrews, Staff Tutor and Senior Lecturer

Georgina Blakeley, Senior Lecturer in Politics and International Studies (Module Team Chair)

Vivienne Brown, Emeritus Professor of Intellectual History

Jovan Byford, Senior Lecturer in Psychology

John Clarke, Emeritus Professor of Social Policy

John Dixon, Professor of Social Psychology

Umut Erel, RCUK Academic Fellowship

Ieman Hassan, Senior Faculty Manager

Catriona Havard, Lecturer in Psychology

Kevin Hetherington, Dean and Director of Studies

Steve Hinchliffe, Reader in Geography

Eluned Jeffries, Associate Lecturer

Juliet Landau-Pope, Associate Lecturer

Jenny Meegan, Senior Faculty Manager

Mel Nettle, Associate Lecturer

Rajiv Prabhakar, Lecturer in Personal Finance

Parvati Raghuram, Reader in Human Geography

George Revill, Senior Lecturer in Geography

Matt Staples, Staff Tutor (Deputy Module Team Chair)

Stephanie Taylor, Senior Lecturer in Psychology

Joan Vickers, Associate Lecturer

Kath Woodward, Professor of Sociology

External assessor

Professor Dale Southerton, University of Manchester

Production team

Roshni Amin, Sound and Vision Assistant Producer

Melanie Bayley, Media Project Manager

Katie Belcher, Media Assistant

Wendy Chalmers, Learning and Teaching Librarian

Sian Contell, Sound and Vision Assistant

Dale Harry, Copy Editor

Matthew Holley, Sound and Vision Media Developer

Joanna Mack, Sound and Vision Producer

Katie Meade, Licensing and Acquisitions Executive

Lesley Moore, Curriculum Assistant

John O'Dwyer, Editorial Media Developer

Eileen Potterton, Curriculum Manager

Emma Sadera, Editorial Media Developer

Ann Tolley, Curriculum Manager

Howie Twiner, Graphics Media Developer (Graphic Art)

The module team would also like to thank the following freelance staff: Mandy Anton (cover design), Julian Clark-Lowes (software), Isobel McLean (indexer), Joanne Osborn (proof-reader), Margaret McManus (copyrights) and Salia Nessa (book editor).

Video production

Mark Galloway, Series Producer, Evans Woolfe Media

Chris Guiver, Camera/Director, Evans Woolfe Media

Harvey Woolfe, Executive Producer, Evans Woolfe Media

Index

advertising 189–202, 267
  and atmospherics 203
  and individual lives 45
  logos 189–90
  and nudges 247
  online advertising 189, 191, 192–6
    banner ads 194–6
    profile based targeting 195
    surveys on 194
  and persuasion 190, 192–201
  seduction of 191, 192, 196–200, 213–16
    evidence for 279–80
  and waste 232
affect
  and advertising 195–6
  and atmospherics 203–4
affective associations
  and advertising 198–9
affluence
  and consumption 275
  shopping and affluent young women 206–8
  and waste 226, 230–7, 273
Africa
  connections with City Road 20, 22, 27
age
  and background music in shops 208–9
  differences and inequalities 25
    in City Road 26, 27
  and identity 75
  making and remaking society 52
  and social order 100
    public/private spaces 93, 94
agency of people
  making and remaking society 272
Akram, Naveed 97
Aldi 161, 162, 165
already made society 265, 268, 269–71, 272
  and differences and inequalities 274
anarchist squatters in City Road 20
  and social ordering 88–9, 98
antisocial behaviour
  and social ordering 97
arguments in social science 282–5
  and behavioural economics 283, 284–5
  claims made in relation to 282, 283, 284–5
  and consumption 283–4

  and evidence 282, 283, 285
  questions asked 282, 283, 285
  and supermarket power 182–3, 283
Arthur, John 26, 29, 65–6, 73, 76
Asda 151, 152, 155, 156, 163, 165
  and garment workers in Bangladesh 173–6, 179
  George fashion range 170
  market share 161, 162
atmospherics
  advertising and shopping 202–5
  mood music in shops 191, 202, 204–10, 247, 279
audios
  and banner ads 195

Bangladesh
  garment workers 173–80, 269
  Rana Plaza disaster 178
  wages and supermarket power 153, 172
banner ads 194–6
Bauman, Zygmunt
  on consumption 125–6, 129–31, 136–7, 139, 267, 279
    and the devalued self 141–2
    and patterns of differences and inequalities 178, 275, 276–7
Beckham, David 45
Beeton, Mrs
  Book of Household Management 138
behavioural economics 226, 238–55, 256
  bounded rationality 241, 284
  choice architecture and 'nudge' principles 245–7
  differences and inequalities in individual behaviour 252–4
  information overload 240
  loss aversion 240, 242
  mental accounting 242
  and overconfidence 241
  and recycling 226, 243, 250–2
  social science arguments on 283, 284–5
  status quo bias 242, 243
  see also nudging
Behavioural Insights Team (Cabinet Office) 244
Belcher, Sophie 206–8, 209, 211, 212, 213
Blythman, Joanna 163, 164
Booth, Charles
  Life and Labour of the People in London 9–11, 12